Black America Series

Columbia
South Carolina

BLACK AMERICA SERIES

COLUMBIA
SOUTH CAROLINA

Vennie Deas-Moore

ARCADIA
PUBLISHING

ISBN 978-0-7385-0665-4

Published by Arcadia Publishing
Charleston, South Carolina

Printed in the United States of America

Library of Congress Catalog Card Number: 00-108965

For all general information contact Arcadia Publishing at:
Telephone 843-853-2070
Fax 843-853-0044
E-mail sales@arcadiapublishing.com
For customer service and orders:
Toll-Free 1-888-313-2665

Visit us on the Internet at www.arcadiapublishing.com

To my mother, Eugenia Powell Deas,
for her financial, spiritual, and emotional support.
Her belief in my work made this book possible.

CONTENTS

AUTHOR'S PREFACE

Author Vennie Deas-Moore, a cultural historian, was hired by the Historic Columbia Foundation to do research while archaeologist Chris Clement was unearthing the backyard of the Mann-Simons Cottage, a historic house museum managed by the foundation. This African-American home belonged to Celia Mann, a free black woman who was a professional midwife and helped to establish First Calvary Baptist Church soon after the Civil War. The church first met in her basement.

As a research writer, I found this work intriguing and very challenging. When I first started this project, I thought I would supply family history related to the archeological dig. I quickly found that this was not a rational approach. In the pits, Chris and his team were digging up artifacts from the late 1800s, artifacts used by the family in daily life. At best, I could corroborate these lives through family lore, inconsistent governmental documents, and very scarce family records, such as Celia Mann's will, which she signed with an "X." Though Celia was well respected in her community, records indicate that she was illiterate. Therefore, diaries and correspondence written by Celia would not be found.

Secondly, from the inception of the project, this family's history reached beyond the backyard. From early on Celia Mann was a midwife throughout this prominent white community. The founding of the First Calvary Baptist Church began in the basement of her cottage. I found her yard to be a complex space of family and community activities.

At this point, I completely ripped off the pages of my yellow legal pad. As an oral historian, the obvious next approached was to trace the family history. Mrs. Regina Monteith, the director of education and interpretation for the Historic Columbia Foundation, made the family tree available to me. This gave me one branch of descendants still living and working in Columbia to research.

Sometimes the unexpected happens. The week before my interview with Mrs. Robbie Atkinson, the great-great-granddaughter of Celia Mann, Mrs. Atkinson's mother died. Her mother was the oldest surviving member of this branch of the family.

I then set my goal to record at least five hours of interviews. I started by tracing previous research on the cottage. Historic Columbia had considerable research, including a 1975 master's thesis, "An Inquiry into the Mann-Simons House," by Julia Taylor Burr.

As I began the oral history taping and archival research, an unexpected story started to be unveiled. Six months into the project, and nearing my deadline, I was resisting any changes to the work. But I began to realize this family was a part of a bigger picture, a picture of black society in Columbia and an integral part of the state capital. I then renamed my report: "Black Society in Columbia."

The results of this smaller project led me to Arcadia Publishing, and proudly I present to readers *Black America Series: Columbia, South Carolina*.

INTRODUCTION

In the late 1700s, Surveyor General John Gabriel Guignard surveyed Columbia. This planned capital city was laid out in a 2-mile-square grid. North-south streets were named after state militia heroes on one side, and Continental Army heroes on the other side. Adjoining streets were named after agricultural products—wheat, rice, blossom, tobacco, indigo. The State House was erected in the center of the city.

The demographics of the city influenced African-American society in Columbia. Research in city directories and census records showed almost equal black and white populations pre-Emancipation. Free blacks and urban slaves lived throughout the city. The 1850 census recorded free blacks as stable keepers, shoemakers, musicians, carpenters, tailors, cabinetmakers, and barbers. In surrounding rural area, slaves hoped to become a part of this urban community and worked to become skilled tradesman.

According to John Hammond Moore in *Columbia and Richland County: A South Carolina Community, 1740–1990*, "The complexities of urban living of the 1850s . . . presented countless dilemmas. No set of rules could control slaves who, after work, gathered in homes, churches, and grog shops where they often acquired new ideas and strange notions."

Columbia was greatly changed by the Civil War. On February 17–18, 1865, Sherman's troops made a direct hit on Columbia. His men blazed a fiery trail through the city. Black Columbians ran for their lives and tried to protect their properties. A free black family passed down a story that recalled an ancestor who "hid in the woods with buckets of water determined to save the old house."

Another dramatic historical dilemma for Columbia was Reconstruction. For a decade, in the 1870s, the federal government took over the state capital, and for the first time, African Americans were in control of the state government. Others were in prominent positions across the city. These early days set the stage for a unique and interesting period in Columbia's black history.

THE CELEBRATION OF EMANCIPATION AT THE SOUTH CAROLINA STATE HOUSE IN 1870

The early morning sun of January 1, 1870, was rising in the winter sky behind the magnificent granite of the South Carolina capitol. Like a phoenix, the State House rose out of the ruins of Sherman's march through Columbia.

It was about 11 a.m. when a crowd of blacks began forming a procession blocks away from the capitol in front of Janney's Hall. There was not a white man in the procession.

Before the start of the parade, the drums echoed through downtown Columbia. Distinguished political officials led the procession. Religious leaders followed carrying Bibles and hymnbooks. What a day of jubilation for freedmen of Columbia and the surrounding vicinity. Marching in a drill formation was a large brass band. There was a high-stepping procession, gathering a crowd as it moved through principal streets toward the capitol grounds.

In front of the building, a large platform had been erected, arched with evergreens and patriotic banners. The national flag stood center stage. It was the day to commemorate Abraham Lincoln's signing of the Proclamation of Emancipation on January 1, 1863.

On the stage were representatives of the Reconstruction legislature. Seated were Governor Robert K. Scott, Simeon Corley, John E. Robertson, William Shiver, Comptroller Neagle, Secretary of State Francis L. Cardozo, and Senator William Beverly Nash.

Representative Thompson, the chairman of the Committee of Arrangements, requested James Davis to preside. Prayer was offered by the Reverend William Johnson, and Assistant Adjutant General Robert B. Elliott read the Emancipation Proclamation. William Beverly Nash, a state legislator of Richland County, was then introduced, and he delivered the main address of the day.

> Friends and fellow-citizens: Seven years ago to-day the proclamation, which announced that freedom had come to our race on this continent, was given to the world. As we stand here celebrating the birthday of freedom to us, all the past with its privations, griefs . . . I want to revive in the memories of those who stand before me a recollection of the longings and cries for freedom that went up from their hearts to God in times past. How they thought that with freedom they would lead better lives; educate their children; build up around them the safe-guards of a well-ordered home, and develop in themselves noble and useful characters. We all cherished such hopes. . . ."

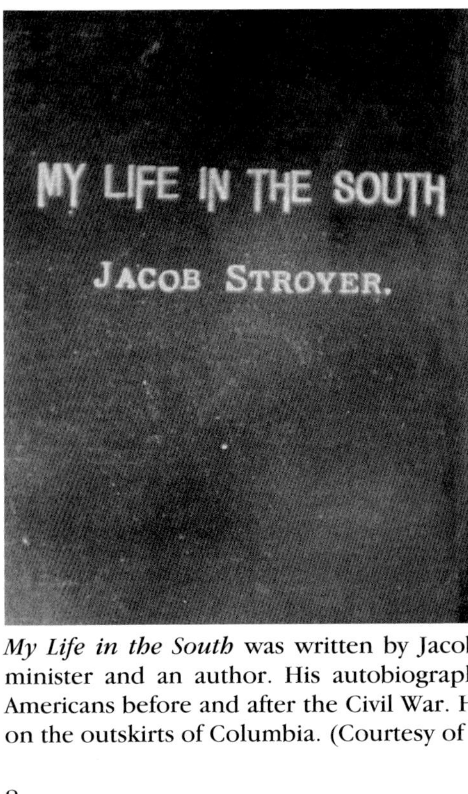

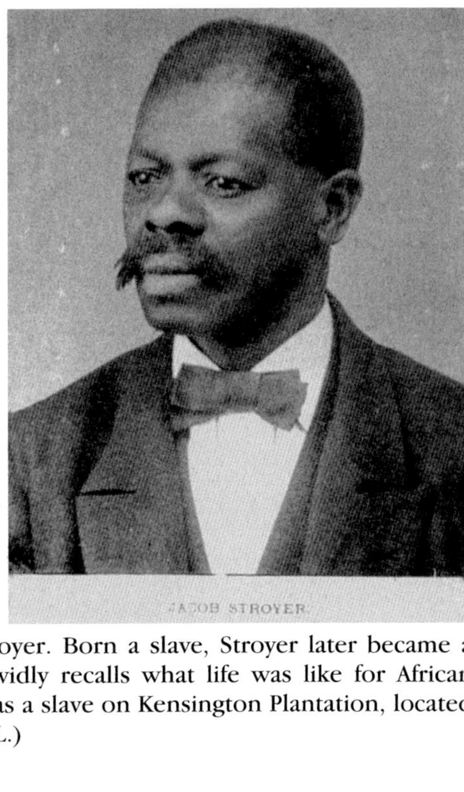

My Life in the South was written by Jacob Stroyer. Born a slave, Stroyer later became a minister and an author. His autobiography vividly recalls what life was like for African Americans before and after the Civil War. He was a slave on Kensington Plantation, located on the outskirts of Columbia. (Courtesy of SCCL.)

One

Politics and Government

One of the results of Reconstruction was that blacks voted, could be elected to office, and could become active members of a national political party. The Reconstruction Acts admitted the states of North Carolina, South Carolina, Louisiana, Georgia, Florida, and Alabama to representation in U.S. Congress. The state legislature in South Carolina consisted of 57 white men and 98 black men. This is the body, and these the state officers, that represented the state of South Carolina.

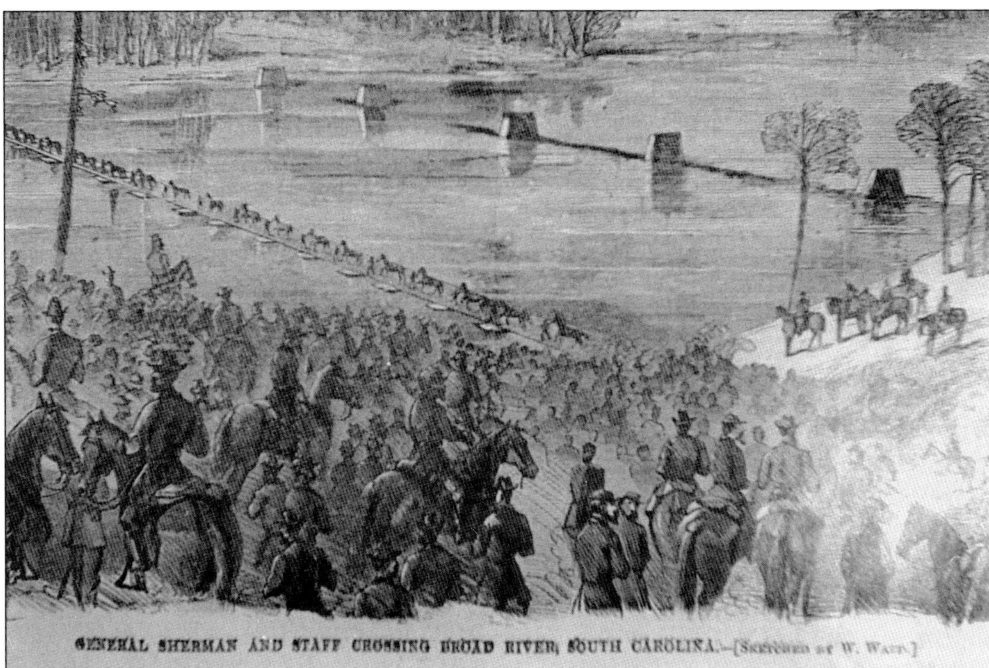

General Sherman and his staff cross the Broad River to Columbia in February 1865. (Courtesy of the Richland County Public Library.)

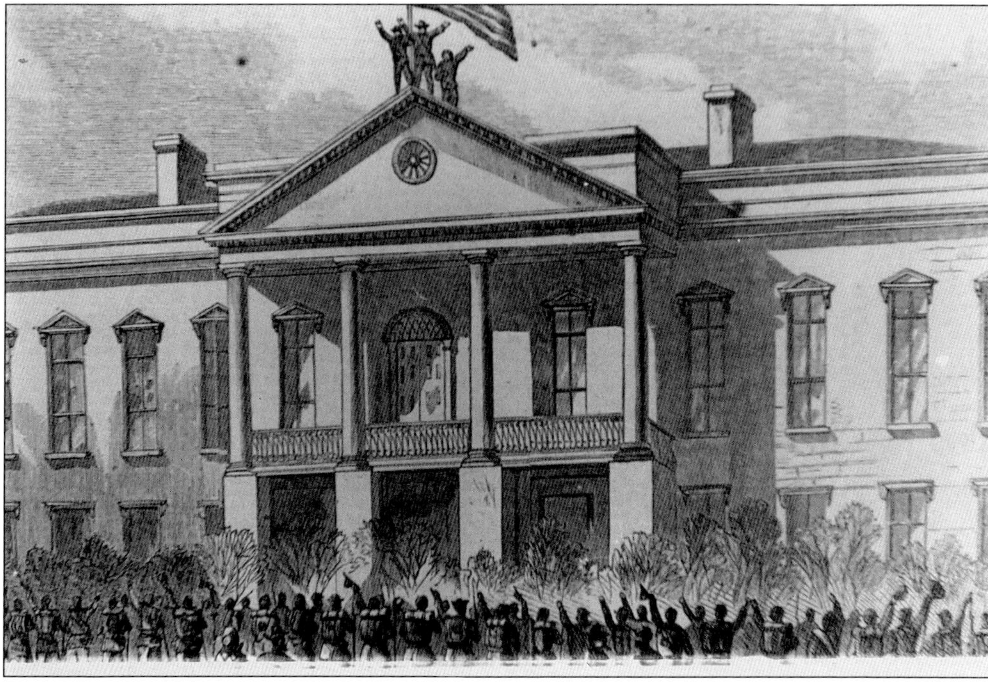

The Stars and Stripes are raised over the Capitol in Columbia. (Courtesy of the Richland County Public Library.)

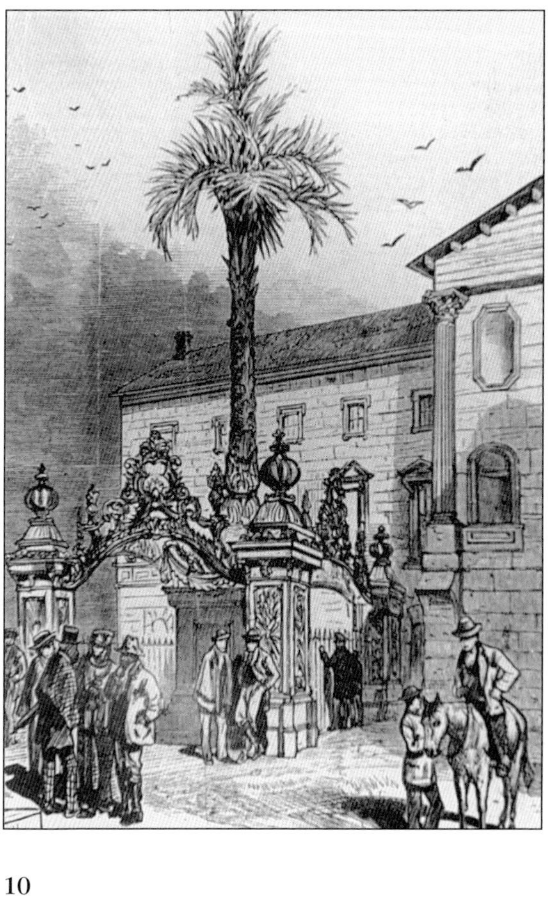

The Palmetto Monument appears in this *c.* 1875 news engraving. Black politicians came from both the Southern black elite and those with "slave" origins. (Courtesy of the Richland County Public Library.)

Pictured here are the radical members of the first legislature in South Carolina following the Civil War. (Courtesy of the South Carolina State Archives.)

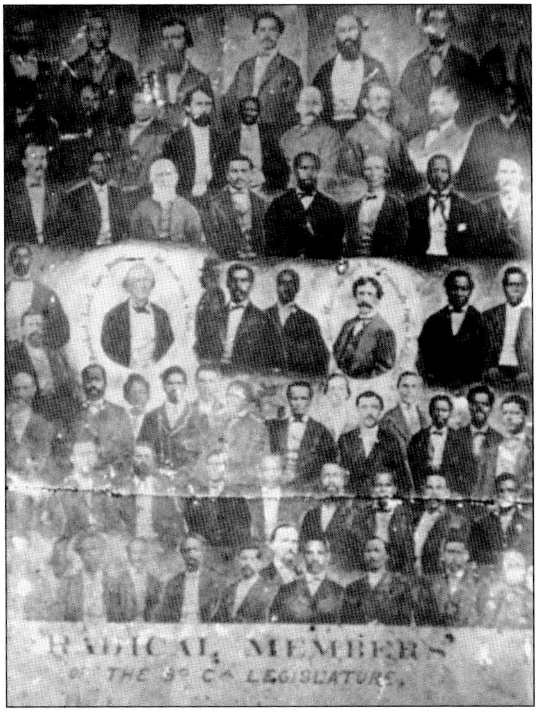

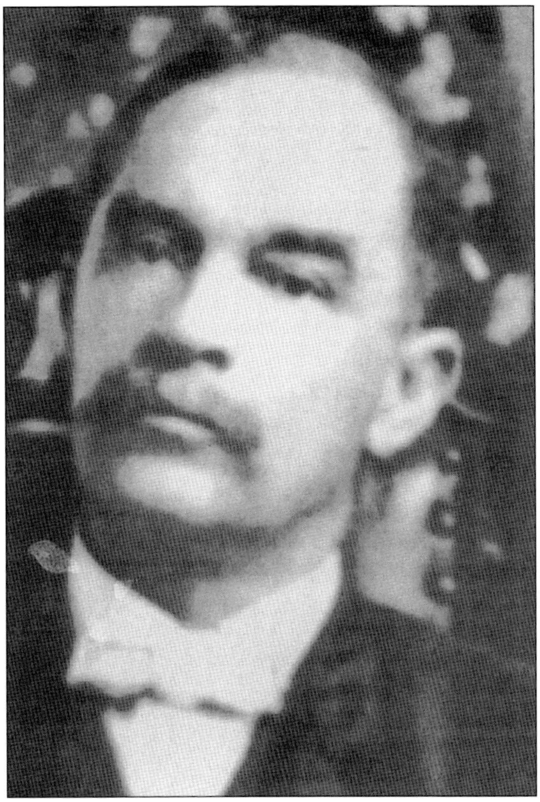

Robert John Palmer was born on January 18, 1849. Palmer served in the House of Representatives from 1876 to 1878 and conducted a business as a merchant tailor on Main Street opposite the old Post Office. Palmer owned property in Washington, D.C., and Columbia. (Courtesy of the Palmer family.)

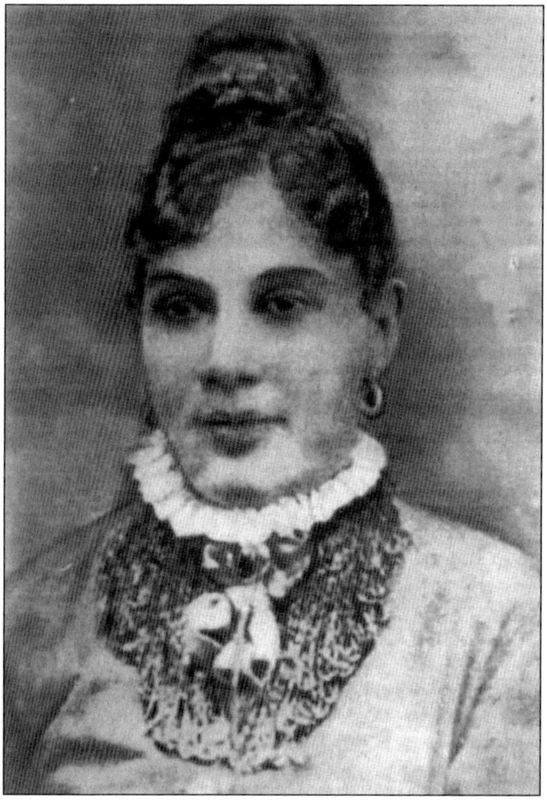

Palmer married Miss Adelaide Perry, and the couple had eight children. They were Ester E. Palmer, Leonora D.Palmer, Jennie E. Palmer, Adelaide G. Palmer, Minnie L. Palmer, Ella S. Palmer, Myrtle May Palmer, and Edmund P. Palmer. (Courtesy of the Palmer family.)

Pictured below is the "Horseshoe" of the University of South Carolina campus, *c.* 1875. In 1873, the university was opened to students irrespective of their skin color. For a short time during Reconstruction, African Americans attended the university, and some, like William M. Dart, were graduates. William Dart became the first principal of Howard School in Columbia. The entrance of the first black student in October 1873 resulted in the resignation of some members of the faculty and student body. (Courtesy of the USC Collection.)

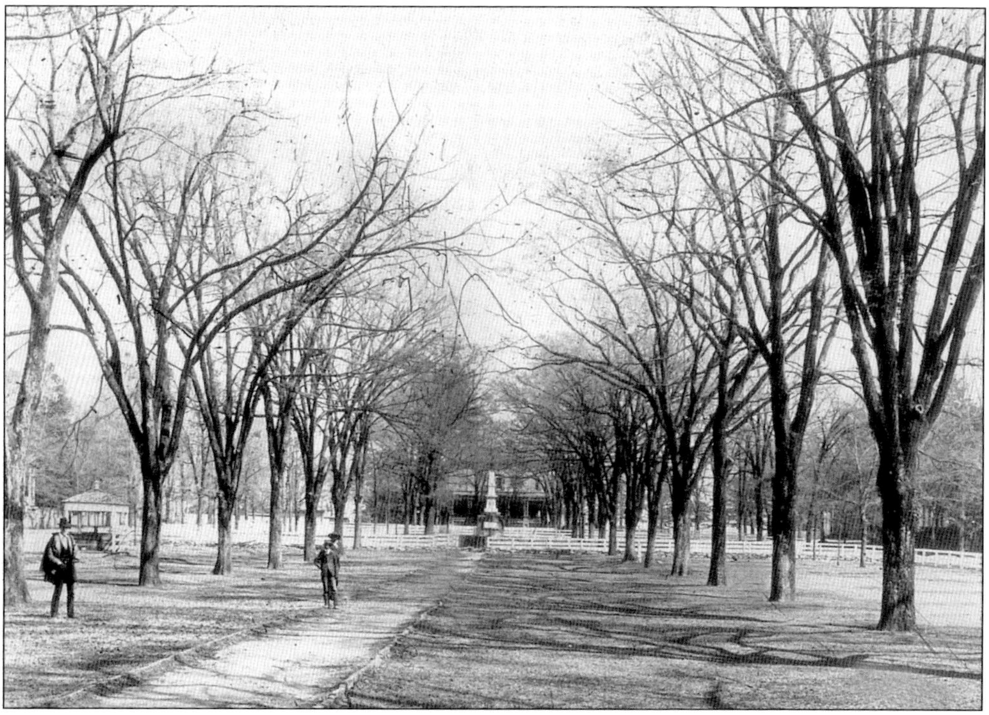

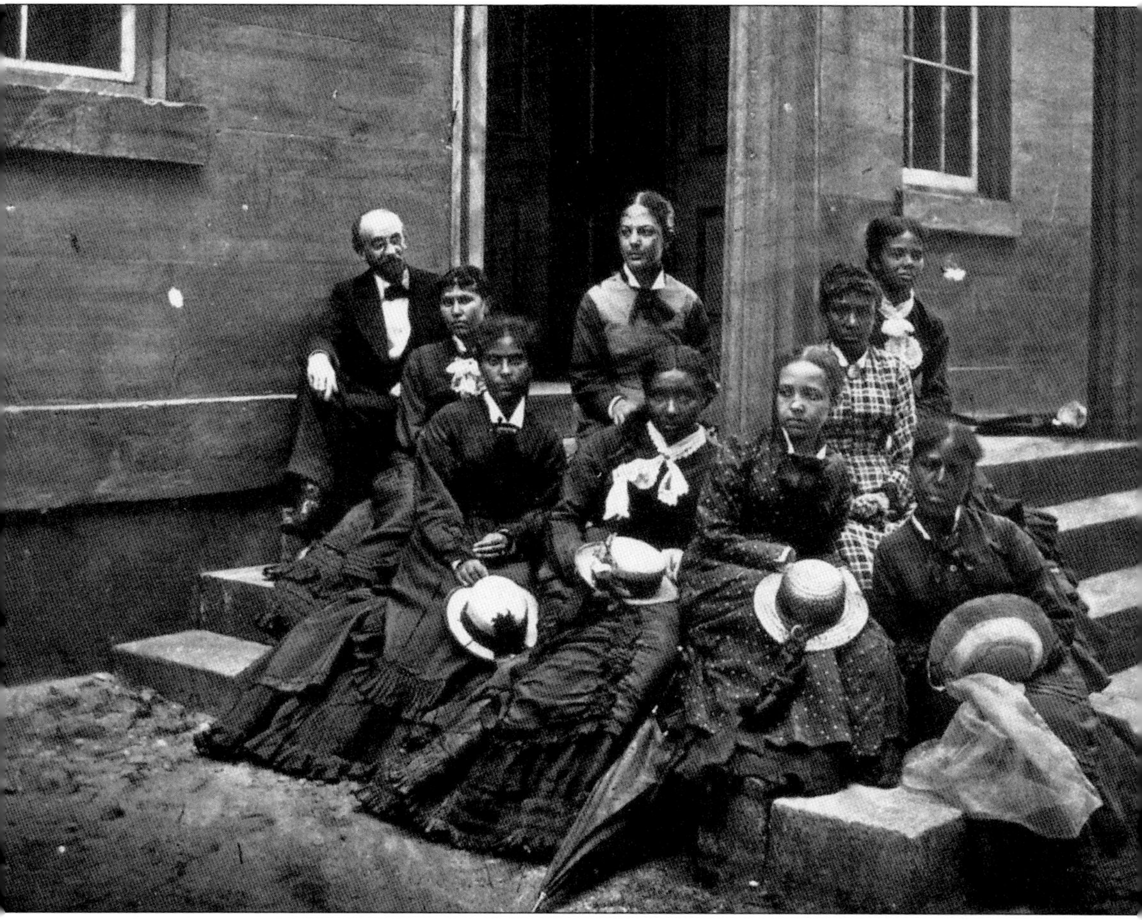

These eight women, probably students in the Normal School (1873–1877), were among the first blacks and the first females to attend classes on the USC campus. The Normal School was a college preparatory department located on the university's campus. In this department, Professors Brewer and Greener taught the classics. College students also assisted in the teaching at the school. Mortimer A. Warren, formerly the principal of Avery Normal Institute in Charleston, came to Columbia as principal of this State Normal School for girls and young women. (Courtesy of the USC Collection.)

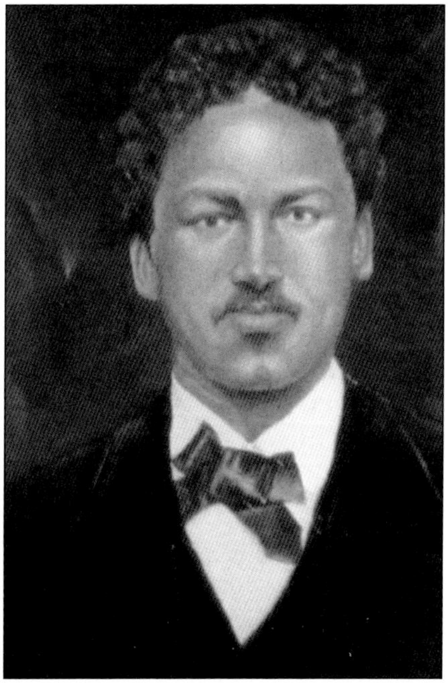

Richard T. Greener is seen here in a painting by Larry Lebby. In 1875, Greener was the first African American to serve on the faculty of the university, then South Carolina College. The first colored graduate of Harvard University, he was a good all-around scholar, a brilliant man, and a polished speaker; he had an international reputation. When the college's library suffered from acts of vandalism, Professor Greener was the one who rearranged the books and restored the 27,000-volume library to its normal condition. (Courtesy of the USC Collection.)

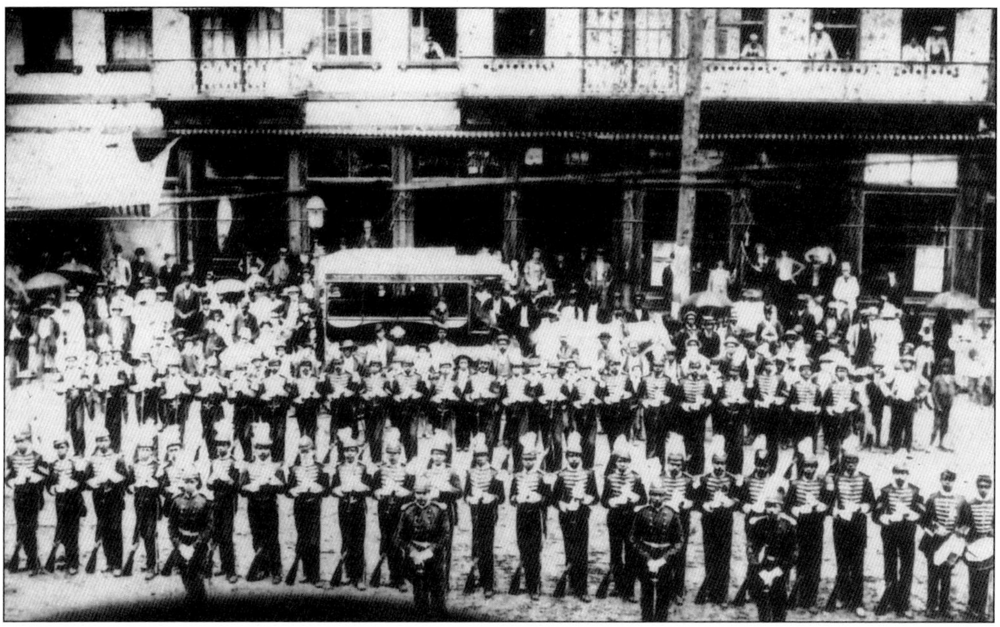

The Capital City Guard, a unit of the state militia, is seen here in the late 1890s. The city of Columbia during Reconstruction never had a Negro mayor, but most of the aldermen were Negroes. One of the aldermen was named Israel Smith. Charles M. Wilder was postmaster for approximately 16 years. At one time there was only one white man on the police force except the chief, Frank Nixon. For some time after Reconstruction, a Negro fire company and two troops of the National Guard served Columbia and the state of South Carolina. The name of the Negro company was the Vigilant, and it was housed on Assembly and Taylor Streets. (Courtesy of the McKissick Museum.)

Two

Columbia: The Capital City

Rapid development was noted during the 1890s in the suburbs of Columbia with the introduction of the electric trolley service. Row construction of bungalow-type houses reflected the trend of living near the trolley line.

Another attraction for growth was the Southern Railway. In the 1890s whites were brought to the area. However, about the early 1900s, both blacks and whites were drawn to the area. Whites were employed in the office of the railroad yards. Blacks came in as rail workers, domestics, laborers, and tradesmen.

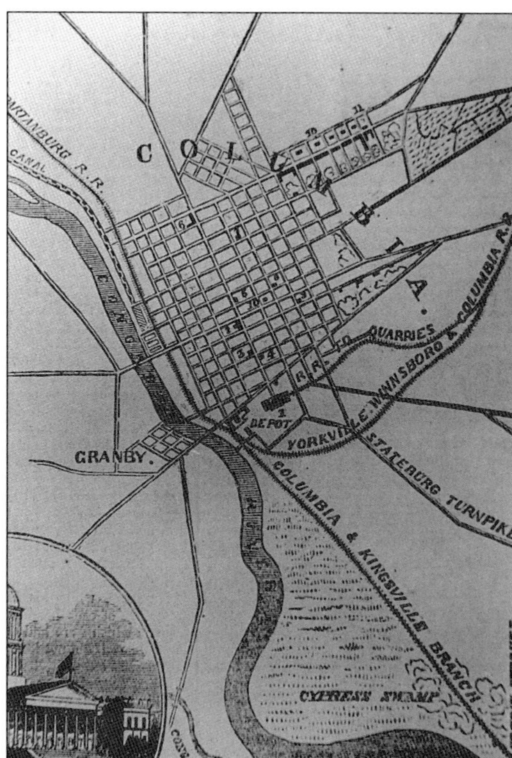

This plan of Columbia shows part of an imaginative view of the State House. (Courtesy of the Richland County Public Library.)

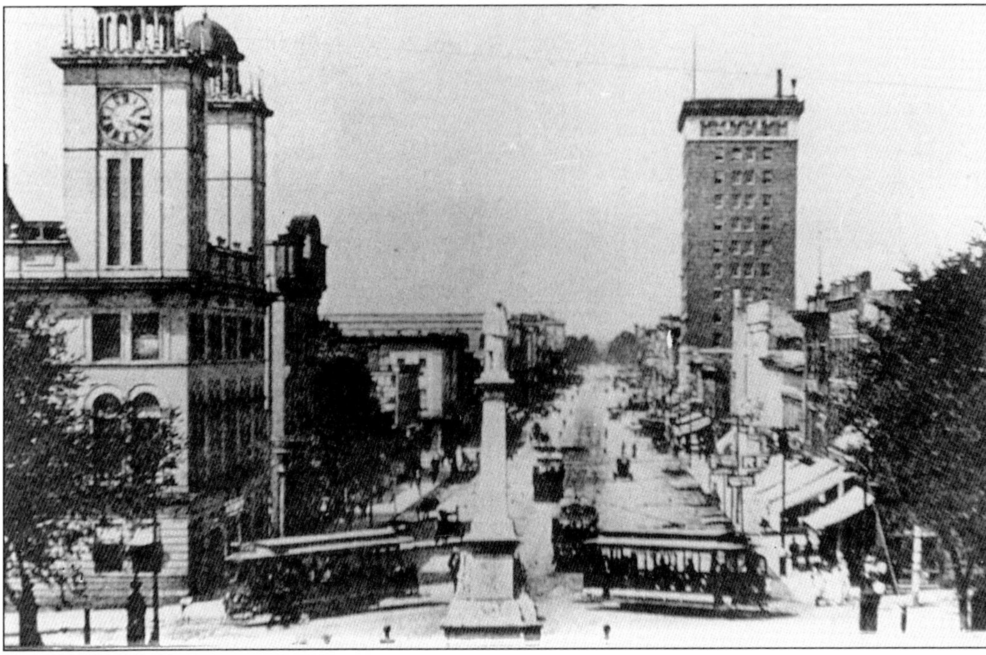

In this early 1900s view of Main Street, looking north, the old city hall is visible on the left. (Courtesy of the Richland County Public Library.)

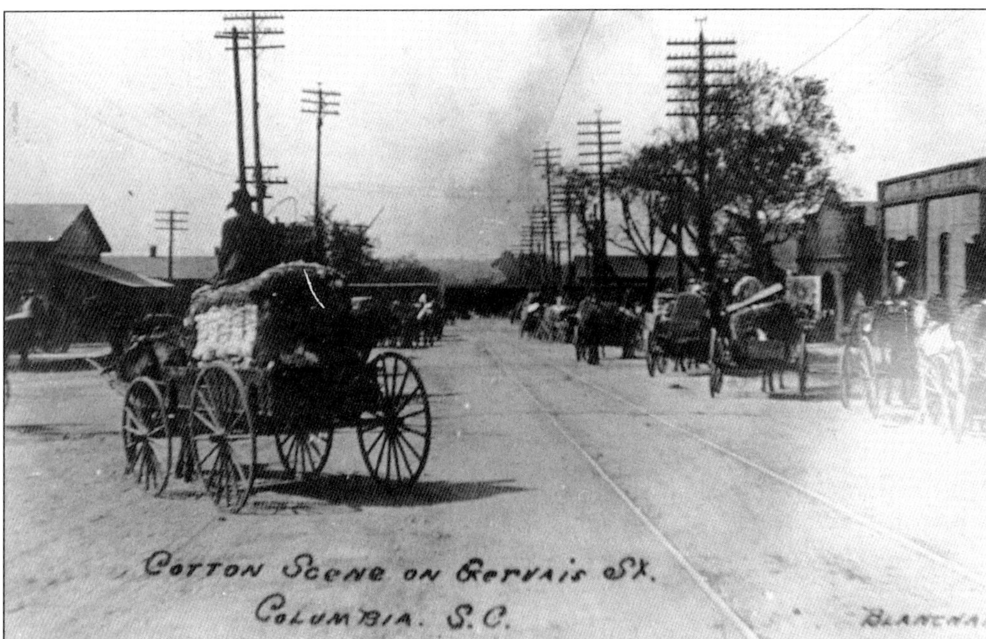

This is a cotton scene on Gervais Street. (Courtesy of the Richland County Public Library.)

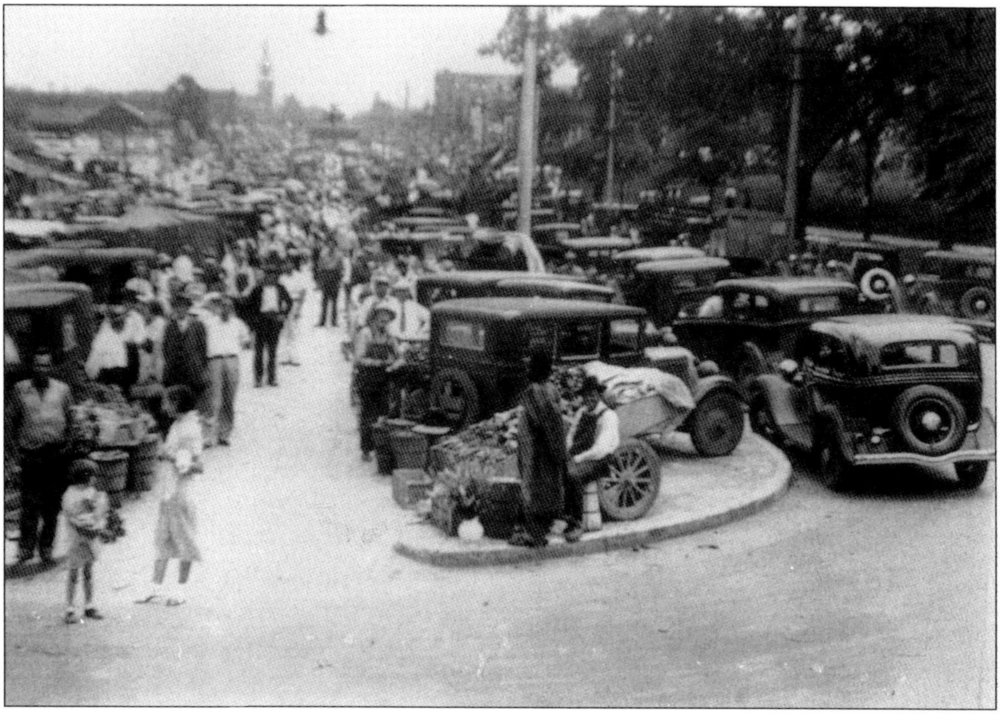

The Assembly Street market is pictured here, *c.* 1940. (Courtesy of the Richland County Public Library.)

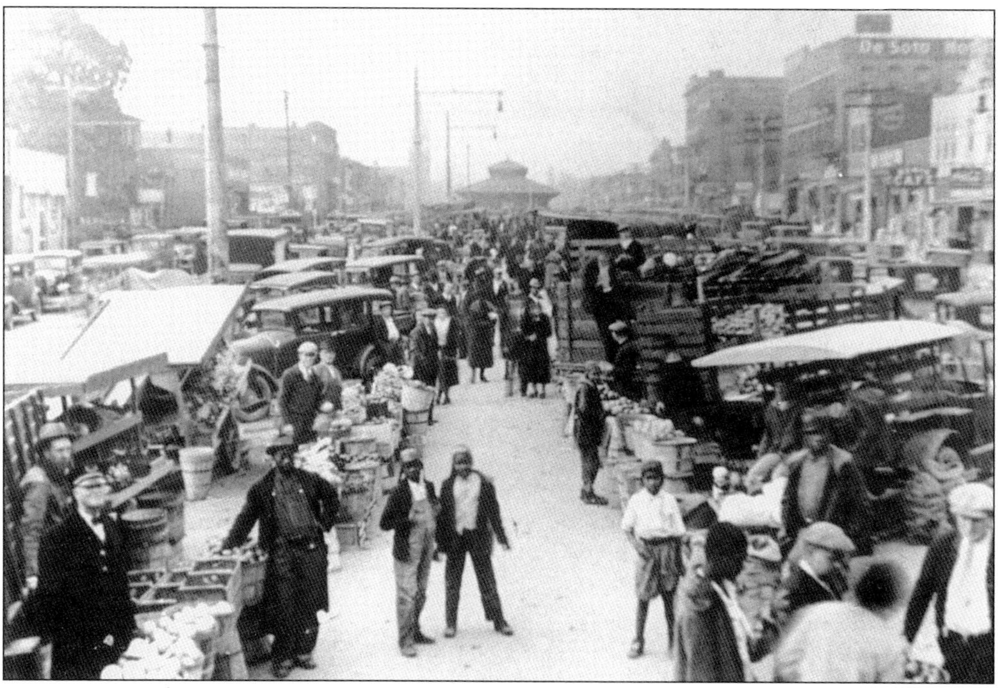

Another busy Assembly Street market scene is pictured here, *c.* 1940. (Courtesy of the Richland County Public Library.)

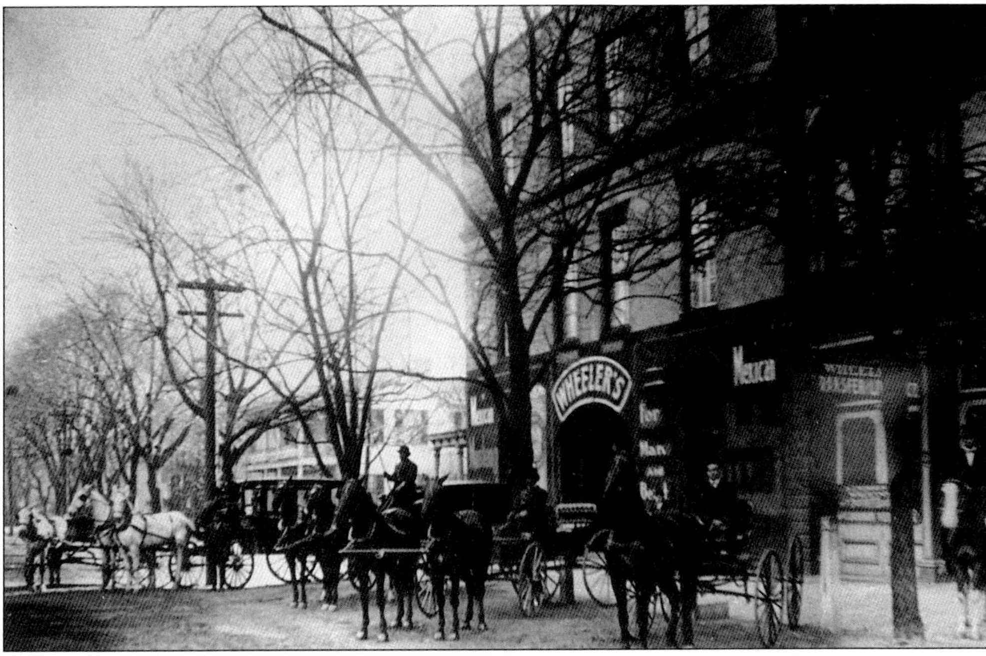

Before the automobile became the king of the road, Wheeler's Transfer and Livery Co. offered Columbians "the most stylish carriages and turnouts" in town during the early 1900s. (Courtesy of the Richland County Public Library.)

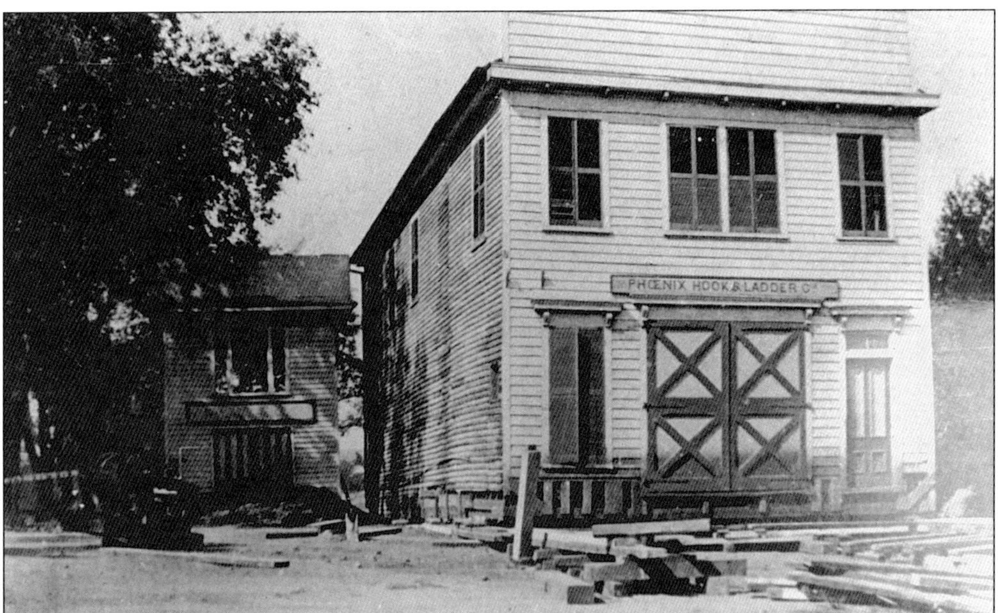

Throughout most of the 19th century, Columbia's fires were fought by a number of volunteer fire companies. One such organization was the Phoenix Hook & Ladder Company, which originated in 1872 and was located on Assembly Street. However, the company closed its doors closed forever in 1893. In 1903, the city organized its own fire department. (Courtesy of the Richland County Public Library.)

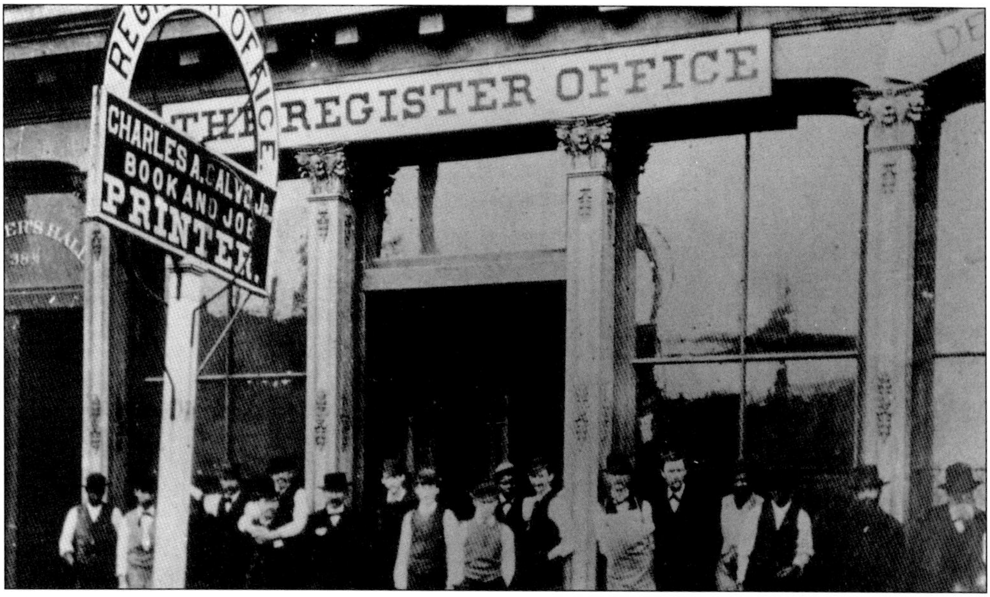

Editors, reporters, and other employees lined up in front of the *Columbia Register* newspaper office on the 1300 block of Main Street for this photo in the early 1890s. Few of them knew that the *Register*'s days were numbered. Begun just ten years after the Civil War in 1875, the *Register* served as a weekly, than a semi-weekly, and finally as a daily, before finally going under in 1898. (Courtesy of the Richland County Public Library.)

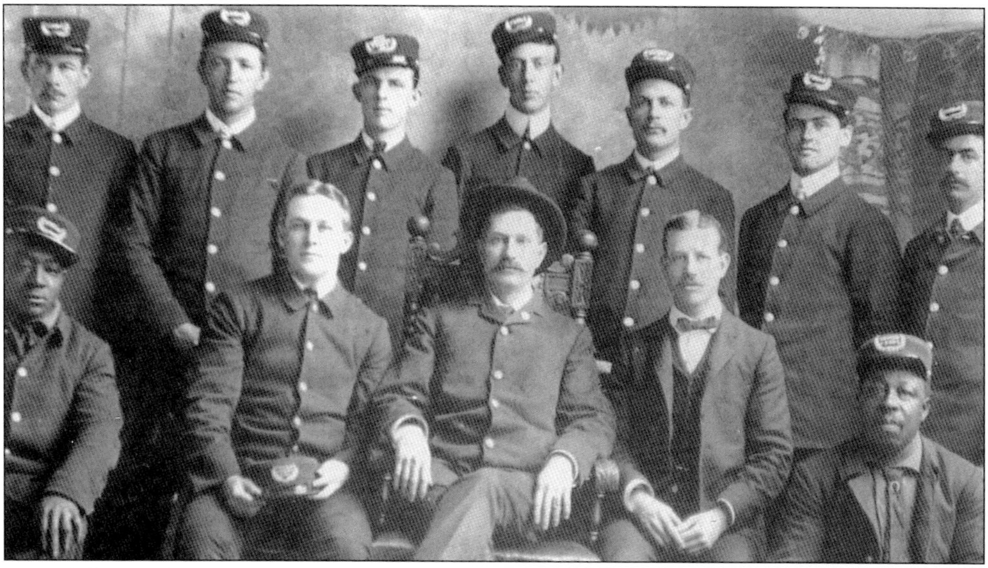

From left to right in this April 1903 photograph are (front row) West Ruff, J.H. Gaston, W.J. May (chief), E.A. Allworden, and Henry Williams; (back row) ? Medlin, J.B. Shroeder, John Carr, William Starling, Harry Garner, ? Cromer, and Bob Dixon. Columbia had two black fire engine companies under the old volunteer system: the Vigilant, organized in 1866, and the Enterprise, founded years later. John Dennison was the first captain of the Vigilant, and Joe Randall was the first captain of the Enterprise. African-American firemen were paid $20 a month. (Courtesy of the Columbia Fire Dept.)

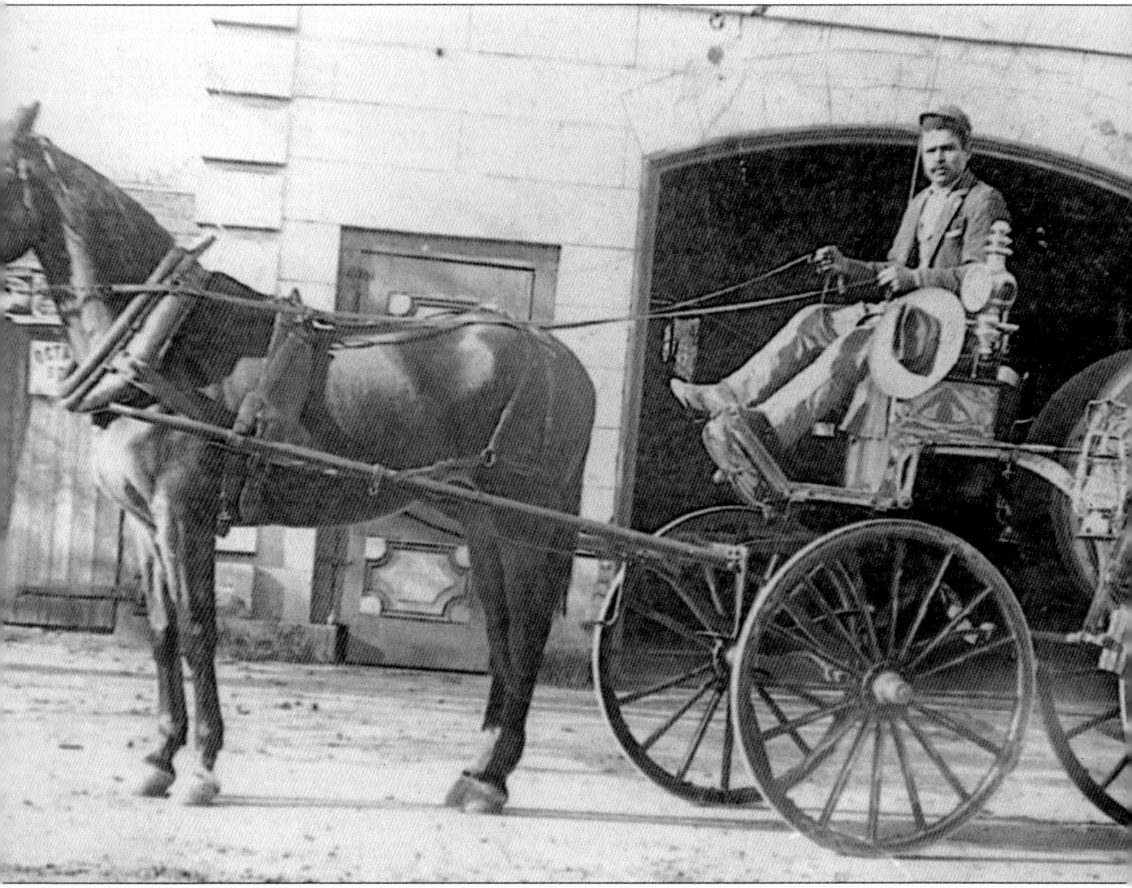

A black man drives a firemen's steamer on Main Street, *c.* 1899. Columbia's fire units engaged in tournaments with other African-American companies throughout the Carolinas and frequently won first prize, competing against companies from Charleston, Greenville, and other towns. These companies competed to see which was the fastest in getting to the scene of a supposed fire and putting its equipment into action. They enjoyed a healthy rivalry, and holidays were frequently made the occasion for these tournaments.

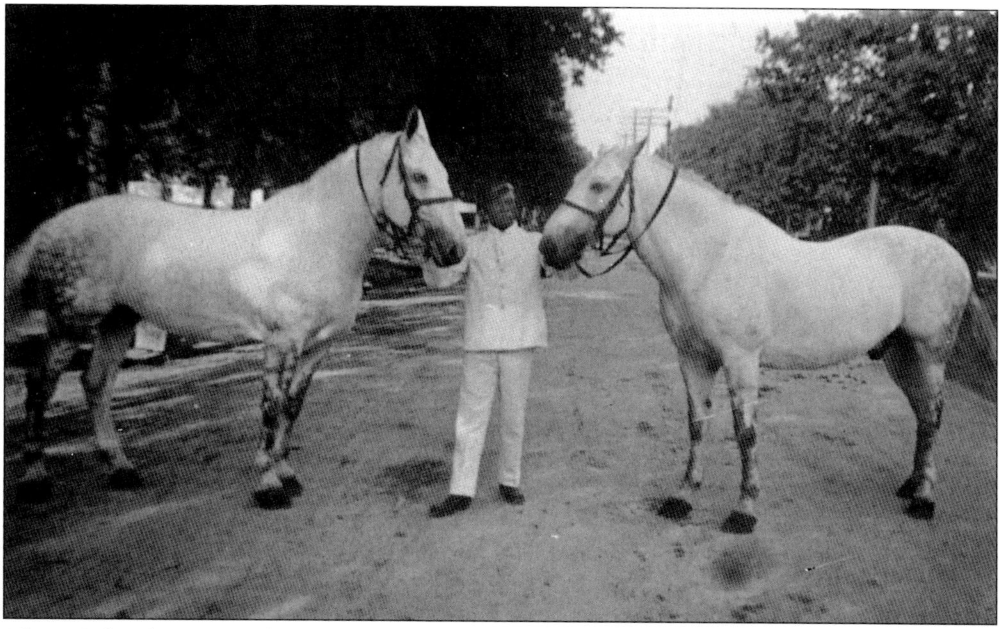

When Columbia opened its paid fire department, African-American firemen were not given the opportunity to prove themselves as only white firemen were hired. However, African-American drivers, like the one above, who diligently drove the horse-drawn fire engines, continued their legacy. (Courtesy of the Columbia Fire Dept.)

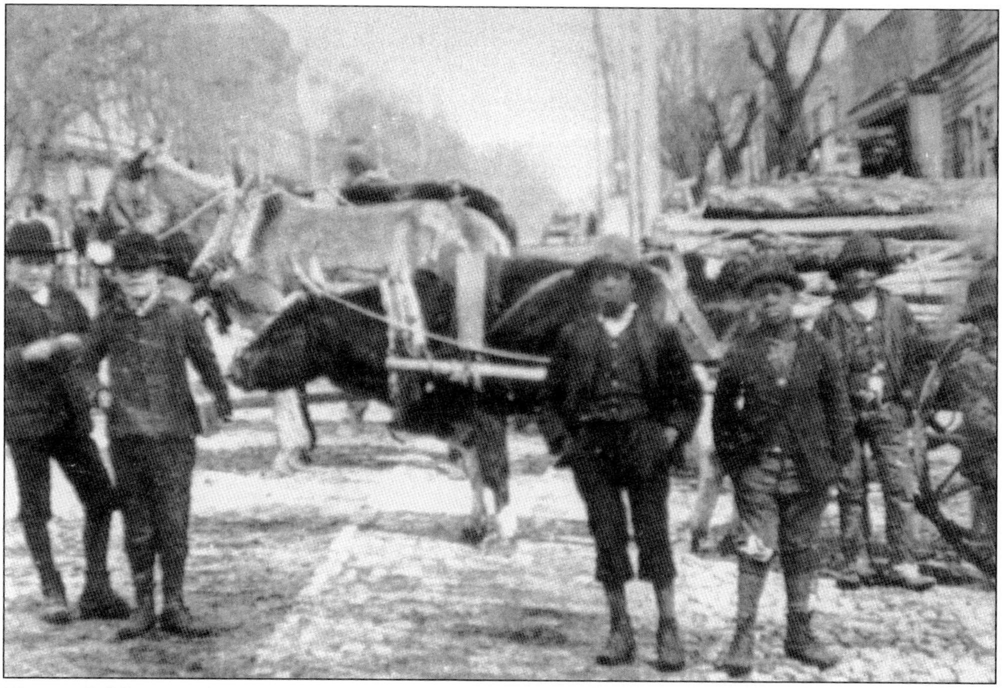

These children make a little extra money by selling firewood on Washington Street in 1887. (Courtesy of the Richland County Public Library.)

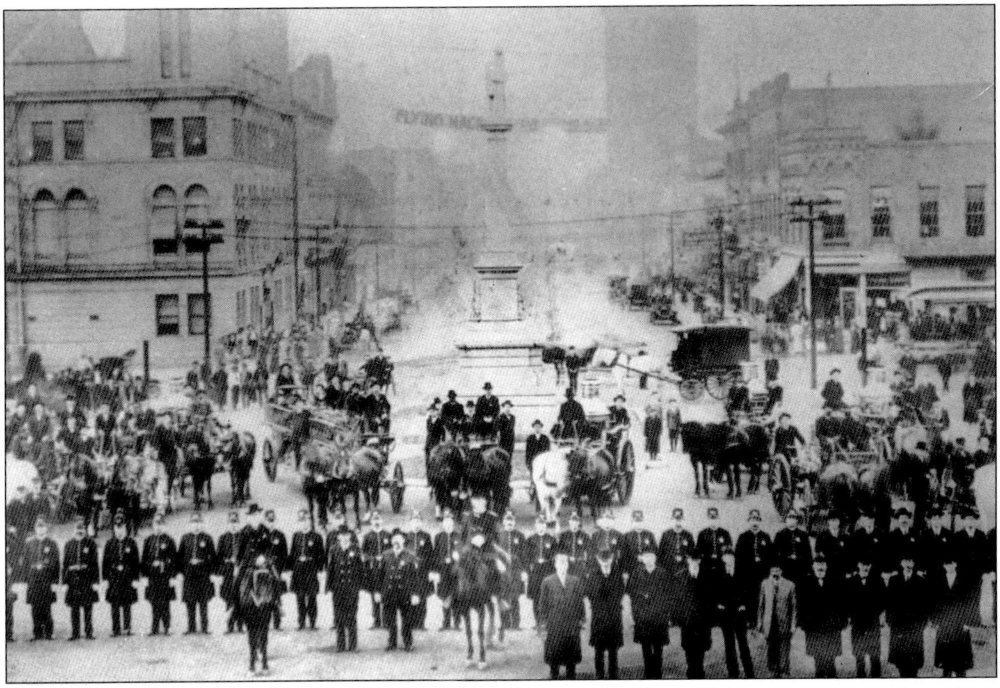

An annual report by the police to the city council in 1906 indicated that two African-American officers were hired by the Columbia Police Department to drive the horse-drawn patrol wagon. (Courtesy of the Columbia Police Dept.)

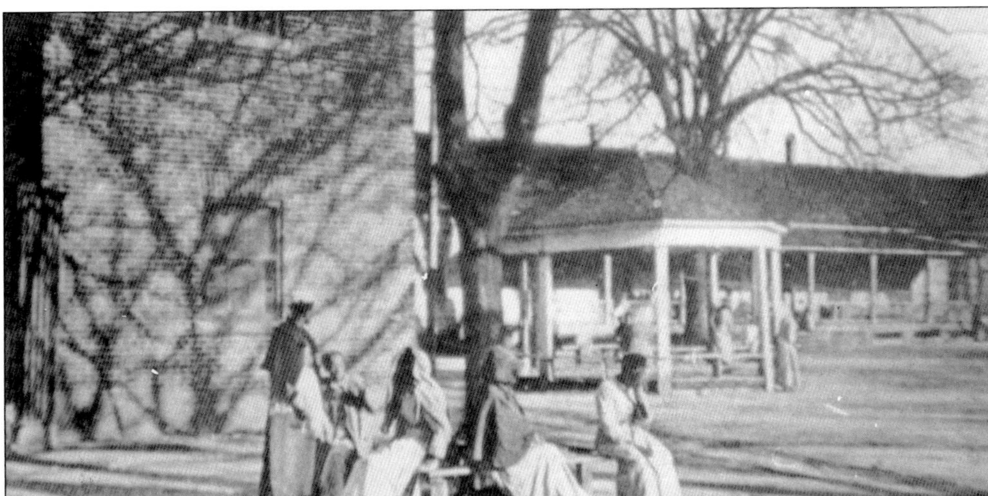

Black female patients and their attendants sit outside the rear wing of the Mills Building in the early 1900s. In 1828 South Carolina opened the South Carolina Lunatic Asylum, one of the nation's first state-supported institutions for people who suffered from mental illness. A few blacks were admitted before 1848, when the legislature officially permitted their entrance. After that, the efforts to admit blacks, mostly slaves, accelerated. Today the South Carolina Department of Mental Health extends across the state with inpatient facilities, mental health centers, and mental health clinics. (Courtesy of the State Dept. of Mental Health.)

Nathaniel Jerome Frederick was an aggressive lawyer of the South. After college, he held a teaching profession and, later, he secured a legal education. In 1913, Frederick was admitted to the South Carolina Bar. Frederick represented many of the famous cases in the annals of South Carolina concerning African Americans. The "Lowman Case," a lynching, was one of these cases. Frederick was a staff attorney for the NAACP and was also a founder and editor of the *Palmetto Leader*, South Carolina's leading black newspaper. (Courtesy of the United Black Fund.)

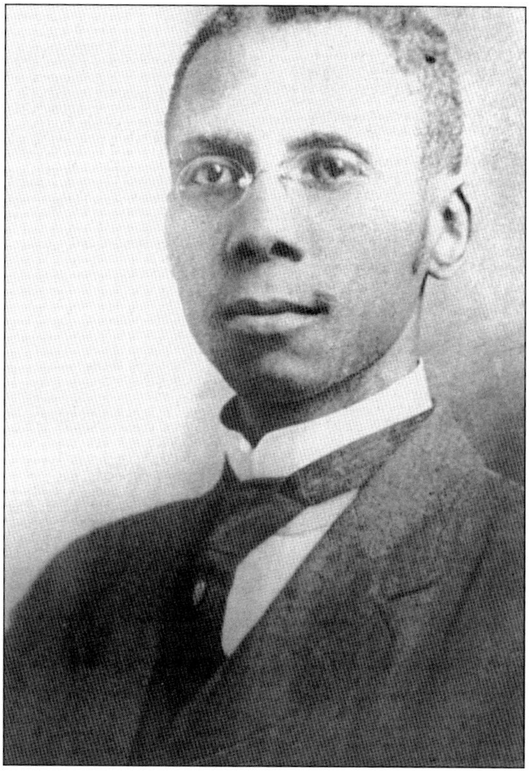

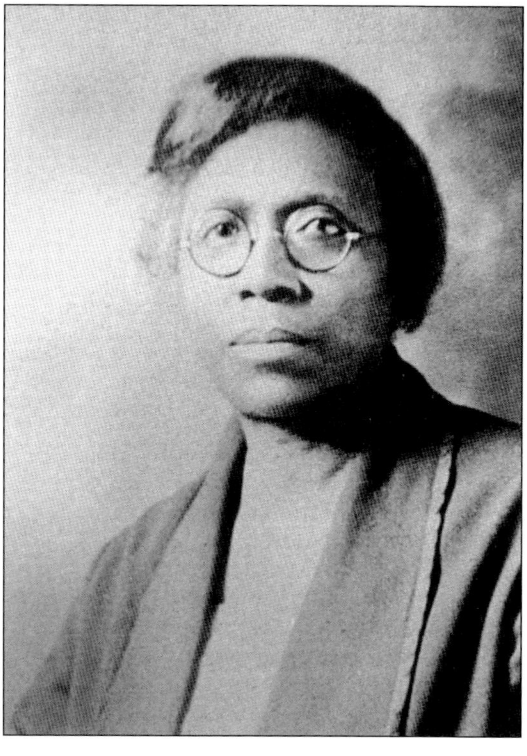

One of Columbia's most noted physicians was Dr. Matilda A. Evans. She was actively engaged in the medical profession for 37 years and founded the Taylor Lane Hospital, the first hospital for African Americans. A number of Columbia's leading surgeons did their first surgical work at this hospital. Evans also founded the South Carolina Good Health Association. (Courtesy of the United Black Fund.)

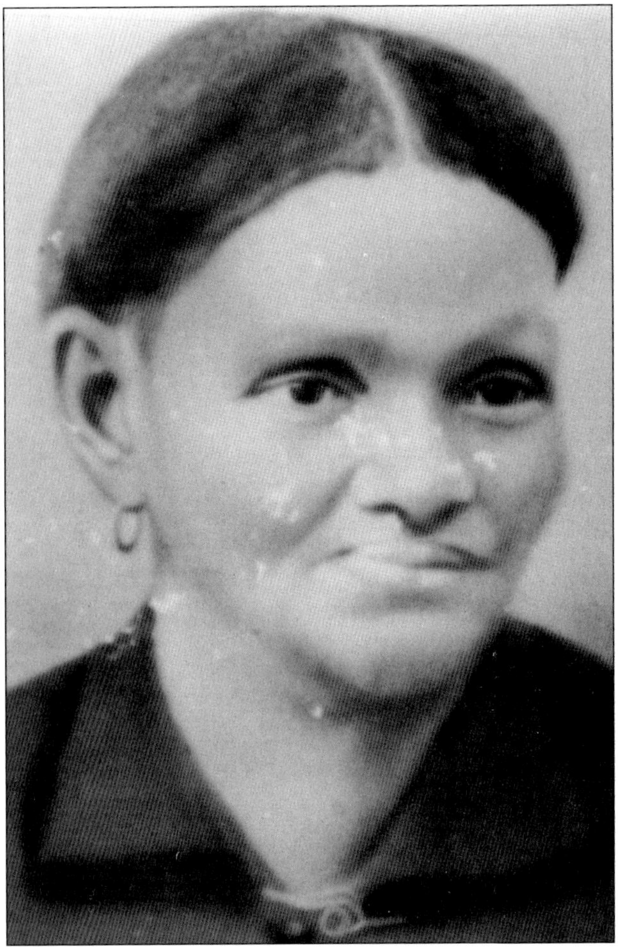

Agnes Jackson Simons (1831–1907), a baker and laundress, was the daughter of Celia Mann. Upon her mother's death, Agnes inherited her mother's house and estate, where she lived for 40 years as the head of a large, multigenerational family.

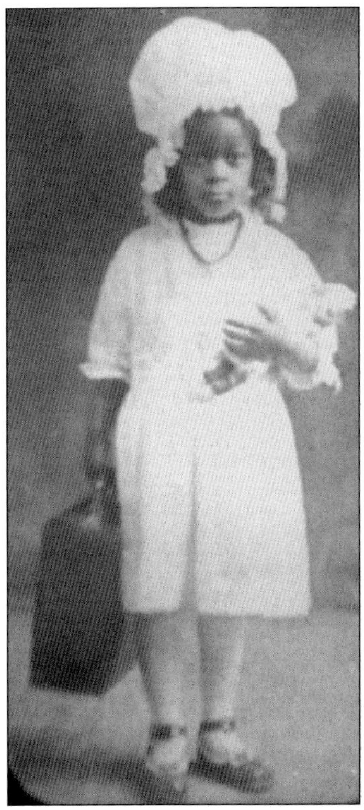

Little Miss Marquerite Summers was born in 1911 and was two years old when this picture was taken. She lived in Scribbers Alley.

Three

BLACK ENTERPRISE

Black entrepreneurships could be found throughout Columbia. Starting in the 1900s through the 1960s, there were many grocery stores, pharmacies, restaurants, sweet shops, barber shops, taxi services, and numerous other businesses. Barber shops were one of the leading categories of personal services in Columbia. Barbers catered mainly to white clientele. Most of these businesses were single proprietorships operated as the major source of income with family labor. An example is a four-generation family, the Leevy-Johnson family, a strong business and political family in Columbia.

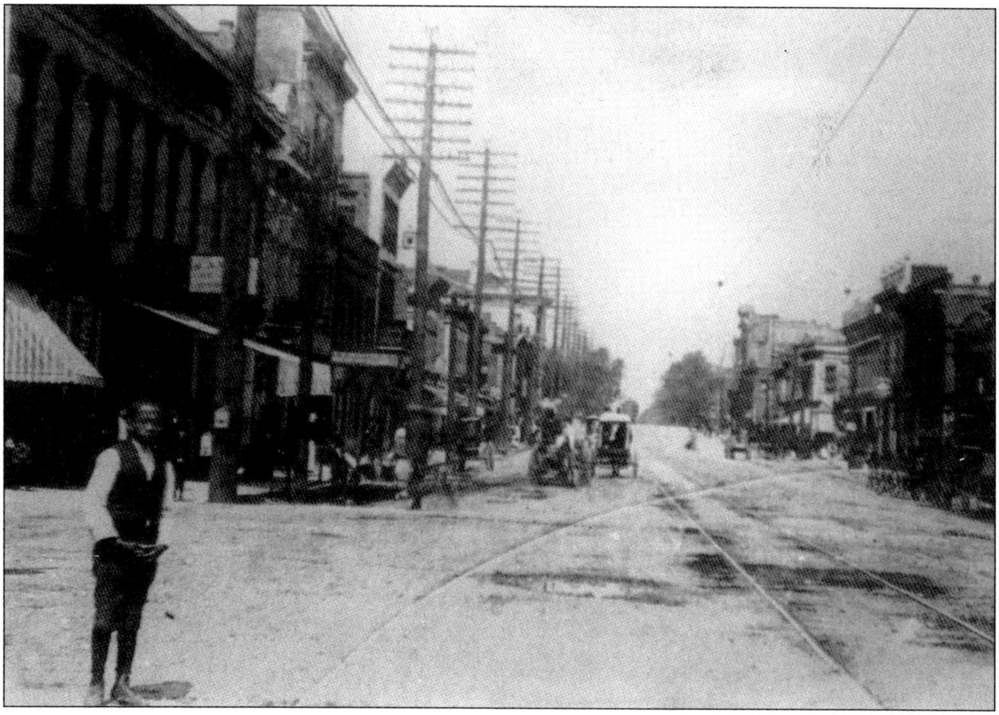

This is a downtown Columbia view of Main Street (Courtesy of the Richland County Public Library.)

14 THE STATE CLASSIFIED DIRECTORY, 1927-28

PINCKNEY'S FUNERAL HOME

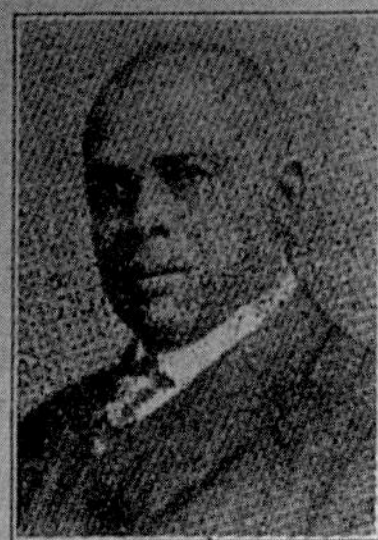

UNDERTAKERS AND LICENSED EMBALMERS

AMBULANCE SERVICE
Complete Motor Equipment

"As good as the best and better than the rest and prices less"

Open All the Time

Office 5707 Res. 7765

1006 WASHINGTON ST. COLUMBIA, S. C.

JOHNSON-BRADLEY FUNERAL HOME

UNDERTAKERS—FUNERAL DIRECTORS

The Best Equipped Establishment Serving Colored People in South Carolina

PROMPT EFFICIENT SERVICE

We Come When You Call—Anytime—Anywhere

PARK and WASHINGTON STS. PHONE 3512

MANIGUALT AND WILLIAMS
UNDERTAKERS
and Funeral Directors

AMBULANCE SERVICE
Courteous and Prompt Attention
First Class Establishment for Colored People
PHONES—OFFICE 8519—RESIDENCE 7242

714 MAIN STREET COLUMBIA, S. C.

OWEN & PAUL

MERCHANT TAILORS

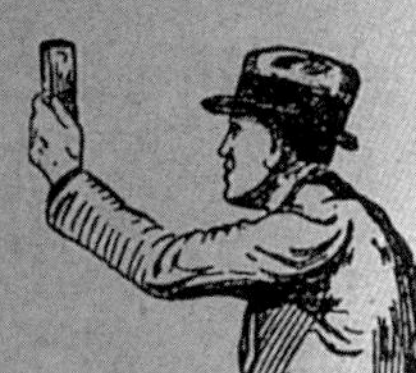

Suits and Overcoats Made To Measurement

ALTERING AND REPAIRING

CLEANING—PRESSING

HIGH CLASS WORKMANSHIP

1117 WASHINGTON ST. PHONE 6963

This page of advertisements was taken from the 1927–1928 State Classified Directory. (Courtesy of the Five Points Book Shop.)

I.S. Leevy was born in 1876 and was a very successful businessman in Columbia. Leevy was a merchant tailor in the early 1900s, during which time he owned and managed a department store. In the 1920s and 1930s, Leevy owned a service station; he was also a retail furniture dealer, farmer, and commercial hog-raiser. He was involved in New Home Development Company Real Estate, Leevy's Barber Shop, Leevy's Beauty Shop, and Leevy's Automobile Garage. His last business investment was Leevy's Funeral Home, which is still thriving today. (Courtesy of the United Black Fund.)

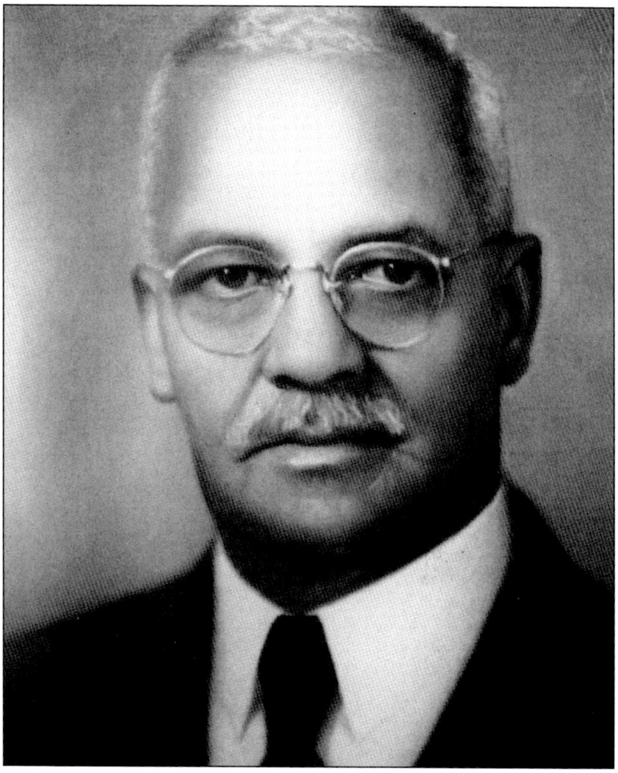

Below is the I.S. Leevy Department Store. (Courtesy of the McKissick Museum.)

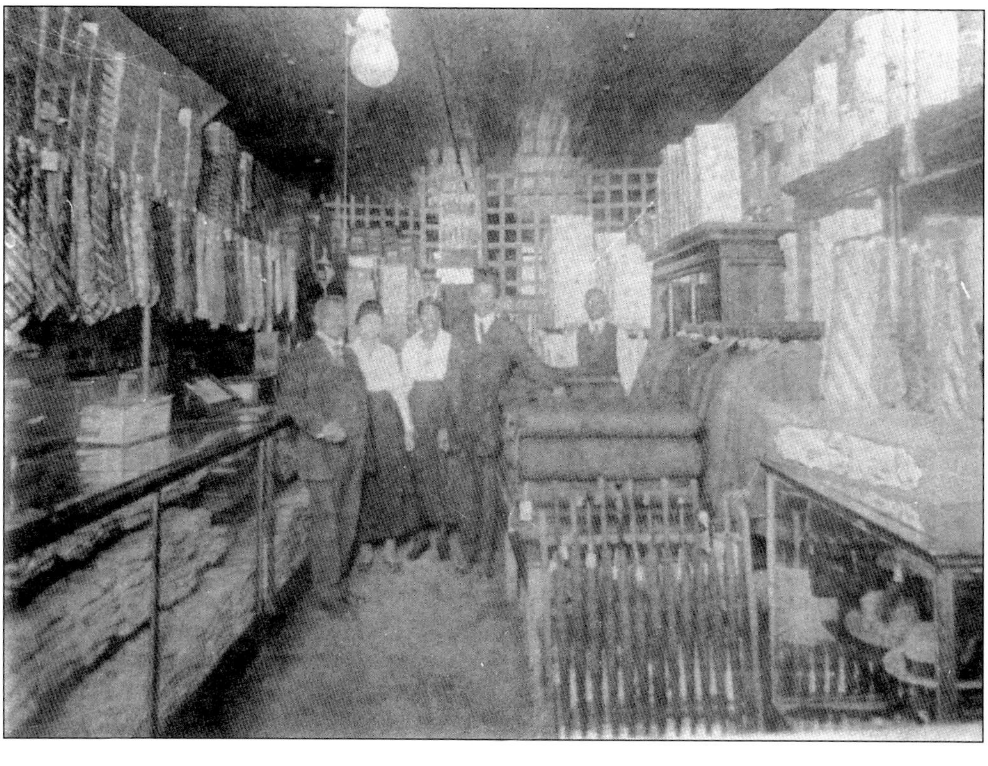

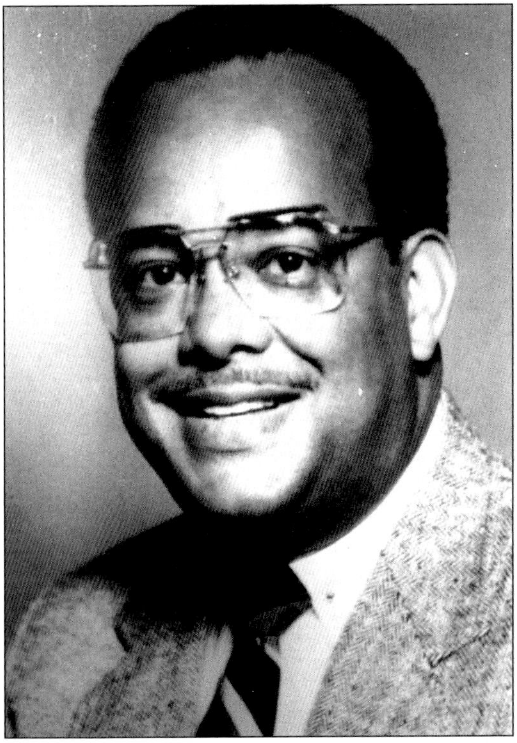

In I.S. Leevy's final years he became blind, but this did not slow him down. His grandson, I.S. Leevy-Johnson (seen at left), made certain his political life continued and carried on his business. I.S. Leevy died on December 9, 1968, at the age of 91. His grandson was later elected to the South Carolina House of Representatives in 1970; he was one of the first blacks elected since the era of Reconstruction. (Courtesy of the United Black Fund.)

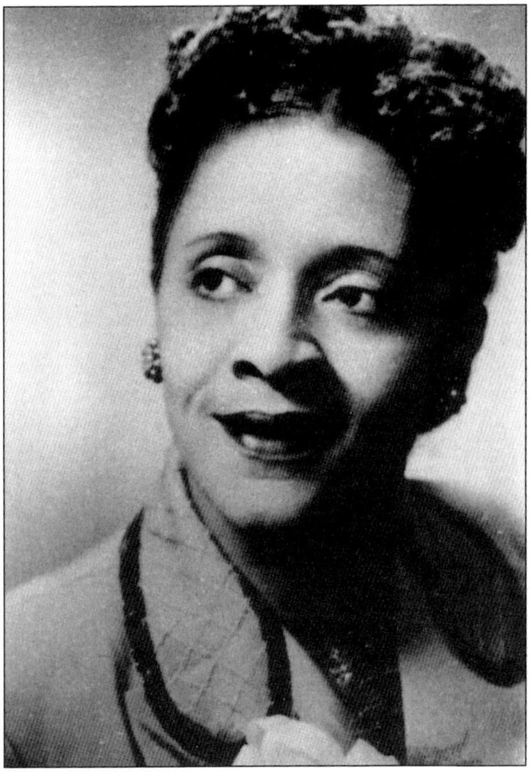

Anna May Manigault Hurley (1907–1976), at a young age, helped her parents run their funeral home. After the death of her father in 1940, Hurley decided to pursue her embalmer's licenses. She ran the Manigault-Hurley Funeral Home for 30 years. She also operated the Congaree Casket Company, which was founded by her father. (Courtesy of the Manigault-Hurley family.)

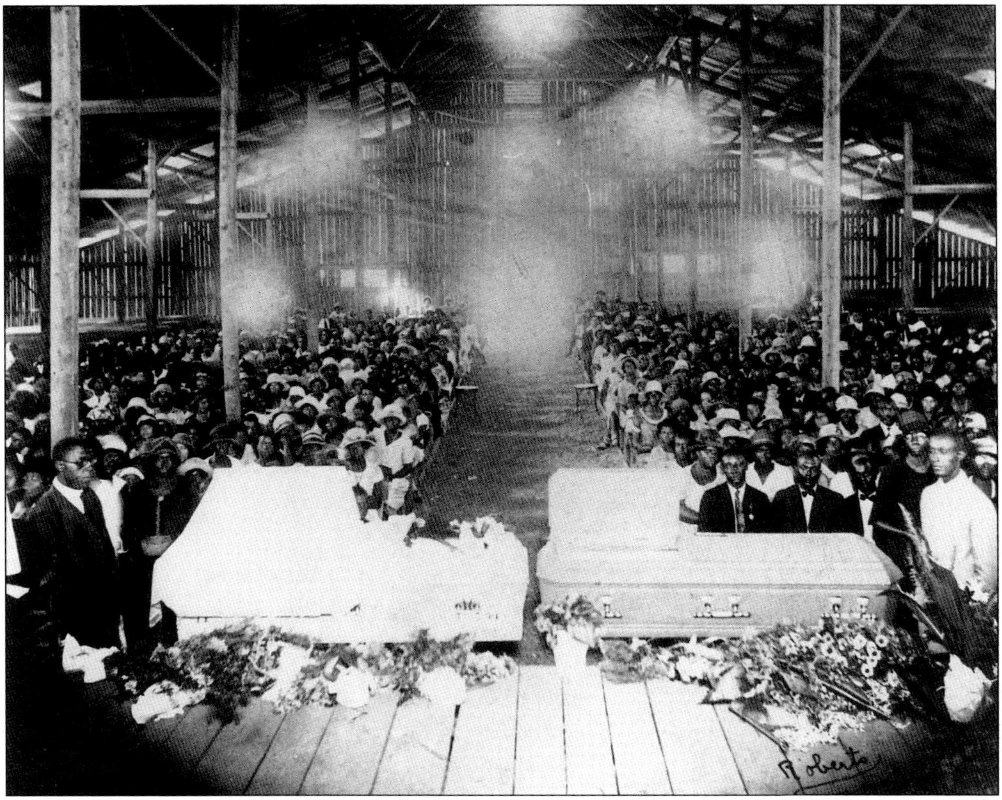

This photograph captures a double funeral, *c.* 1920. (Courtesy of the McKissick Museum.)

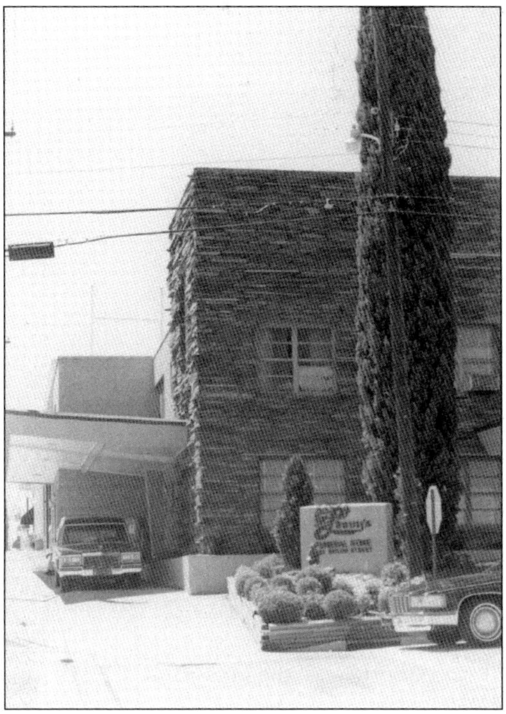

This is the Leevy Funeral Home as it appears in the year 2000.

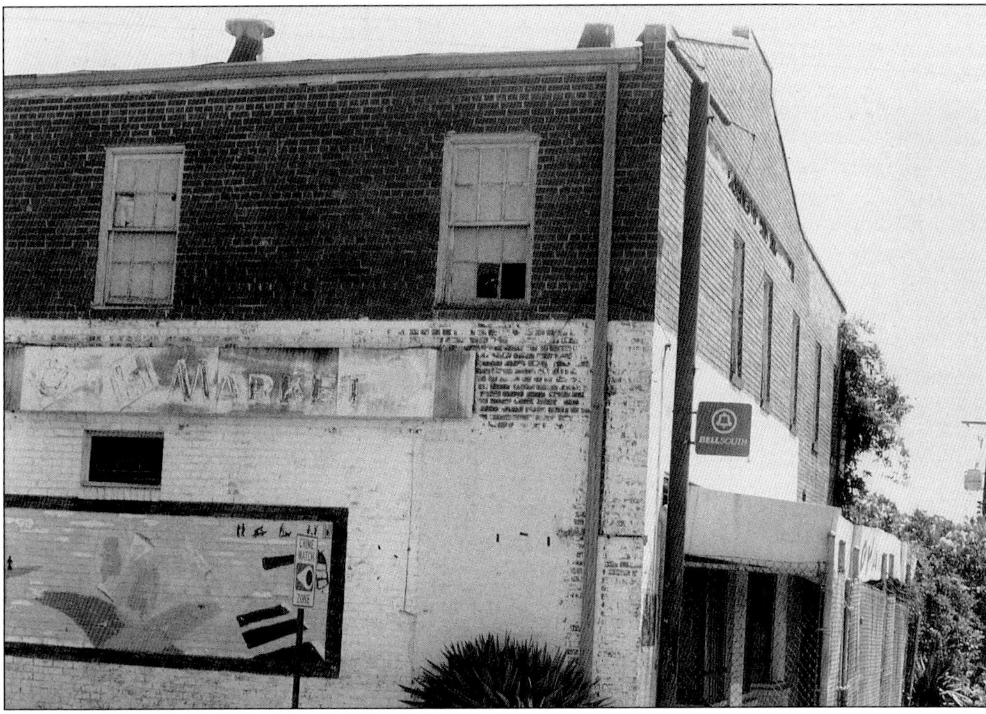

This is the former building of the Carpenter's Union.

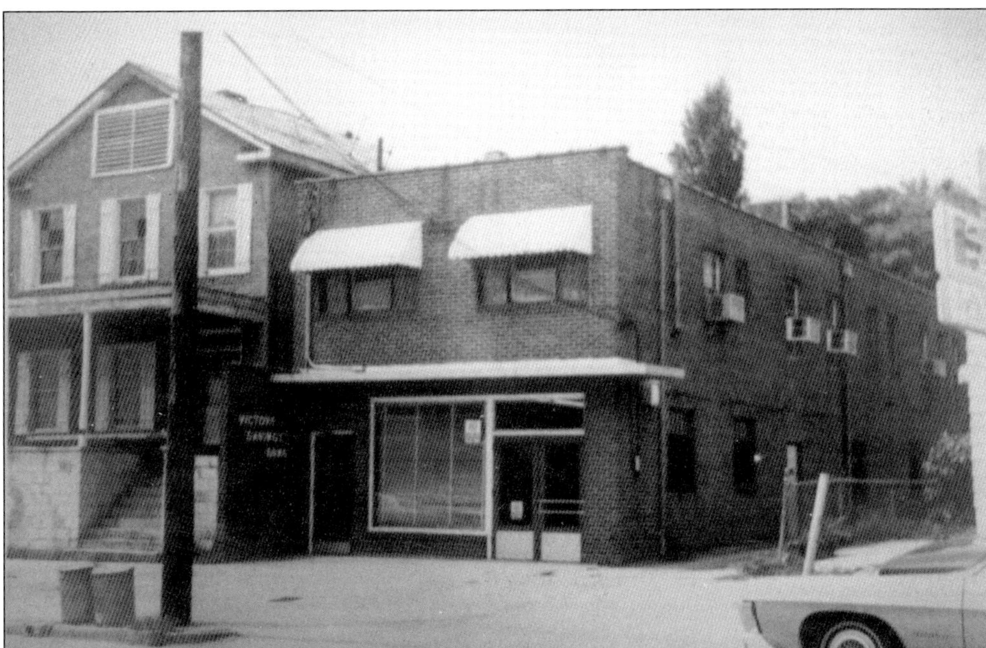

One unique development in Columbia during this time period was the establishment of the Victory Savings Bank in 1921. Dr. H.D.Monteith and members of his family founded this bank, the state's only minority-owned banking institution. (Courtesy of SCCL.)

The North Carolina Mutual and Provident Association built this structure in 1909, and the building became an integral part of the Washington Street business district. Two black physicians had offices in the building during the 1920s and other businesses, professionals, and institutions in the Mutual building provided goods and services to the African-American community. Other prominent businesses in the downtown area included the Blue Ribbon Taxi Company, the Mutual Grocery store, and several restaurants, food stores, and hairdressers.

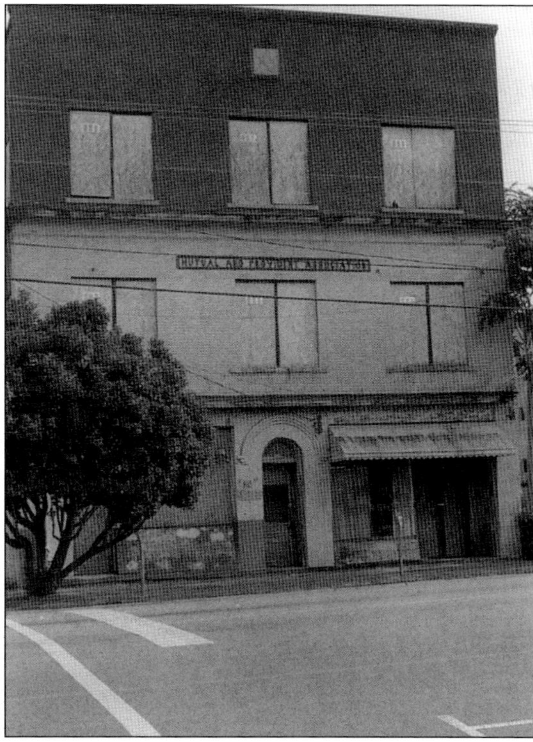

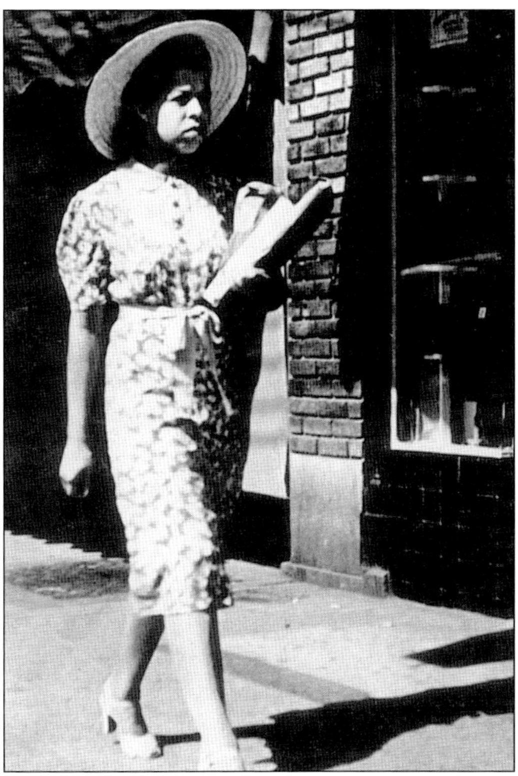

This smartly dressed young woman is walking down Columbia's Main Street. (Courtesy of the Titus family.)

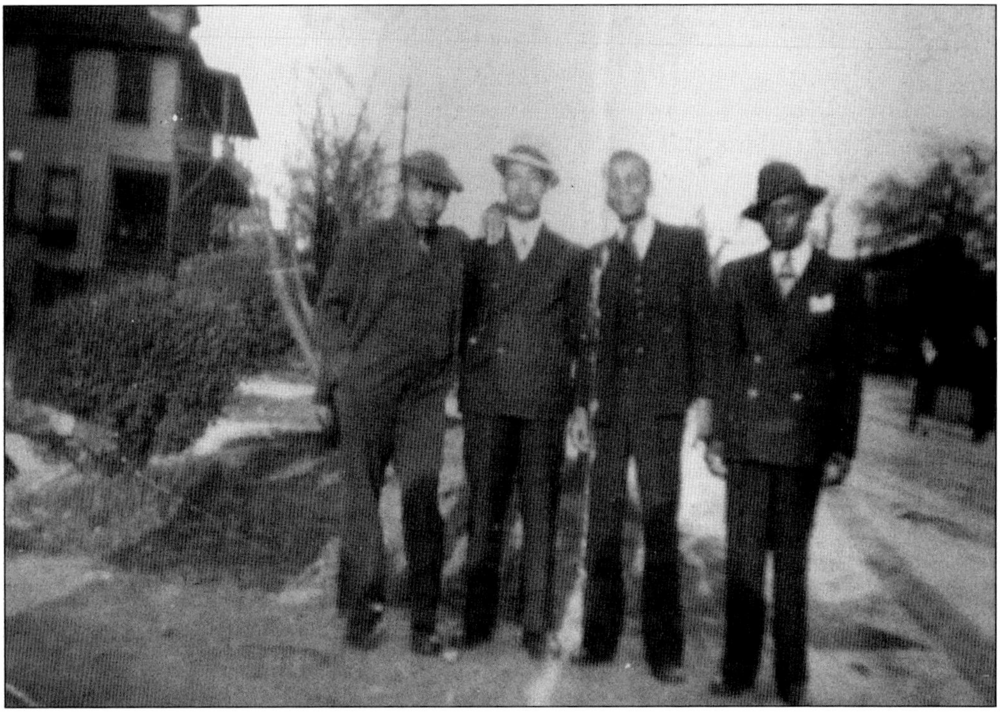

Four friends, dressed in suits and hats, pose for this *c.* 1930 photograph in Black Downtown. Black Downtown was adjacent to a black residential area and was the oldest black business area in Columbia. (Courtesy of Caroline Summers Floyd.)

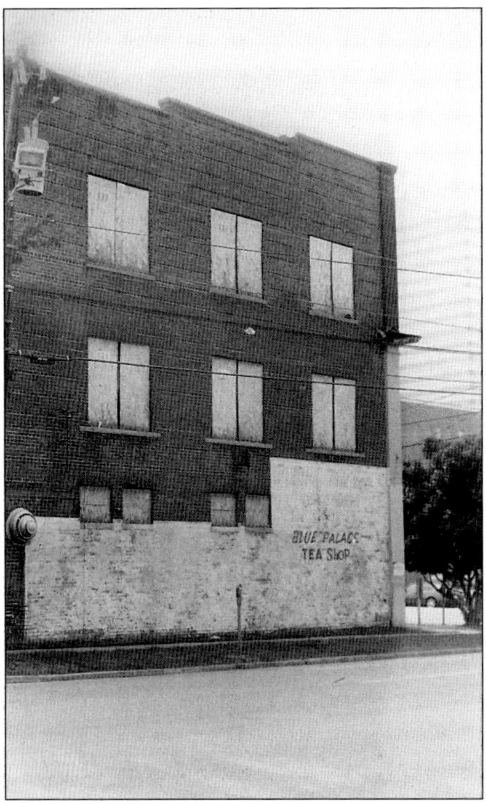

The Blue Palace Tea Shop, seen here in the year 2000, was listed in 1903 City Directory. This building housed various tenants through the years, including restaurants, tea shops, stores, and various offices on the first floor.

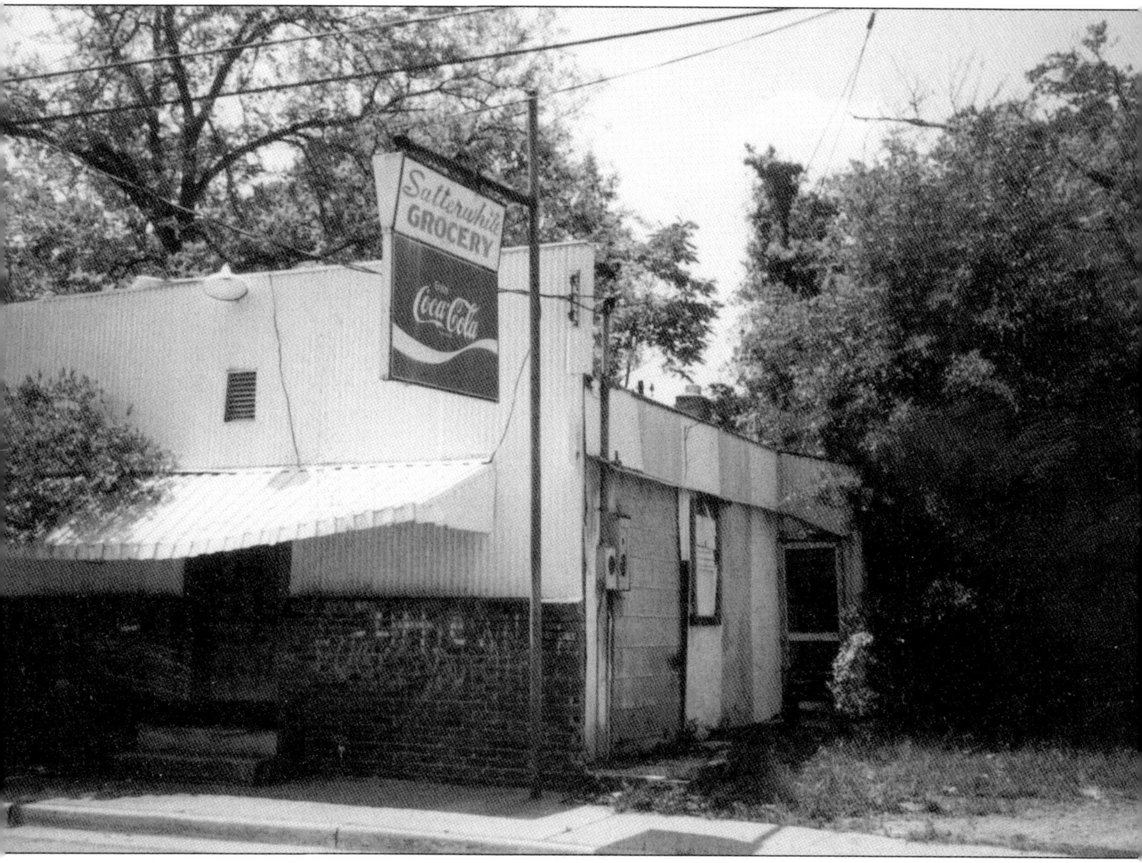

Here is the Satterwhite Grocery in the year 2000.

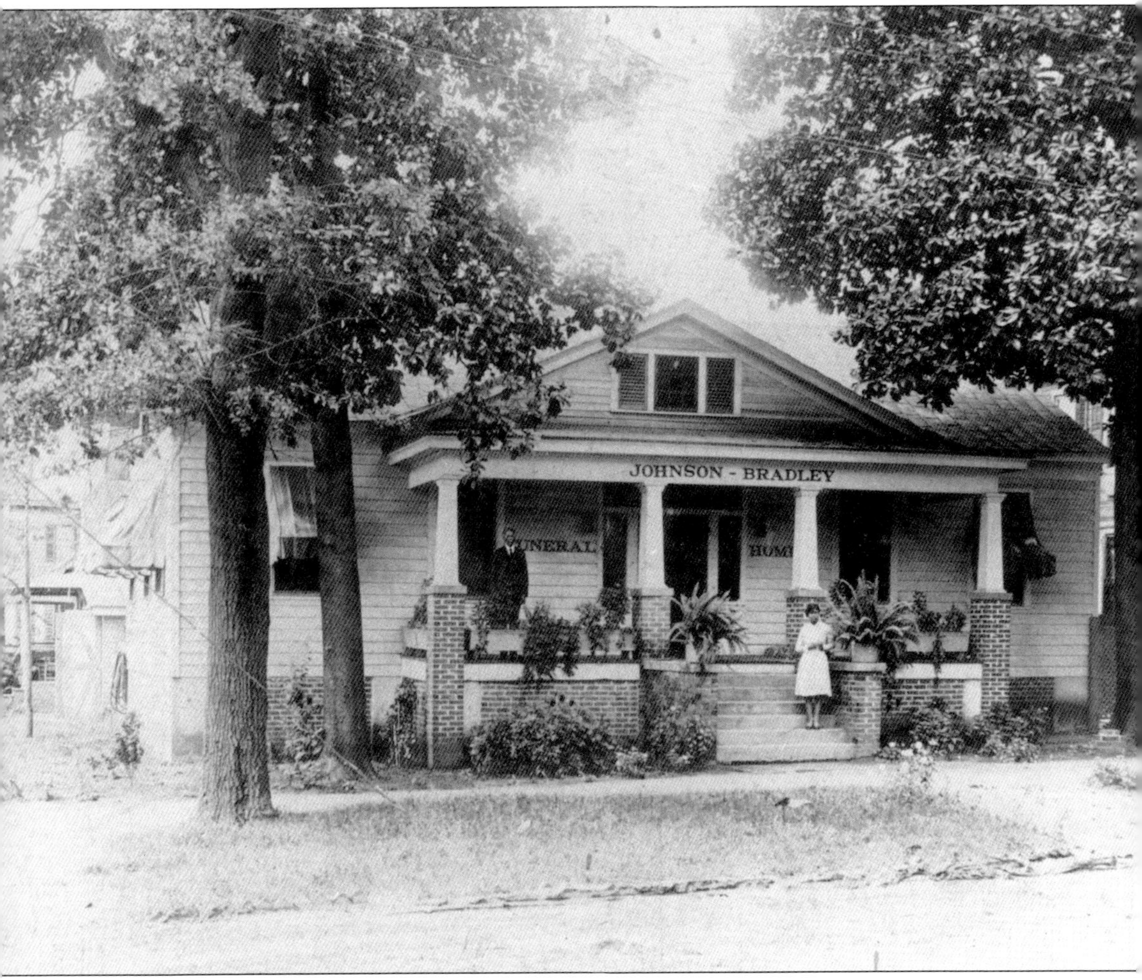

Pictured here is the Johnson-Bradley Funeral Home. The date of this photograph is unknown. (Courtesy of the McKissick Museum.)

Richard Samuel Roberts was a master photographer. (Courtesy of the United Black Fund.)

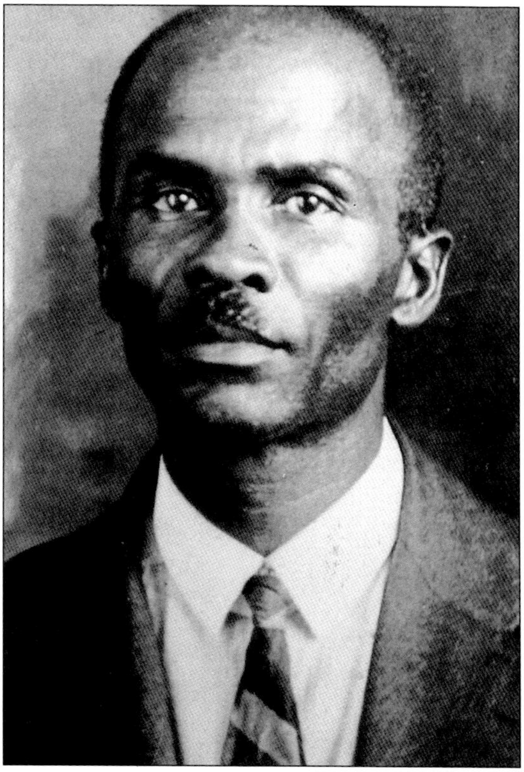

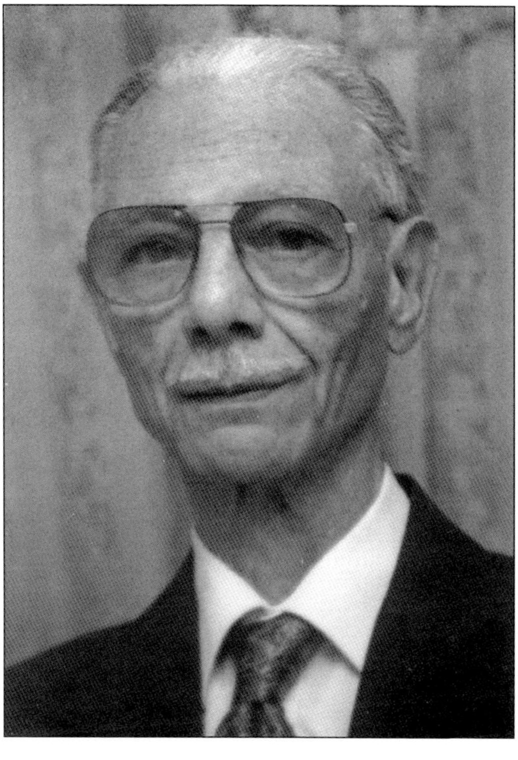

Edwin R. Russell was a nuclear chemist. (Courtesy of the United Black Fund.)

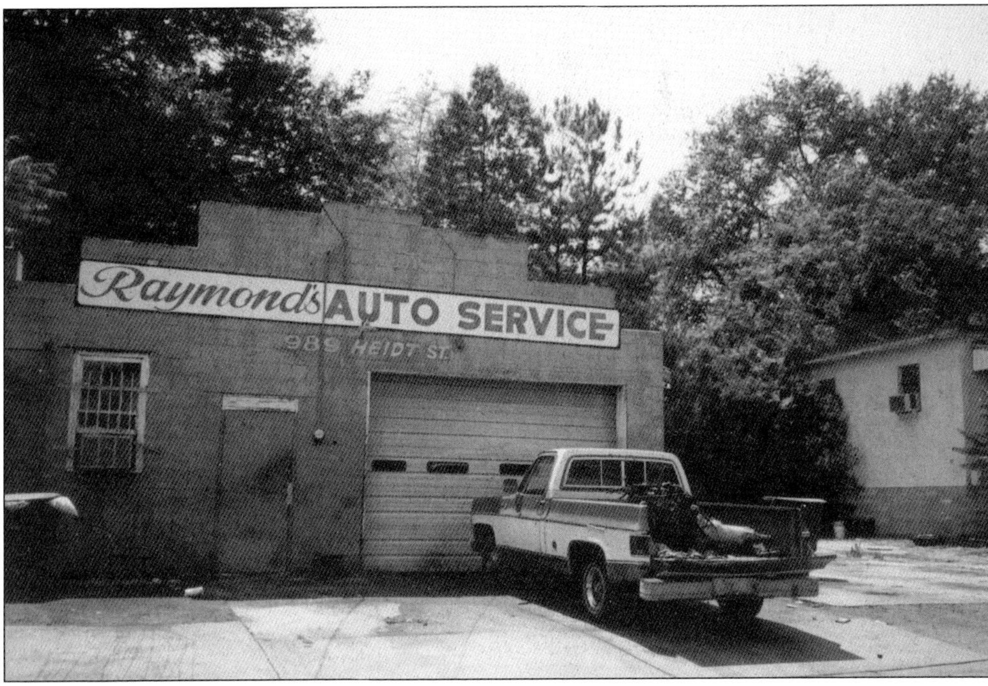

Raymond's Auto Service is seen here in 2000. This shop can be found in the Waverly community.

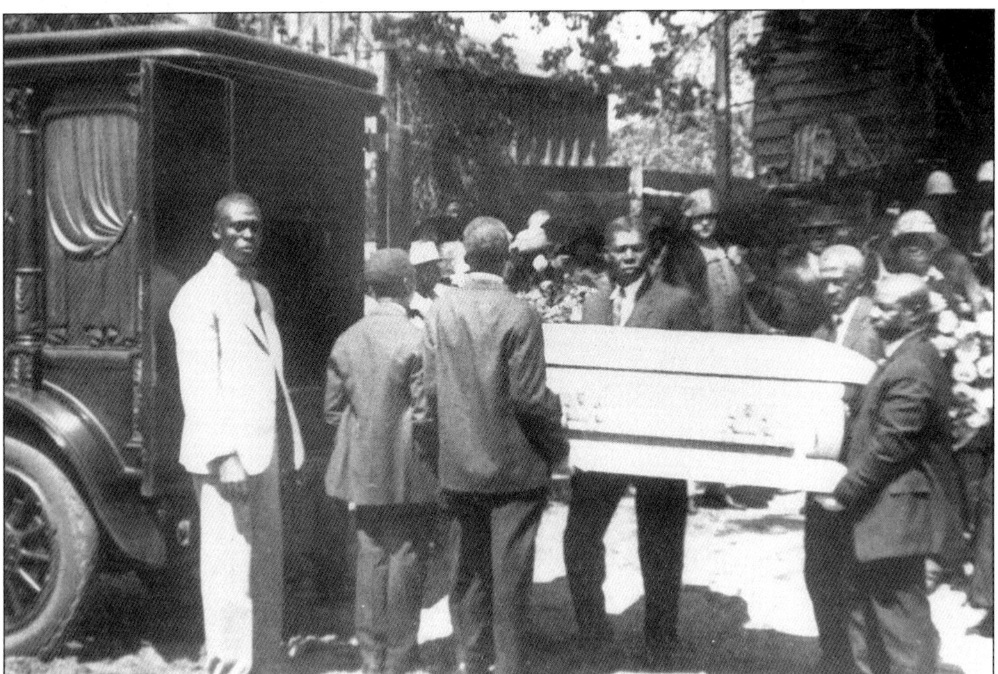

This *c*. 1926 Columbia funeral was conducted by Manigault-Gaten-Williams. Mrs. Manigault is the woman in the hat, center rear. This photograph was taken by Richard Samuel Roberts. (Courtesy of the Manigault-Hurley family.)

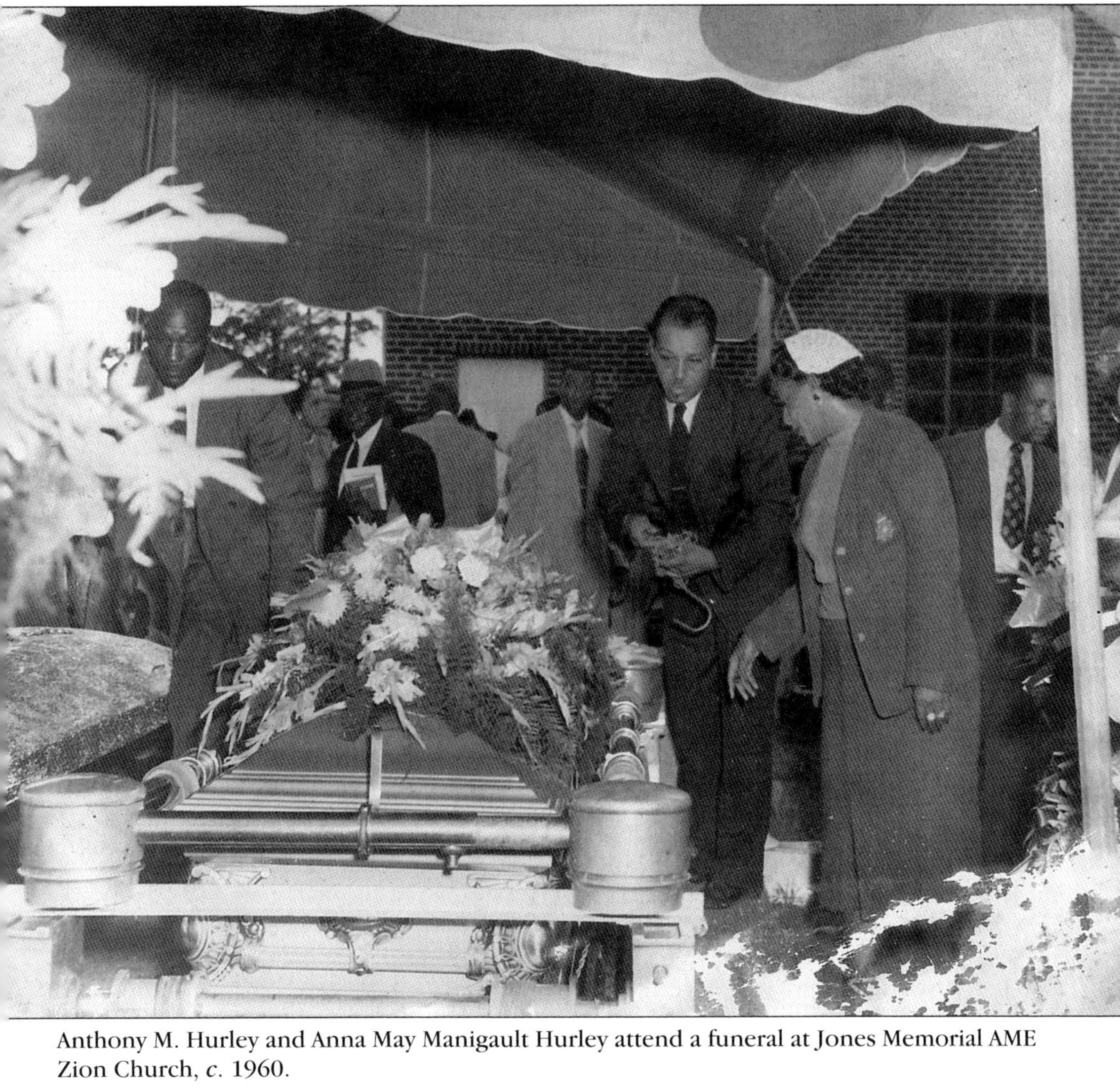

Anthony M. Hurley and Anna May Manigault Hurley attend a funeral at Jones Memorial AME Zion Church, *c.* 1960.

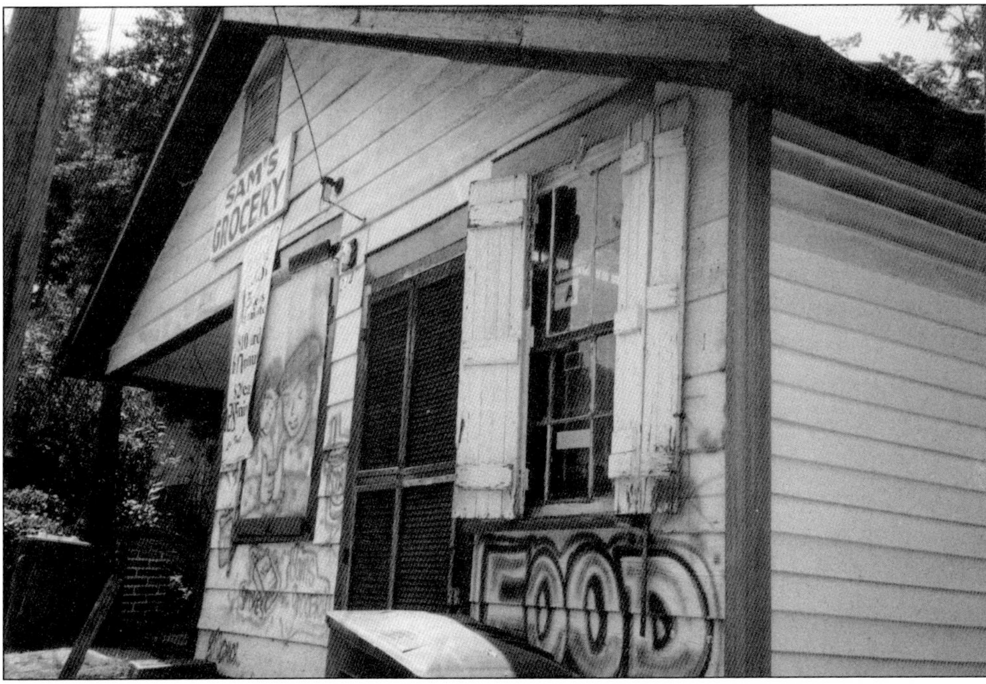

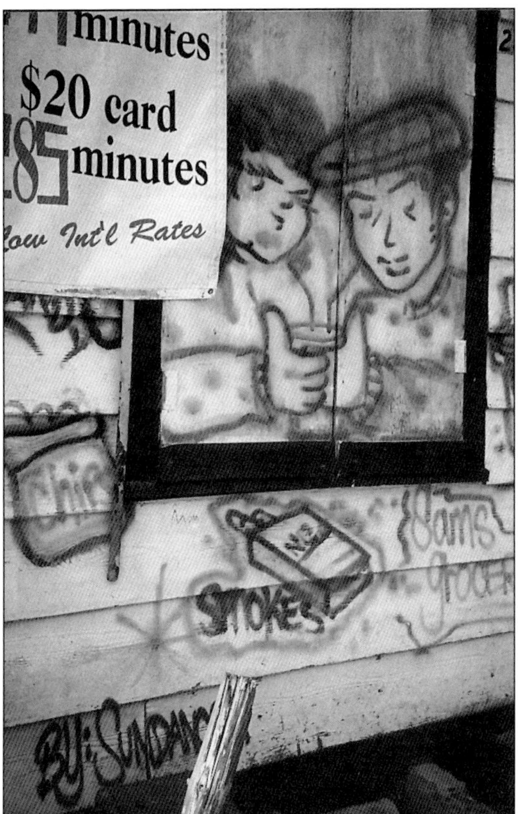

Above and at left are modern-day photographs of Sam's Grocery. The graffiti art by "Sundance," visible on this structure, has become an aesthetic standard for the African-American neighborhood. Driving through these areas, one can spot his work miles away and confirm it by his signature. In the 1980s, however, once-successful black businesses were fading and Sundance's work began to be whitewashed away.

The historically black Read Street neighborhood, located off Harden Street, has been the subject of continuous revitalization efforts throughout the 1990s. Hill's Barber Shop is pictured here in the year 2000.

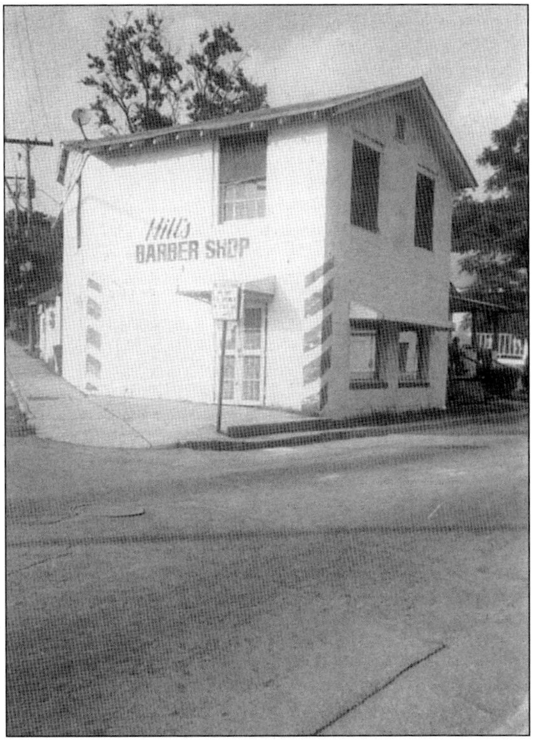

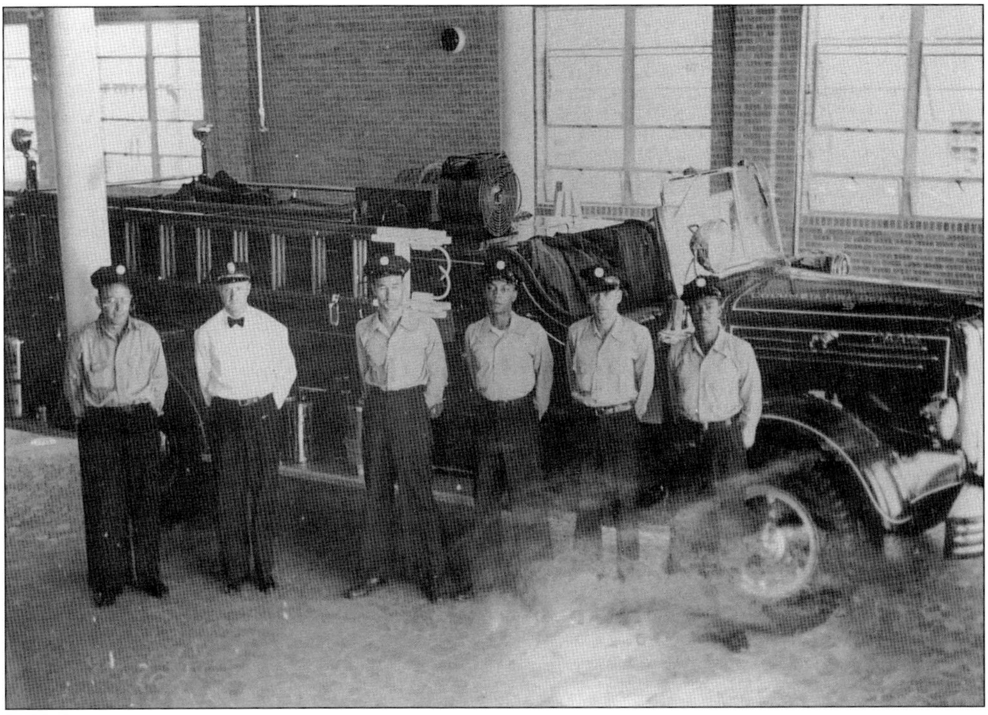

Here, a group of firemen stand by a fire engine on Harden Street. (Courtesy of the Columbia Fire Dept.)

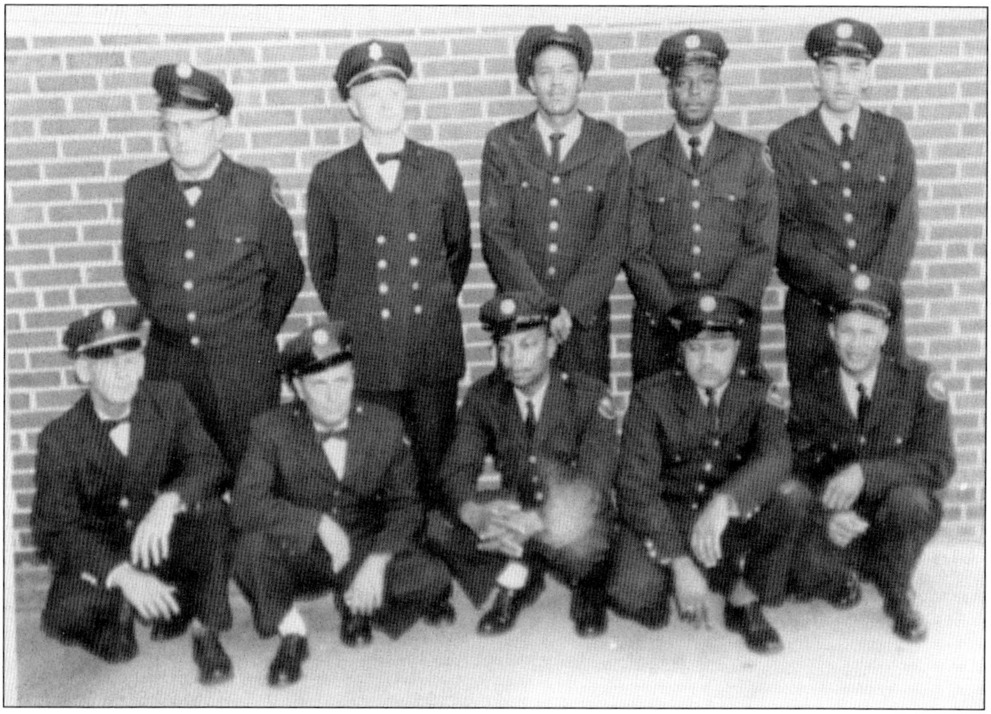

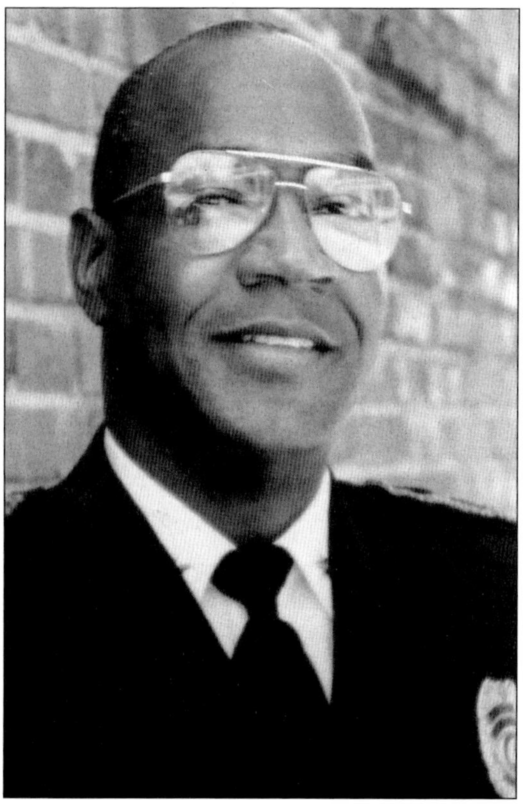

It was not until the 1950s that African Americans were again employed by the Columbia Fire Department as they had been in the early 1900s. However, rather than permitting these black firefighters to work with their white counterparts, the city built a fire station that now stands at 1901 Harden Street. Eight firemen were hired at the new station. Pictured here, from left to right, are (bottom row) Warren Gage, A. Seegars, Lewis Williams, Willie Jones, and A. Coles; (top row) Derrick L. Grover, R.M. Neely, Thomas Jones, Bernie Fraizie, and C.B. Mitchel. (Courtesy of the Columbia Fire Dept.)

Charles P. Austin Sr. has been the chief of police for the city of Columbia since October 1, 1990. (Courtesy of the Columbia Police Dept.)

Born in Edgefield County in 1885, John C. Artemus Sr. moved to Columbia in 1907 following a confrontation with his family's sharecropper landlord over unfair wages. He became deeply involved in the labor problems of blacks. Along with a small group of supporters, Artemus organized Local 2260 of the United Brotherhood of Carpenters and Joiners of America. (Courtesy of the United Black Fund.)

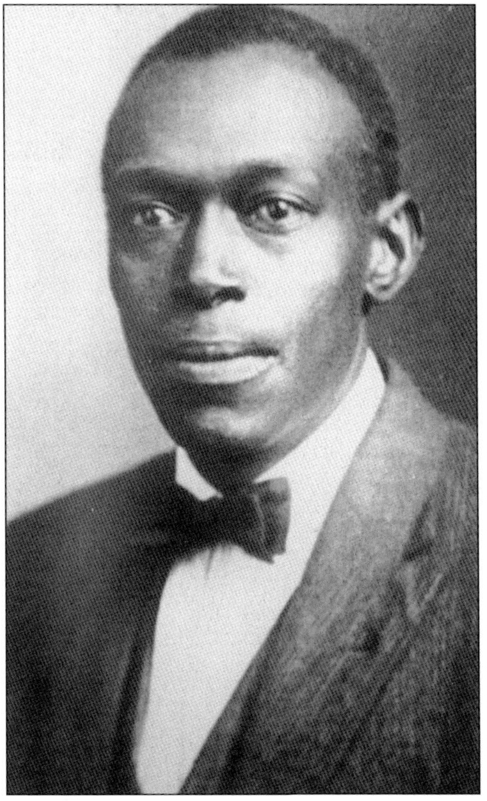

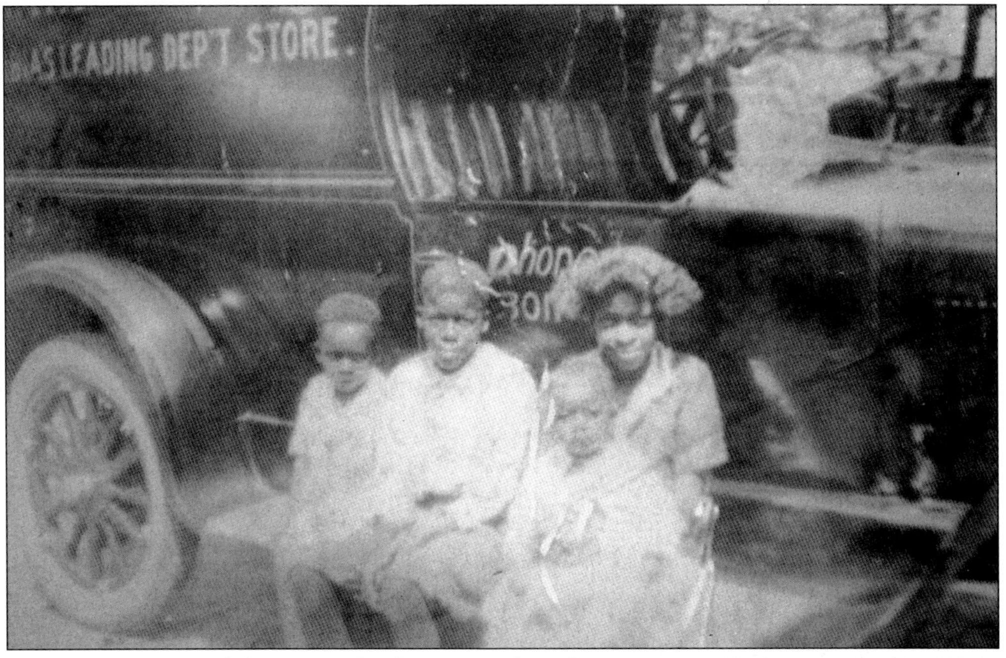

Pictured here is a delivery truck of Mimnaugh, John L. & Co. Clothing parked on Main Street, *c.* 1920.(Courtesy of Caroline Summers Floyd.)

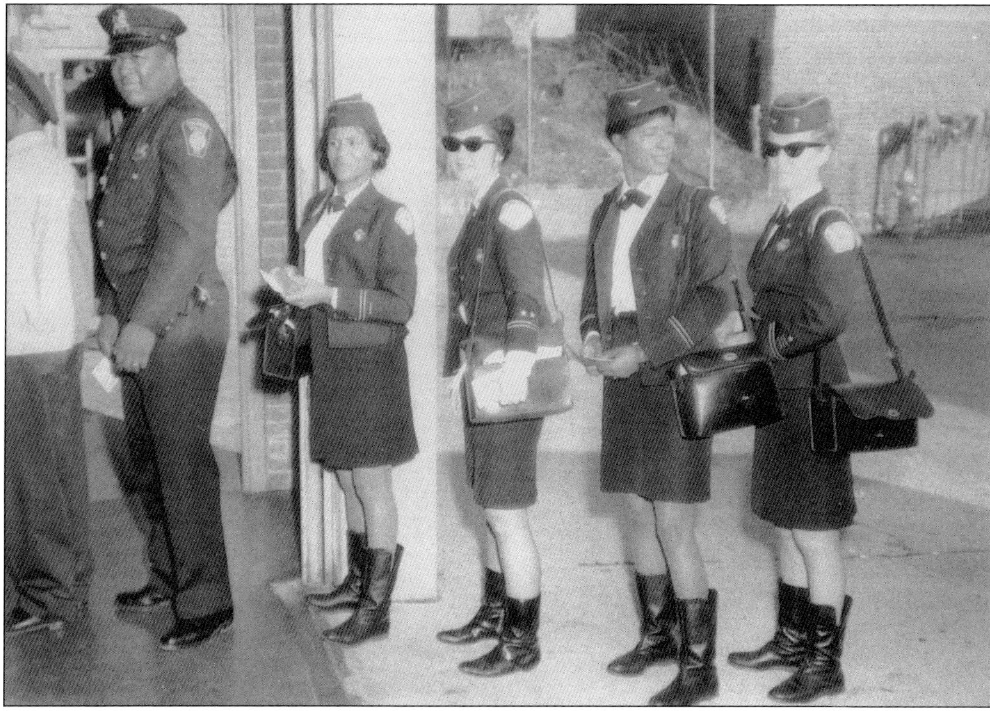

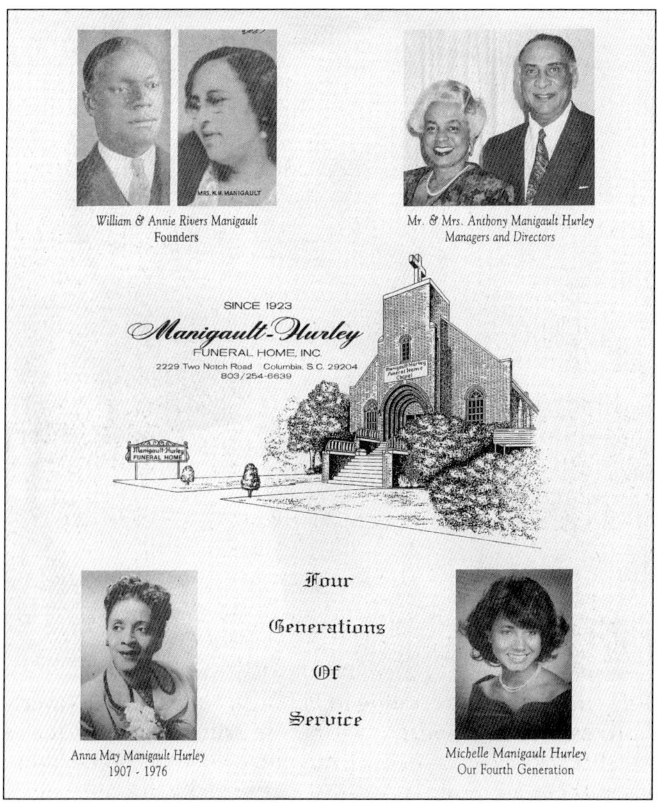

In this group photograph, Sgt. Willie James, the first black police officer on motorcycle duty, is accompanied by Betty Marion, Dessie Higgins, Estelle Trapp-Young, and April Reynolds-Speight. Estelle Trapp-Young climbed the ranks since joining the Columbia Police Department as a meter reader in 1968 to become the first female captain. (Courtesy of the Columbia Police Dept.)

This flyer advertises the family-owned Manigault-Hurley Funeral Home. (Courtesy of the Manigault-Hurley family.)

Four

Neighborhoods

In the early 20th century the Waverly community consisted of both blacks and whites, as well as some people of Jewish descent. But, as the years passed, the white population gradually moved out, and the black residents purchased their vacated property. Waverly then became a predominately African-American community with exception of a few white businesses, mainly grocery stores. The majority of the residents in the the neighborhood were then homeowners.

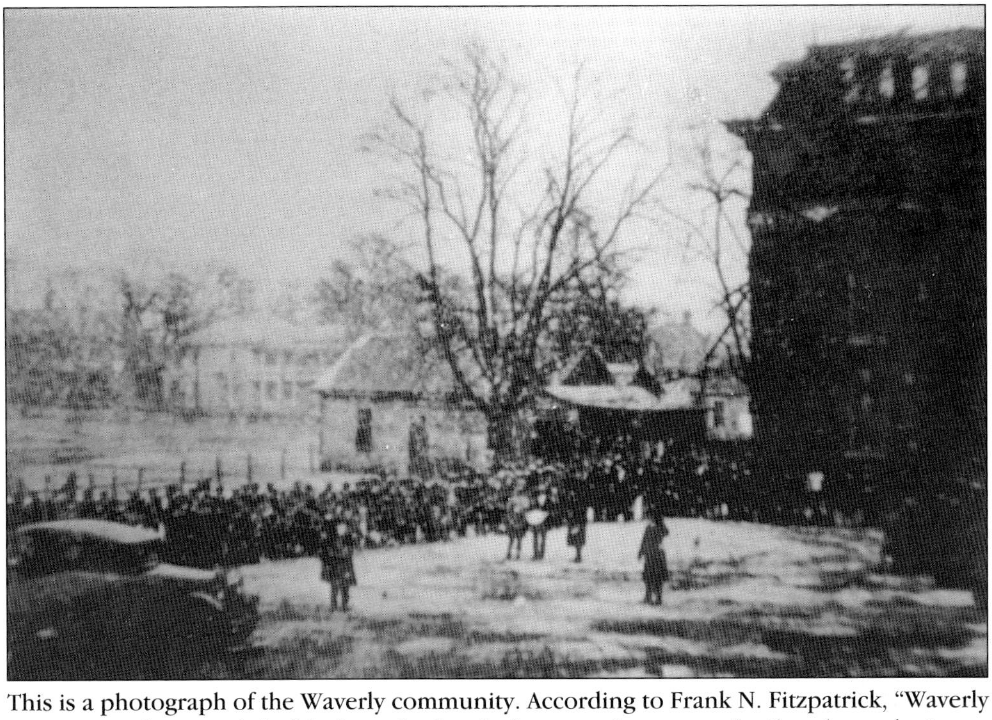

This is a photograph of the Waverly community. According to Frank N. Fitzpatrick, "Waverly was occupied primarily by black professionals, lawyers, doctors, and railroad people. It was beautiful. It was a place where everybody knew everybody. Everyone owned his home; there were not a lot of rental properties as there are now." (Courtesy of the McKissick Museum.)

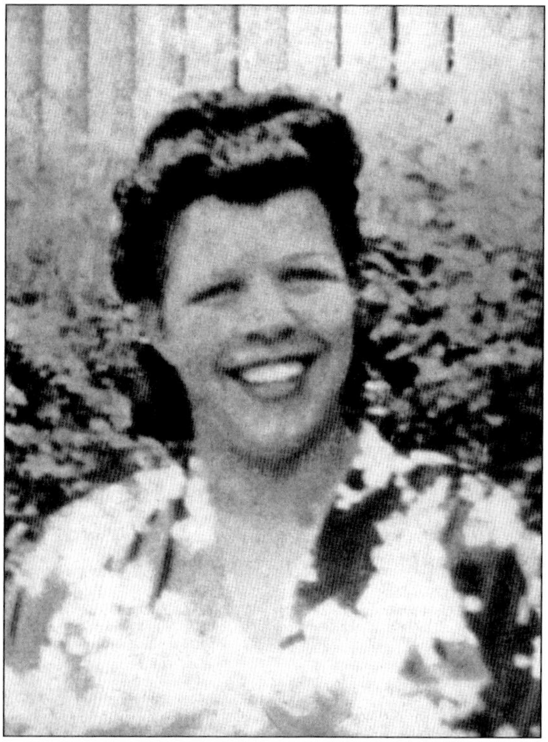

A smiling Harriet G. Titus worked as a hostess at the USO and met her husband there. She was a Columbia businesswoman and also wrote for the *Palmetto Leader*. (Courtesy of the Titus family.)

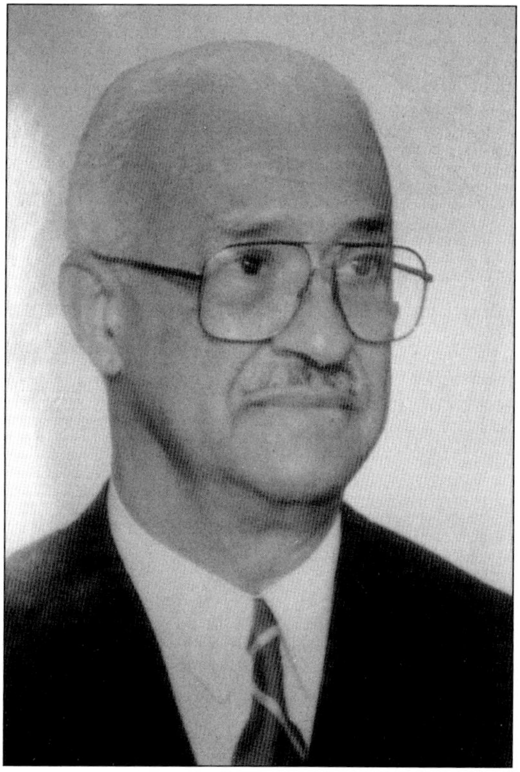

Dr. Noble P. Cooper Sr., a dental surgeon, performed community services that helped to improve the quality of life for many Columbia citizens. He was one of the first black dentists accepted for membership in the South Carolina Dental Association. (Courtesy of the United Black Fund.)

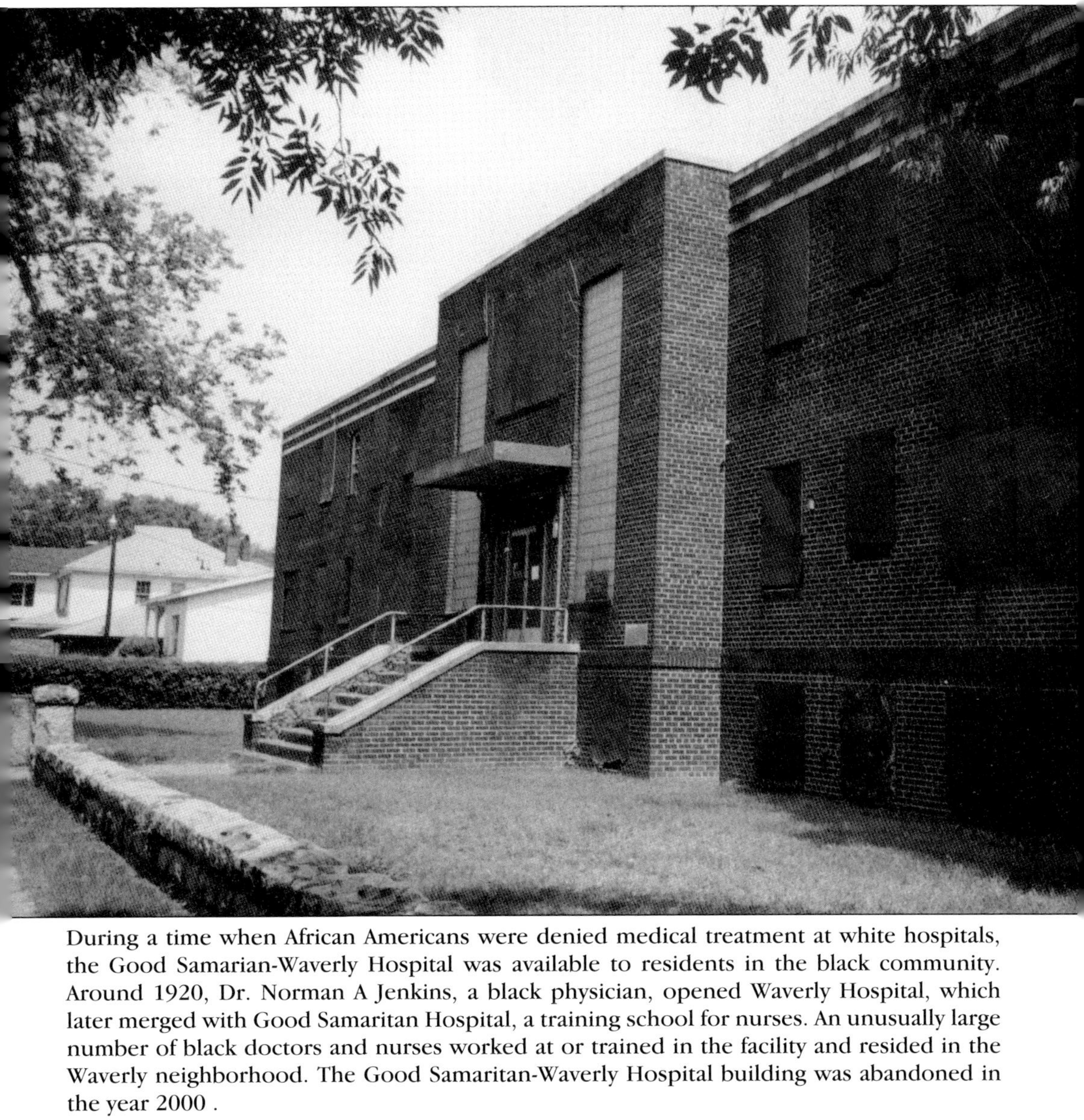

During a time when African Americans were denied medical treatment at white hospitals, the Good Samarian-Waverly Hospital was available to residents in the black community. Around 1920, Dr. Norman A Jenkins, a black physician, opened Waverly Hospital, which later merged with Good Samaritan Hospital, a training school for nurses. An unusually large number of black doctors and nurses worked at or trained in the facility and resided in the Waverly neighborhood. The Good Samaritan-Waverly Hospital building was abandoned in the year 2000 .

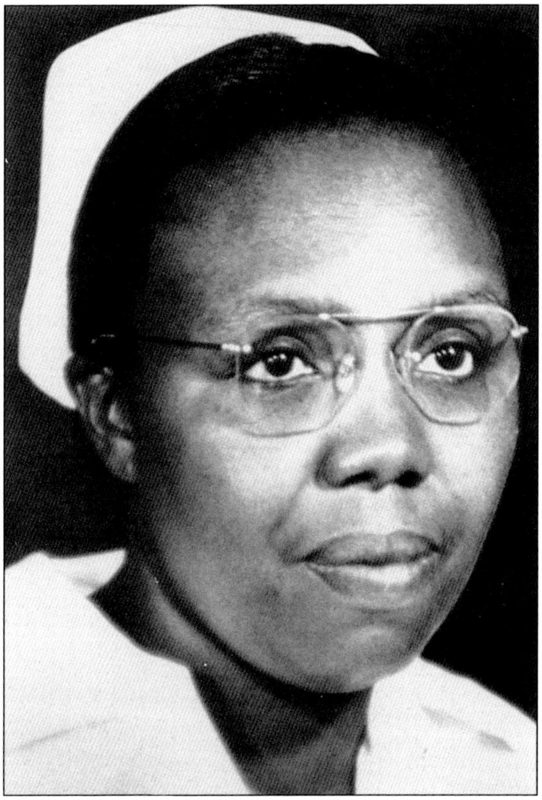

Sadie Felder Nickpeay, pictured here, was the first licensed practical nurse in South Carolina Whaley Hospital. (Courtesy of the United Black Fund.)

Below, Waverly Hospital nurses participate in a training session. (Courtesy of the Columbia Fire Dept.)

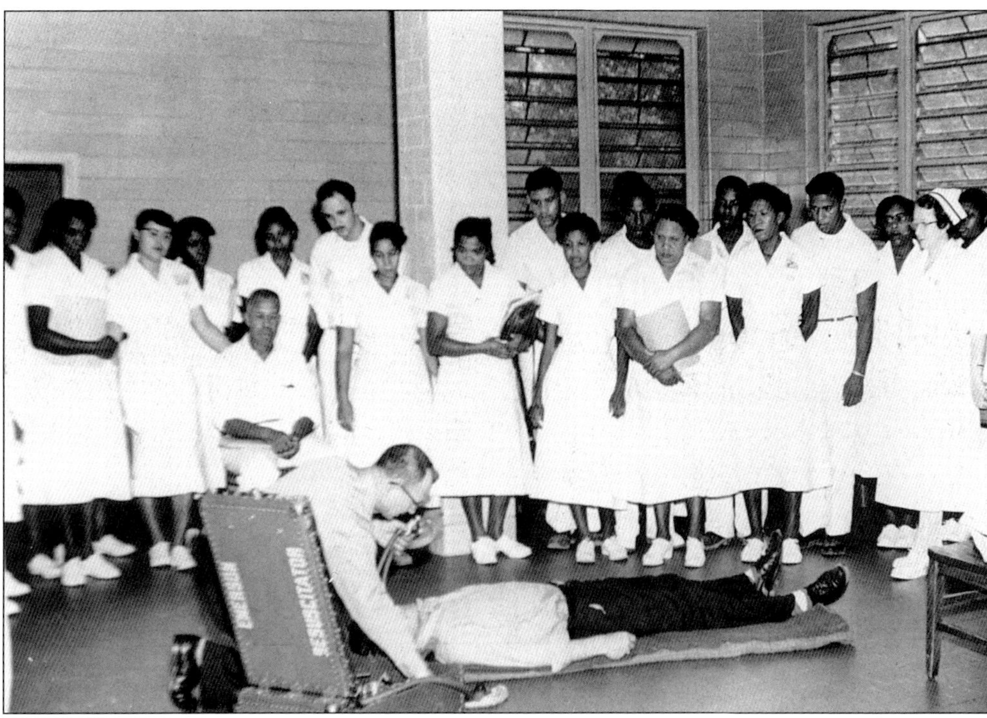

The Carver Theater, seen here in 2000, hosted amateur hour and talent shows. In the 1940s, James Payne, better known as "Mr. Jive," hosted these shows.

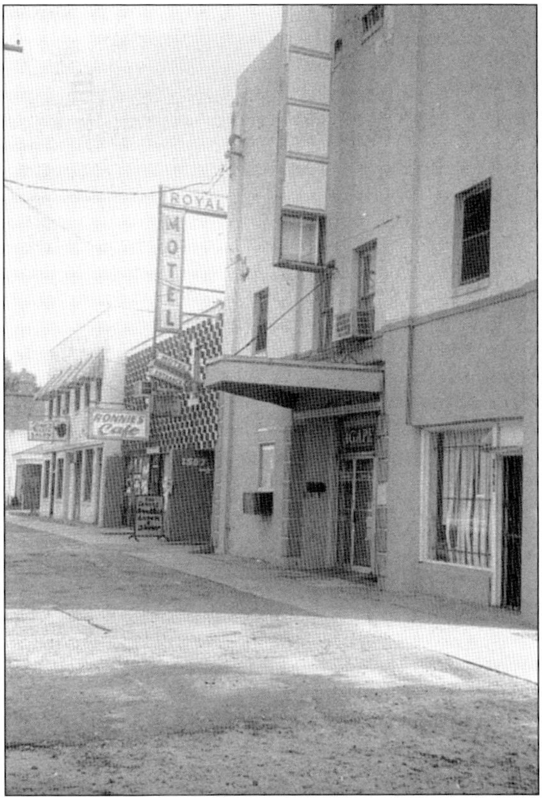

Below, locals enjoy trying their luck at the carnival games at the Palmetto Colored State Fair. (Courtesy of the Richland County Public Library.)

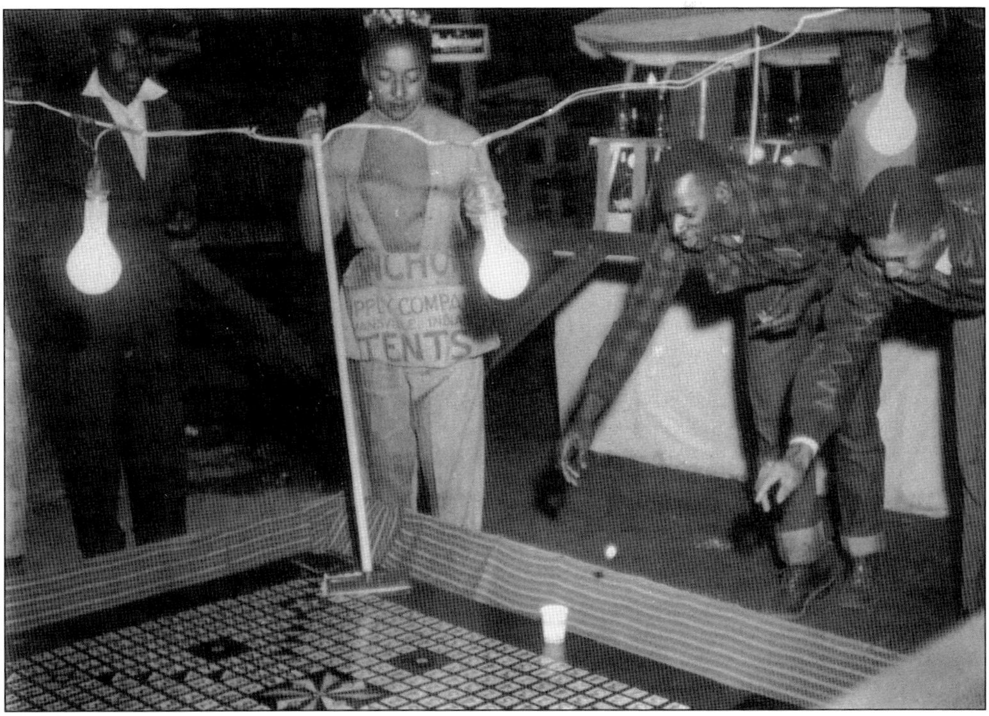

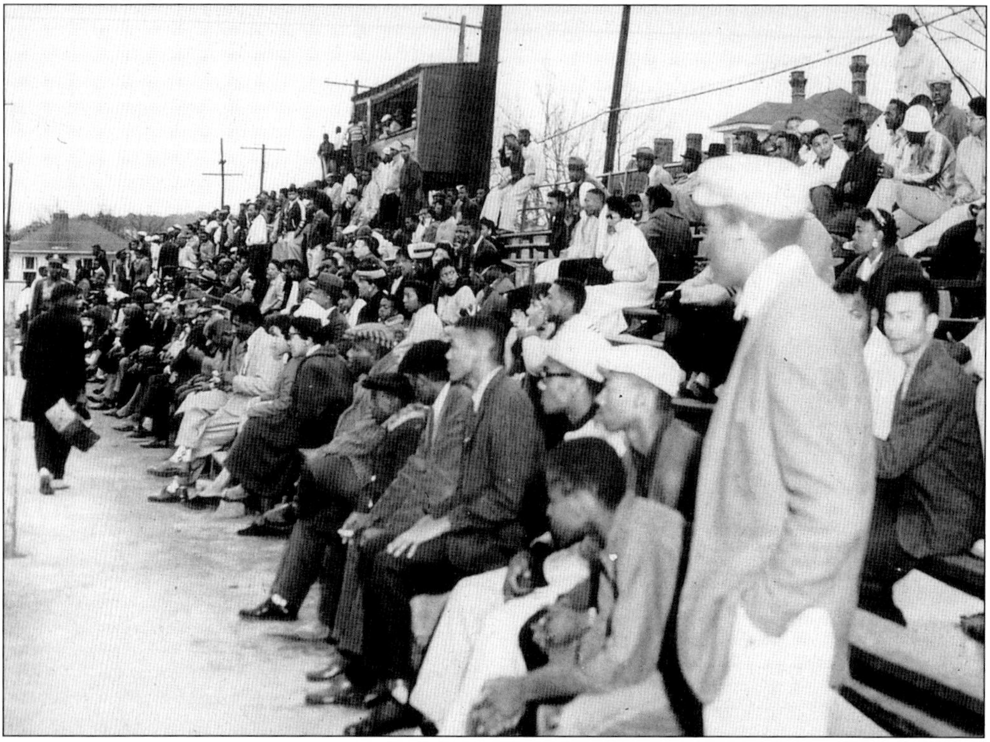

A baseball game is underway at Hurst Stadium in the Waverly neighborhood. (Courtesy of the McKissick Museum.)

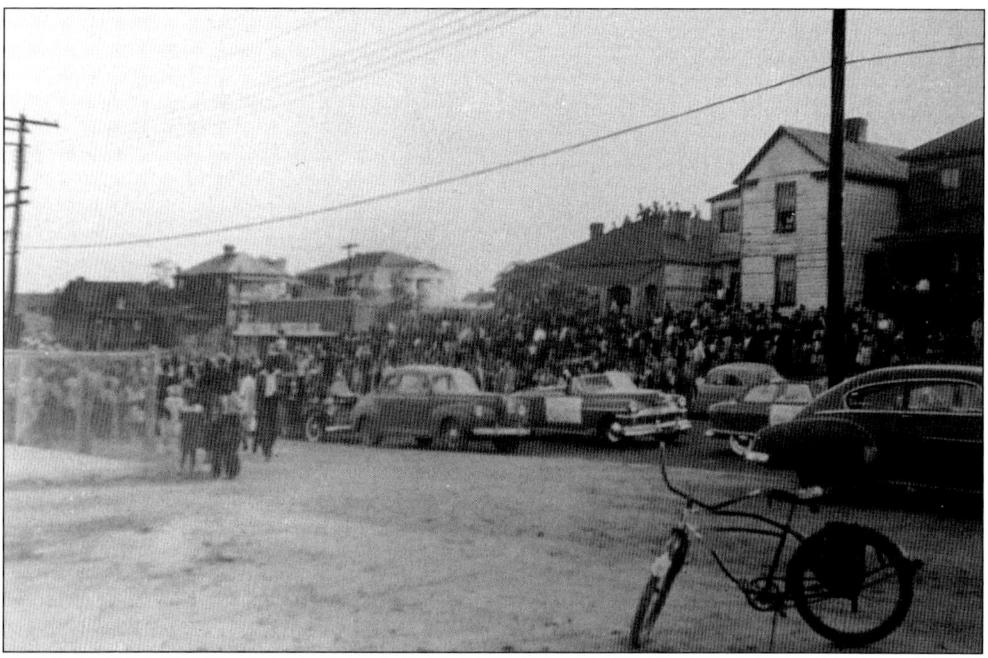

In this neighborhood picture, the Blue Fish and Oyster Co. parade winds through the community. (Courtesy of the Columbia Fire Dept.)

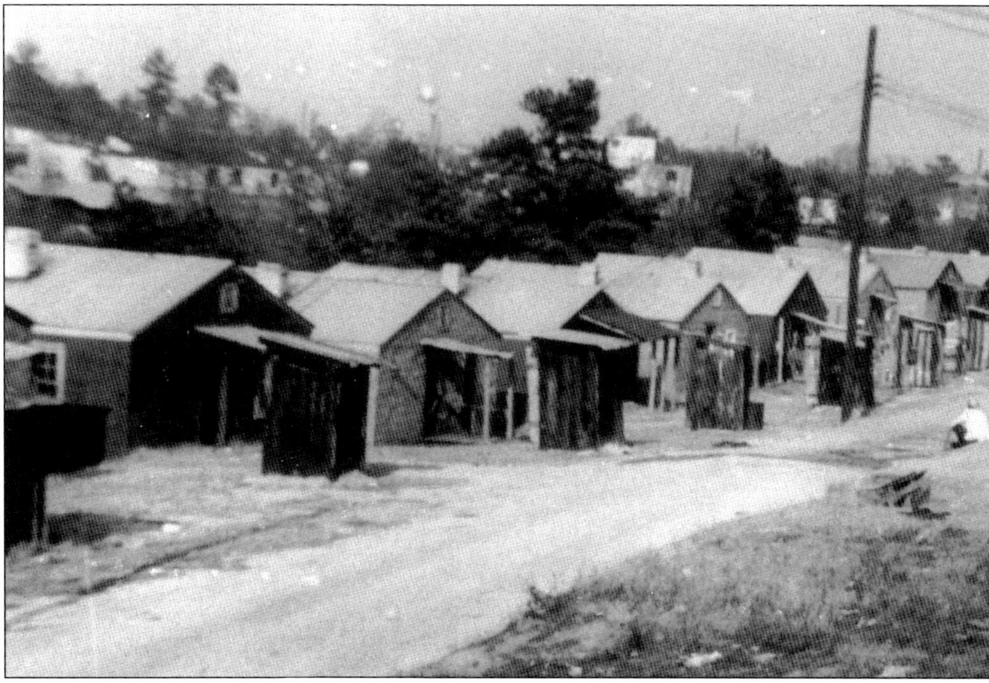

Pictured above is the "Black Bottom" area in northwest Columbia in 1924. "Black Bottom," a section of town between Main Street and the river, was a dismal section around the jails and the penitentiary, where unpaved streets and alleys threaded between rows of weather-beaten shotgun houses. Here lived the whites and blacks of the poorest classes. (Courtesy of the South Carolina State Museum.)

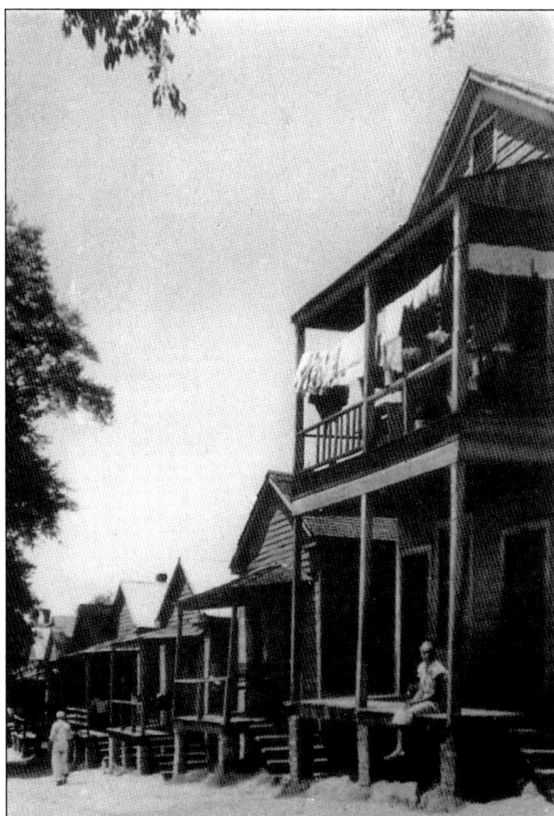

Tenant houses in the Columbia area are seen here. (Courtesy of the South Carolina State Museum.)

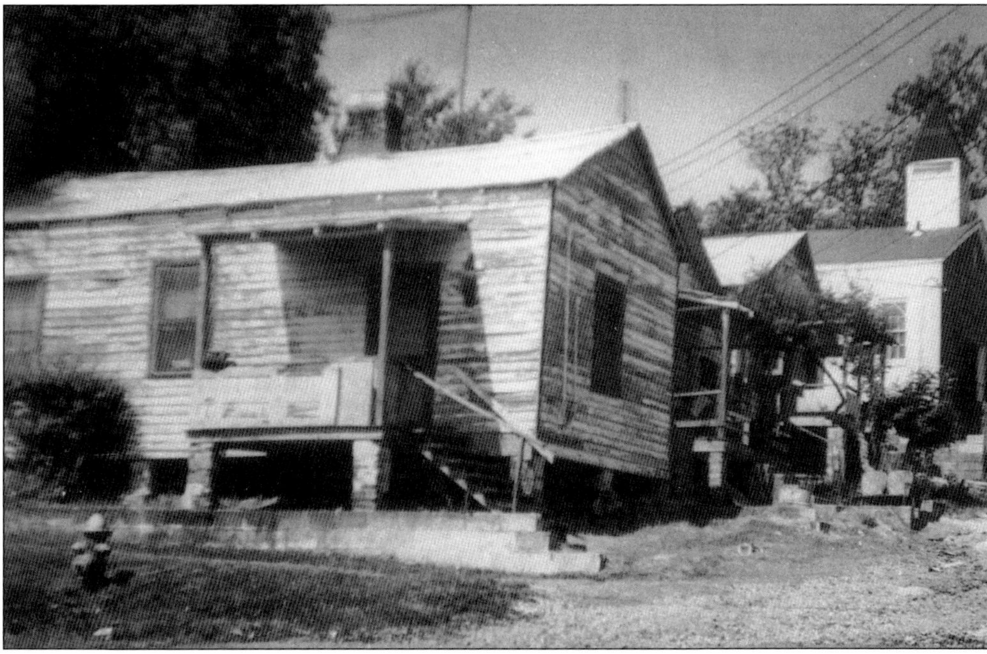

This view shows Pulaski Street, *c.* 1979. (Courtesy of the South Carolina State Museum.)

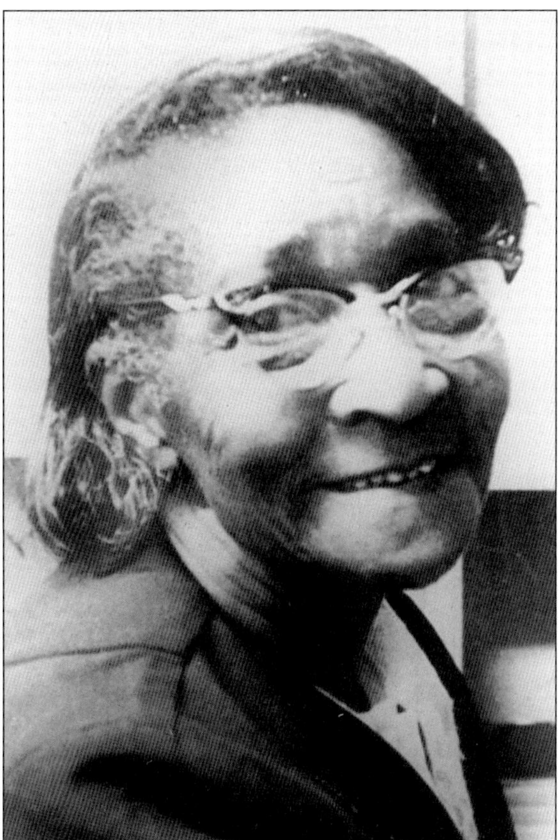

Lugenia Key Hammond made it her mission to revitalize her community. By 1974, "Black Bottom" had become an oasis of hope with affordable public housing, spacious yards, a community center, and health and dental facilities. In 1978, the Columbia Housing Authority dedicated the area and renamed it Lugenia Key Hammond Village. (Courtesy of the United Black Fund.)

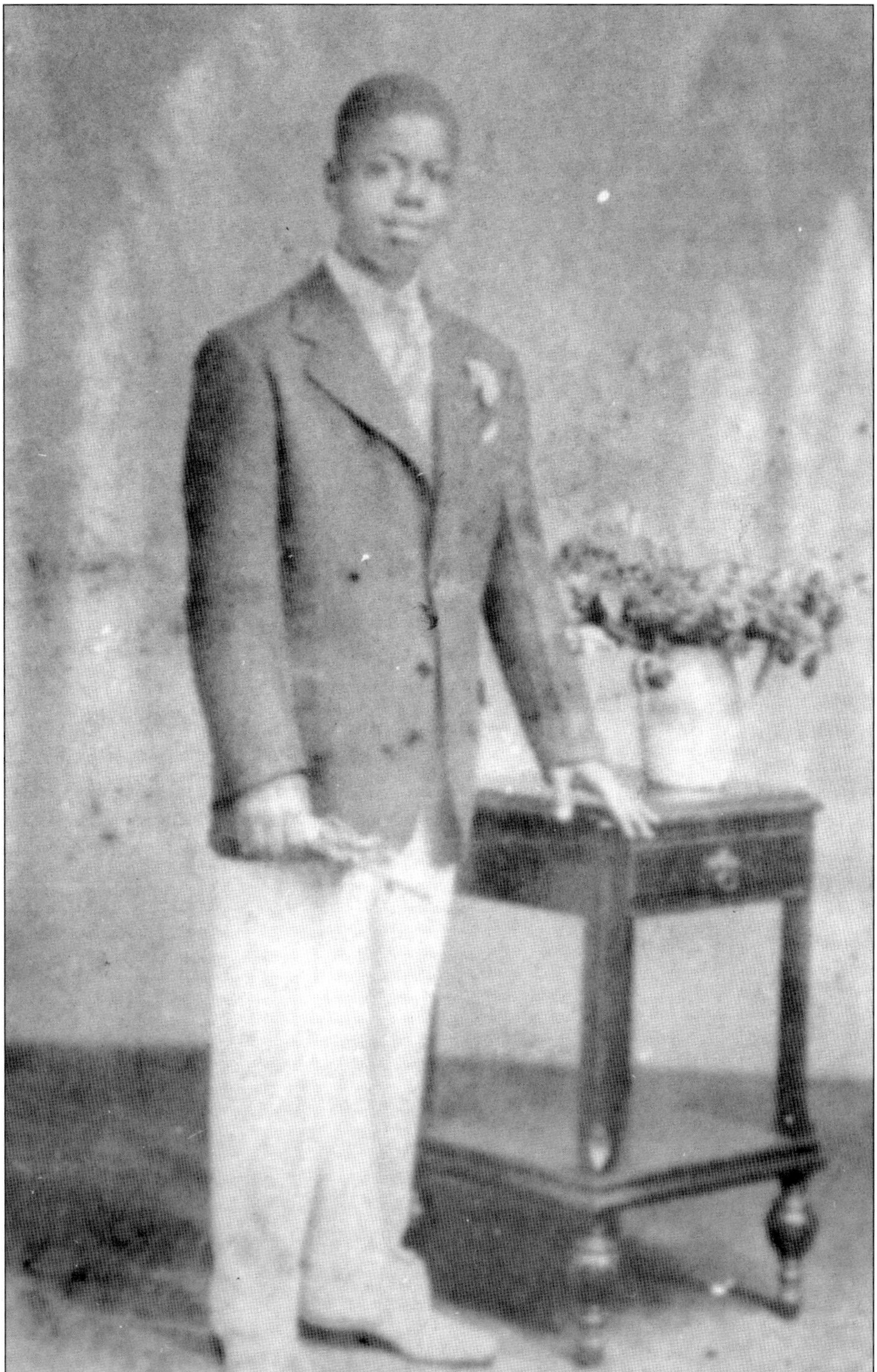

This professionally posed portrait will go "To grandmother and auntie, From Samuel F. Ragin, Age 14, June 26, 1975." The picture was taken at the Dobkins Studio at 884 Columbia Avenue in New York City. (Courtesy of the Eva P. Trezevant Memorial Library.)

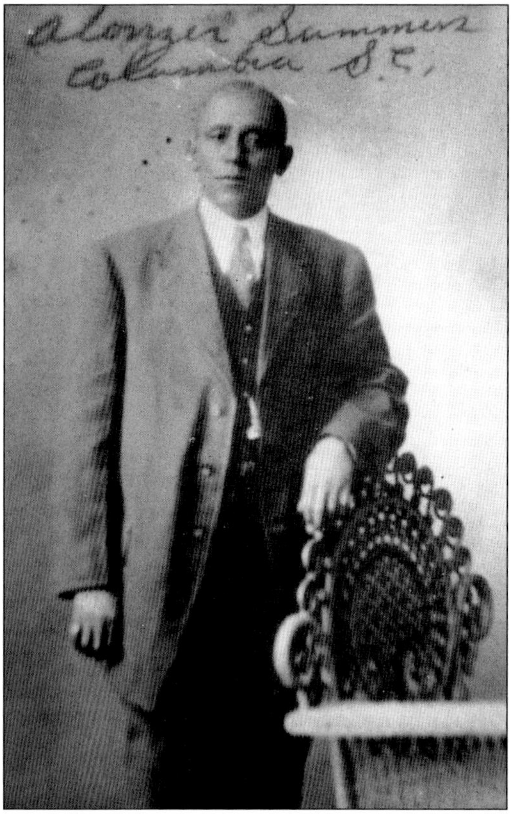

As the years passed, many African Americans started to migrate from the South to the North, to the "land of milk and honey," and Columbians began to develop extended communities in New York, Philadelphia, Washington, D.C., and other major cities. This posed portrait of Alonzer Summers was taken around 1900.

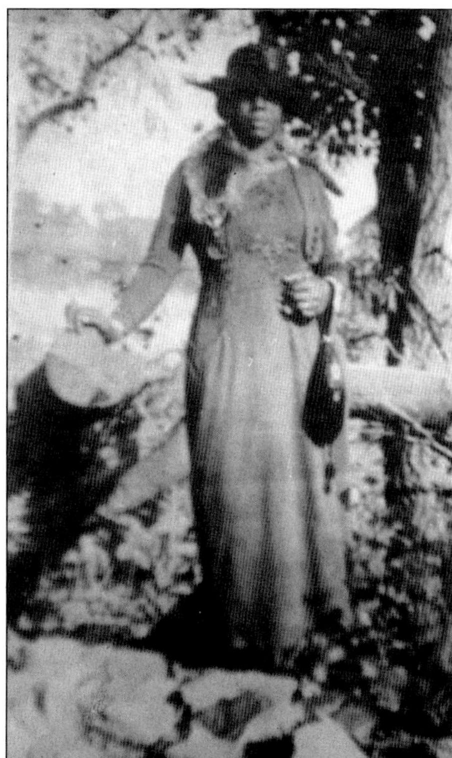

Mary Summers, the daughter-in-law of Alonzer Summers, had this picture taken around 1927.

Five

SOCIAL LIFE

During the Negro State Fair in 1925, that Thursday, some 8700 people passed through the gates. This was the greatest year in its history of eighteen years.

Benedict represented its music, hospital, home economics, literary, and scientific departments. Allen University showed how a kitchen should be arranged through its domestic science department and exhibited its literary department. The Booker T. Washington High School had one of the best exhibits of all. It showed the manual training school, the brick-laying trade, dressmaking, and the domestic science department.

A special feature of that year's festival was the prizefight, Friday afternoon at the football stadium, between "Happy" Hunter of Atlanta, Ga. and Bob Lawson of Pittsburgh, Pa. "Happy" Hunter was no match for the onslaughts of the sledge-hammer blows of fighting Bob Lawson.

—*Excerpts taken from the* Palmetto Leader, *Saturday, October 24, 1925*

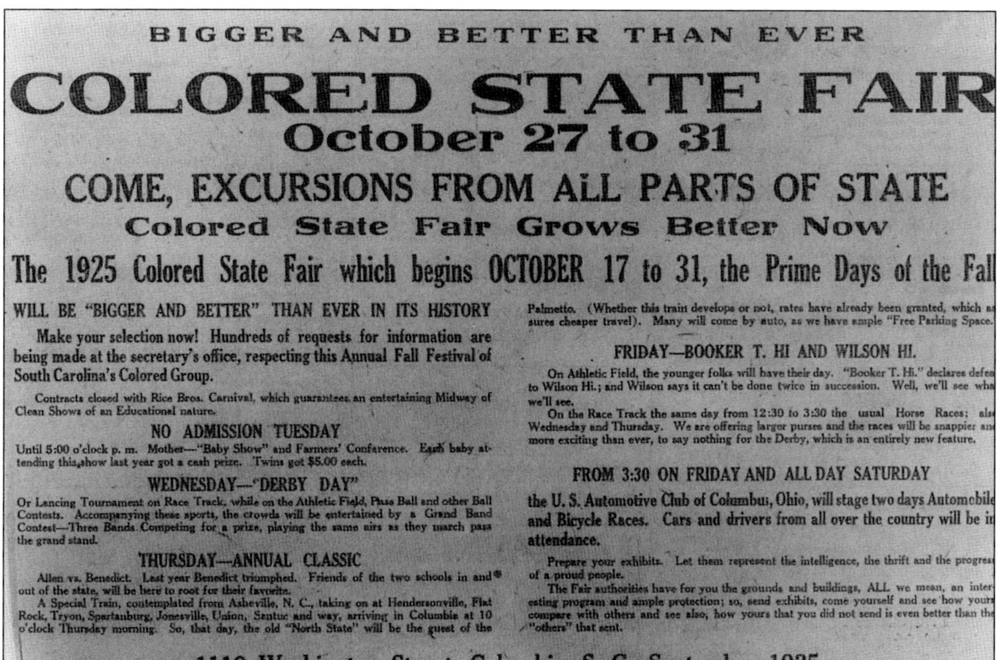

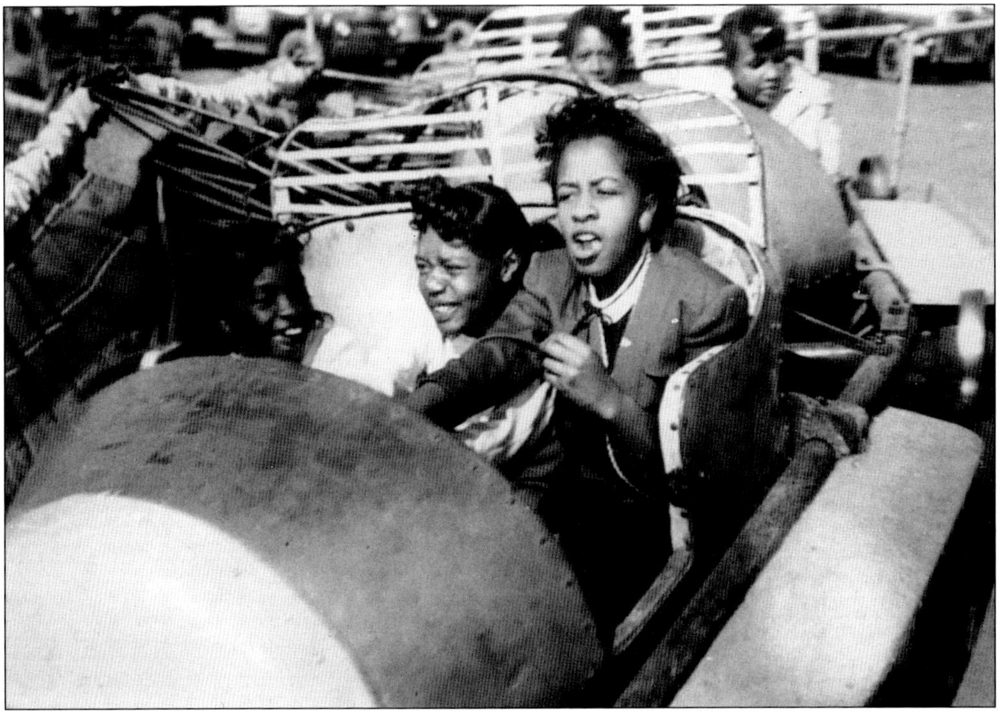

These young girls take a ride at the Palmetto State Fair. (Courtesy of the Richland County Public Library.)

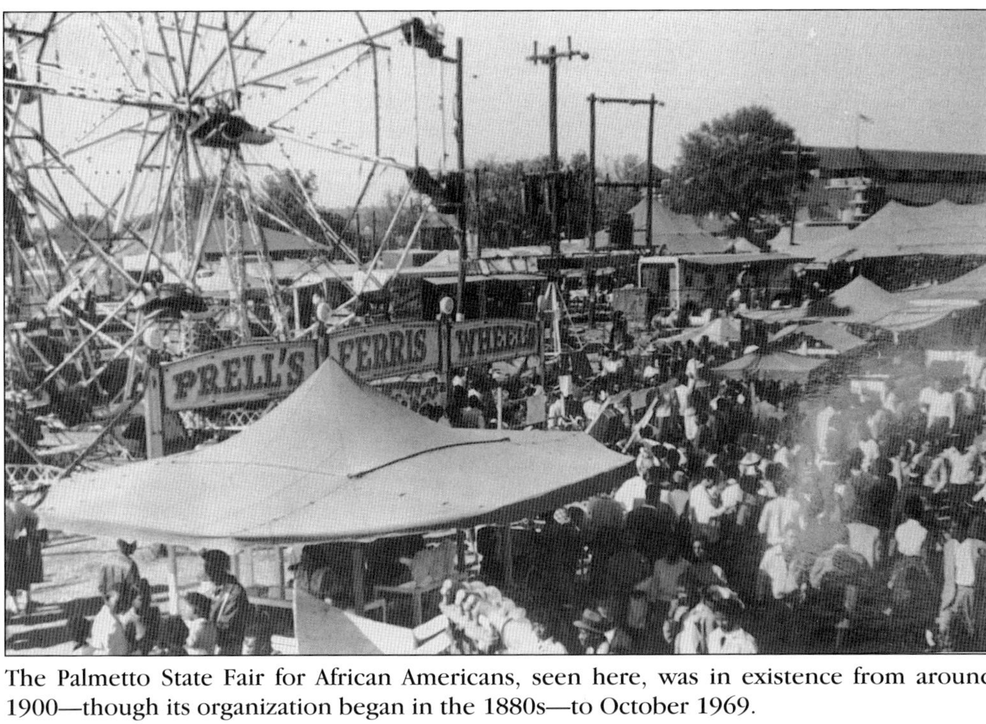

The Palmetto State Fair for African Americans, seen here, was in existence from around 1900—though its organization began in the 1880s—to October 1969.

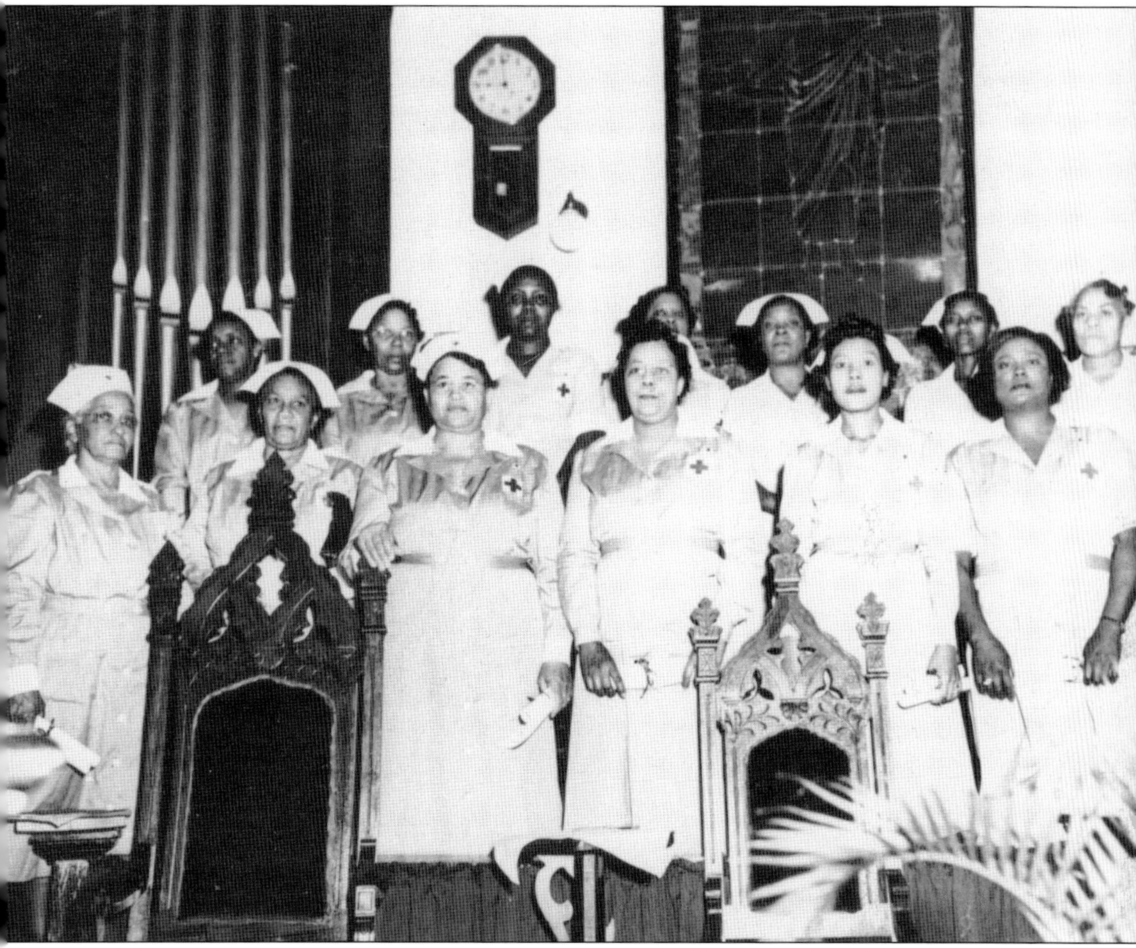

In 1942, the Richland County Chapter of the American Red Cross organized the Negro Auxiliary of the chapter. This was accomplished at a mass meeting sponsored by Professor C.A. Johnson, the supervisor of the Negro Schools of Columbia. At this organizational meeting, Mrs. Ruth Butcher was elected chairman. During the first year, the Negro Auxiliary conducted two home nursing classes and two first aid classes, as well as many knitting and sewing classes. During the Negro State Fair, the auxiliary operated a booth demonstrating the work of the Red Cross and providing first aid when needed. Pictured here is a Red Cross Capping Ceremony. (Courtesy of the South Caroliniana Library, USC.)

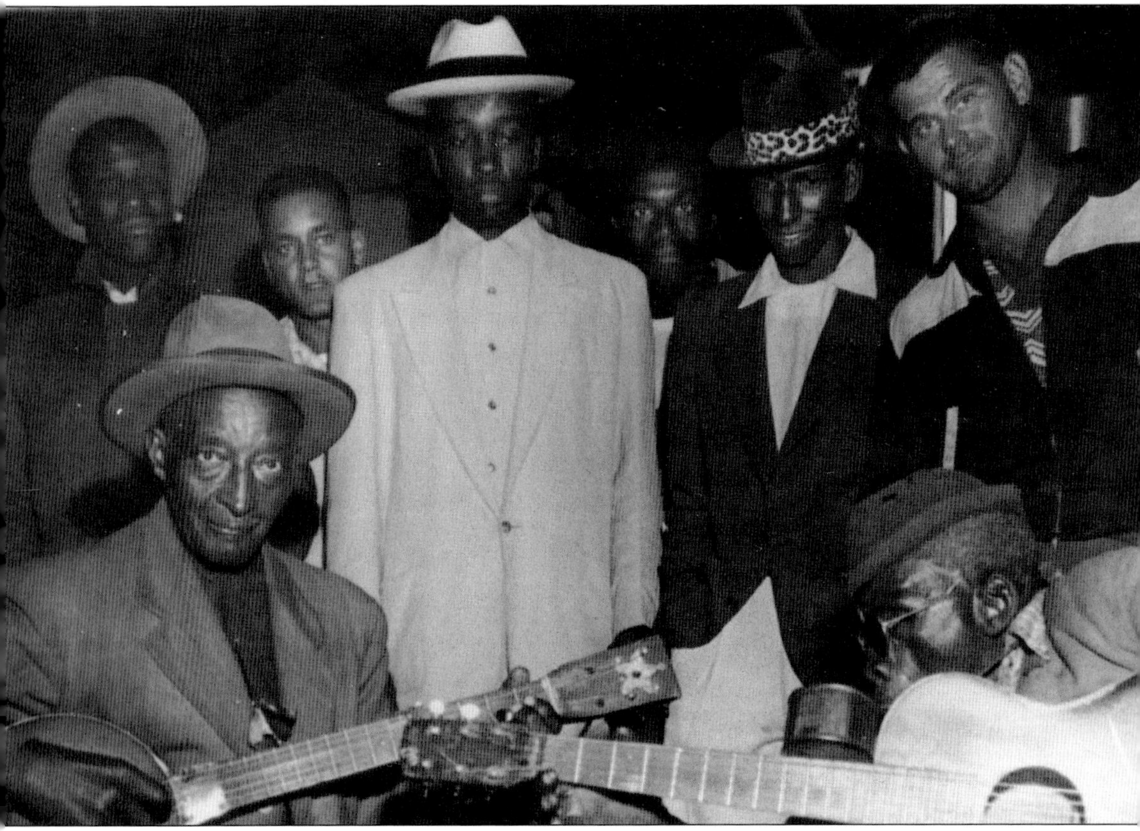

Blues players contributed great music to the Palmetto State Fair, which drew people from across South Carolina, including these two musicians. (Courtesy of the Richland County Public Library.)

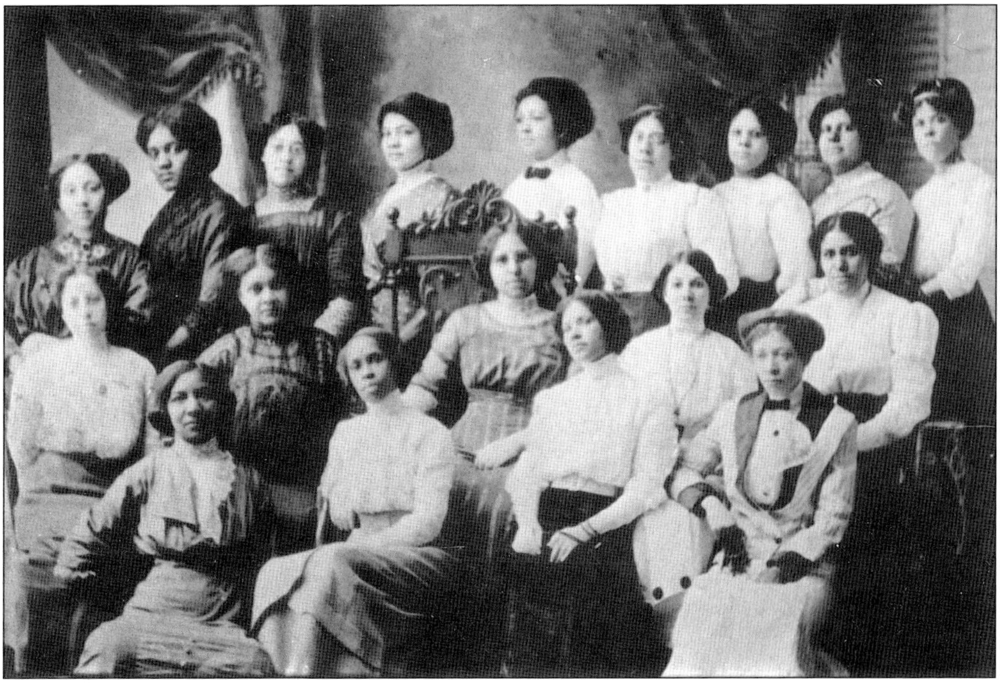

The Tuesday Afternoon Club in Columbia was typical of the literary and cultural organizations formed all over the state at the turn of the 20th century by blacks and whites, males and females. (Courtesy of the McKissick Museum.)

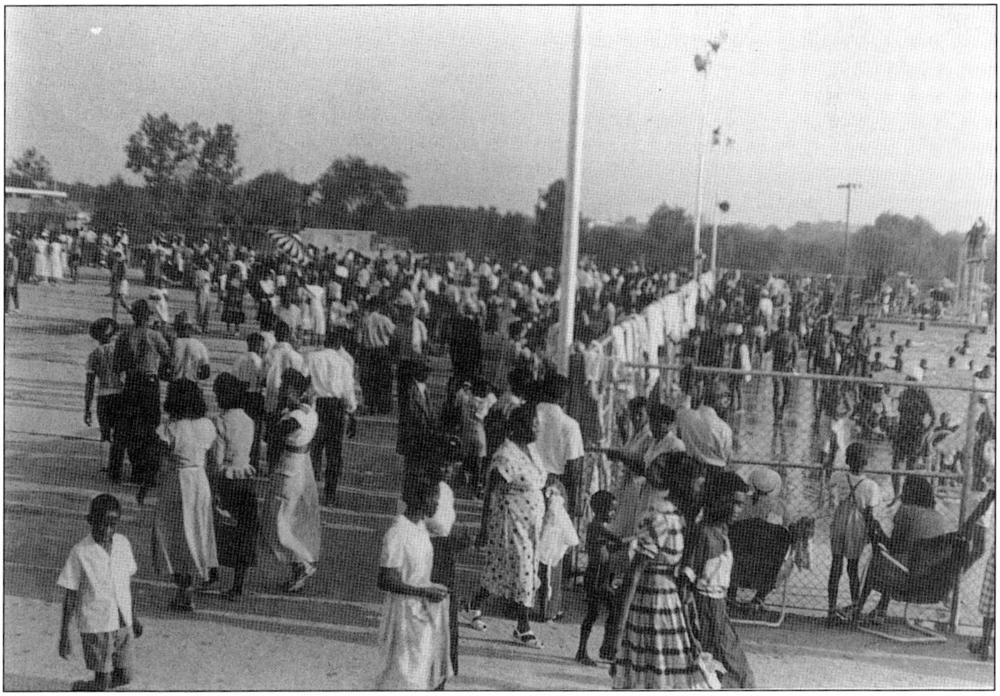

A crowd gathers at Drew Park Swimming Pool. (Courtesy of the City of Columbia Parks and Recreation Dept.)

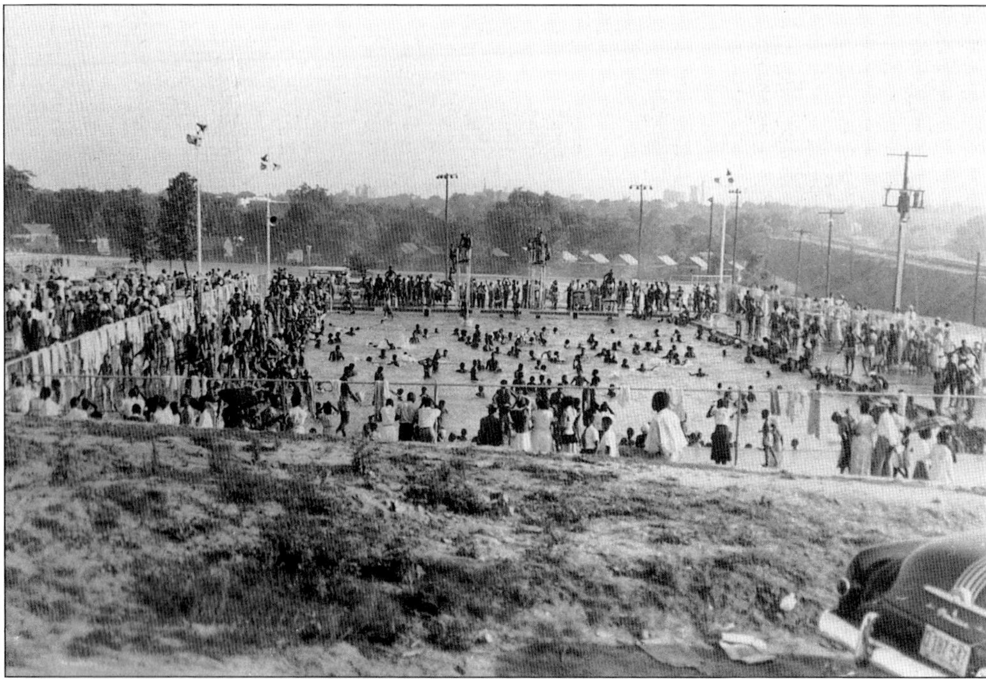

In this photograph, hundreds of people make use of the popular Drew Park Swimming Pool. (Courtesy of the City of Columbia Parks and Recreation Dept.)

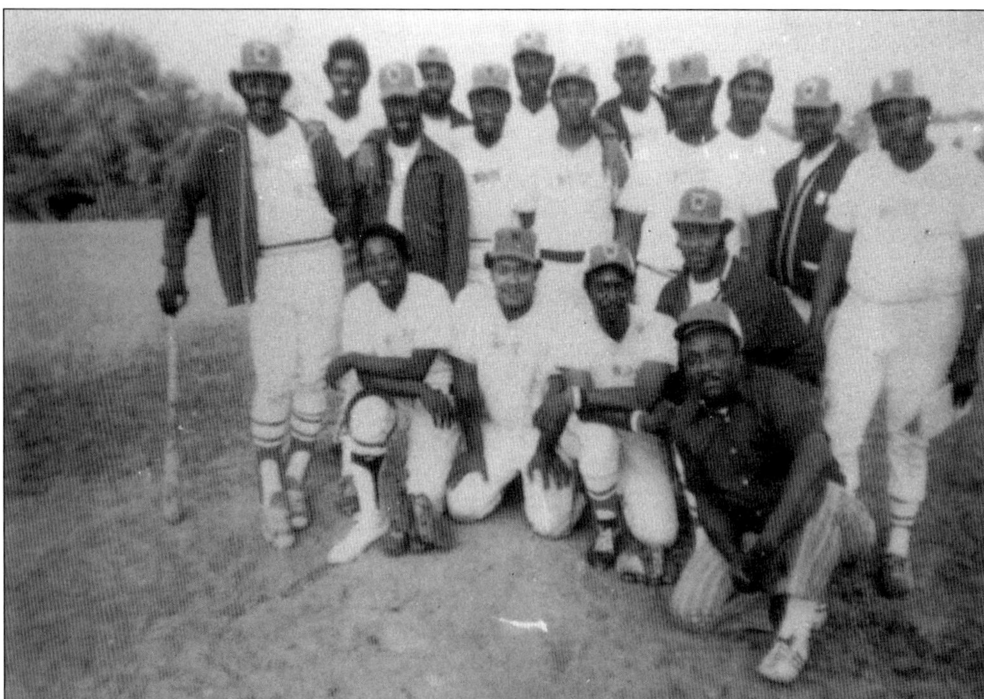

The Columbia Whips baseball team played on a field that was located on Pulaski Street. (Courtesy of the Richard Caughman family.)

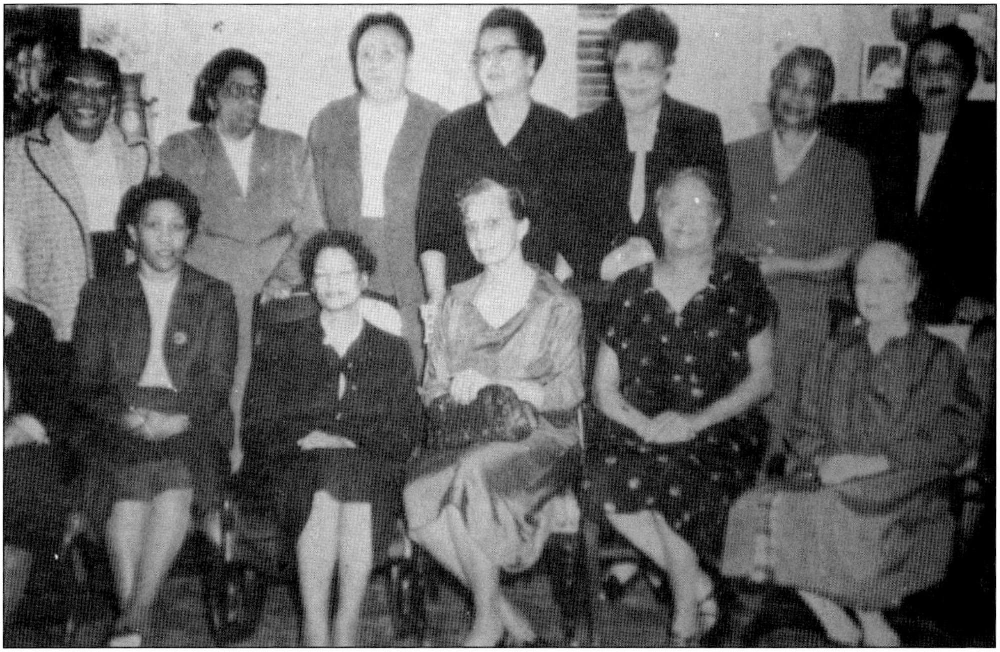

Pictured above is the Culture Club of Columbia. This group was part of the South Carolina Federation of Colored Women's Clubs, which was organized in 1910. (Courtesy of the McKissick Museum.)

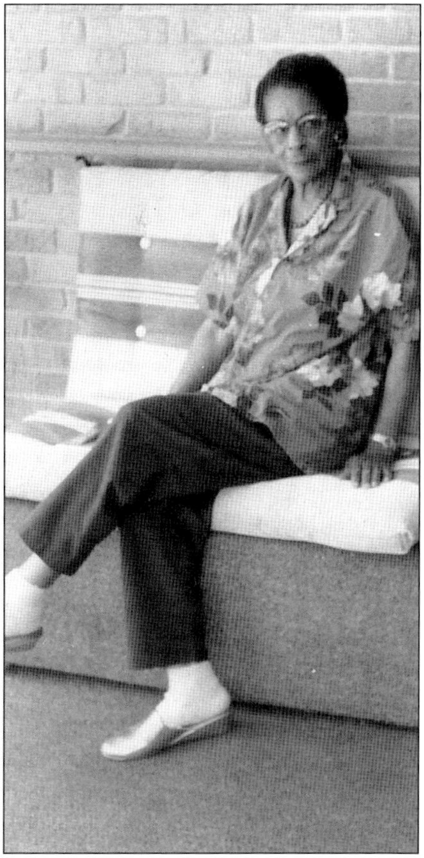

"We would catch hands and high step like chorus girls in New York. We slim girls were thrown through the legs of the tall guys. We would shuffle. We would push out our hands, shuffling across the floor like old people," said Mrs. Cayruth, now 82, remembering her teenage years at the Big Apple Club and other dance clubs around the Columbia area. As she talked, Mrs. Lucretia Cayruth got up in the middle of her living room, moved her hips and kicked her legs to demonstrate the dances she did as a young girl. These black youngsters created the jitterbug, and the Suzy-Q, she remembered, insisting that they created many of their own dances."It was the Big Apple that really caught on. We would go around, and someone would get on the floor. My partner will get on the floor, be the apple, and we would move around him putting our fingers on his head. That would be the Big Apple," said Mrs. Cayruth. Little did they know that the dance they created through their impromptu movements would become the craze in big cities like New York and Chicago.

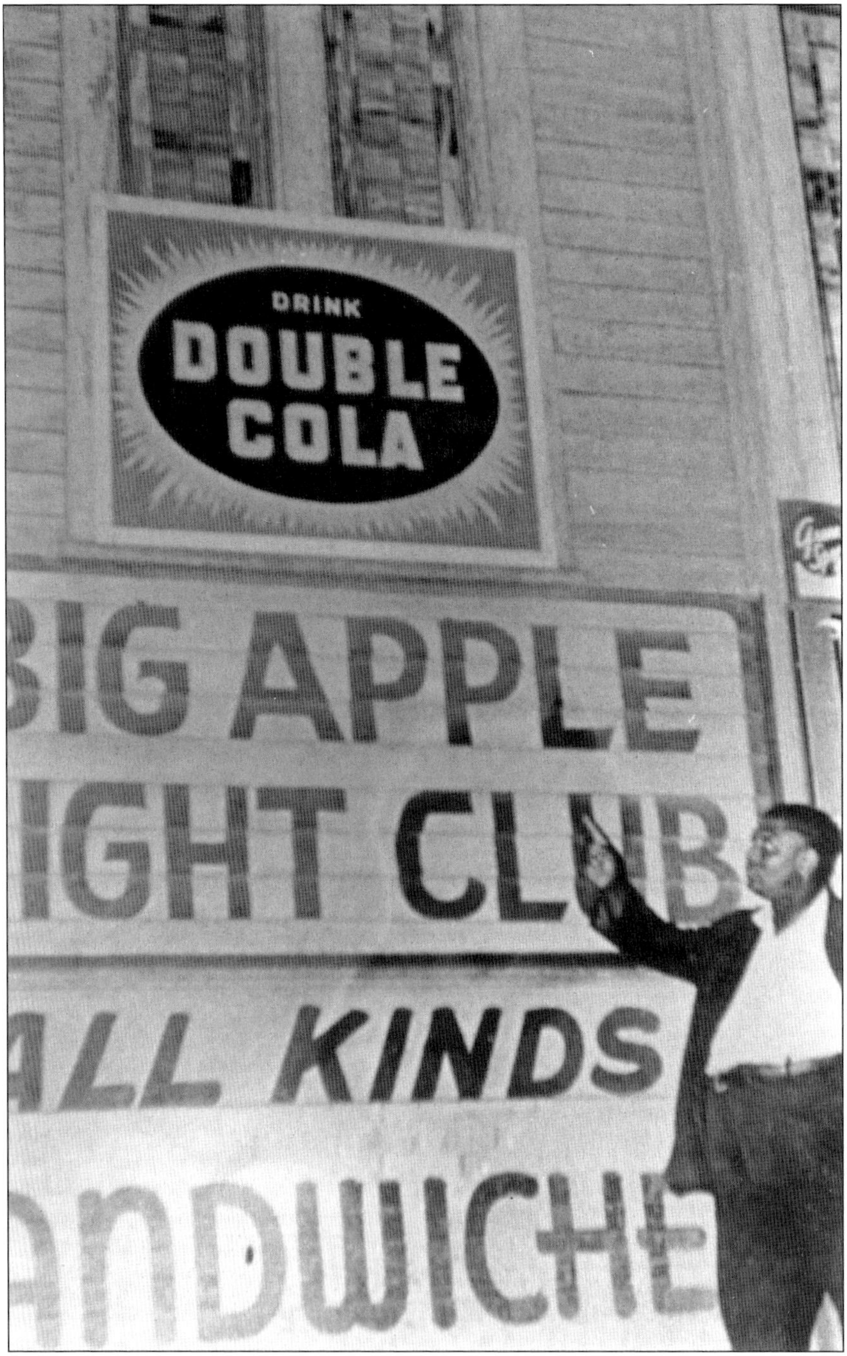

The music coming from the Big Apple Night Club bounced out onto the street, and some white college students from the University of South Carolina were attracted by the bebobic tunes. At first, the students—William Spivey, Donald Davis, and Harold Niles—just hung around the door peering in. But one night, Fat Sams, the owner of the club, permitted them to watch. For a dime, "Big Elliot" Wright, the club's bouncer, would allow them to go to the balcony. (Courtesy of the Richland County Public Library.)

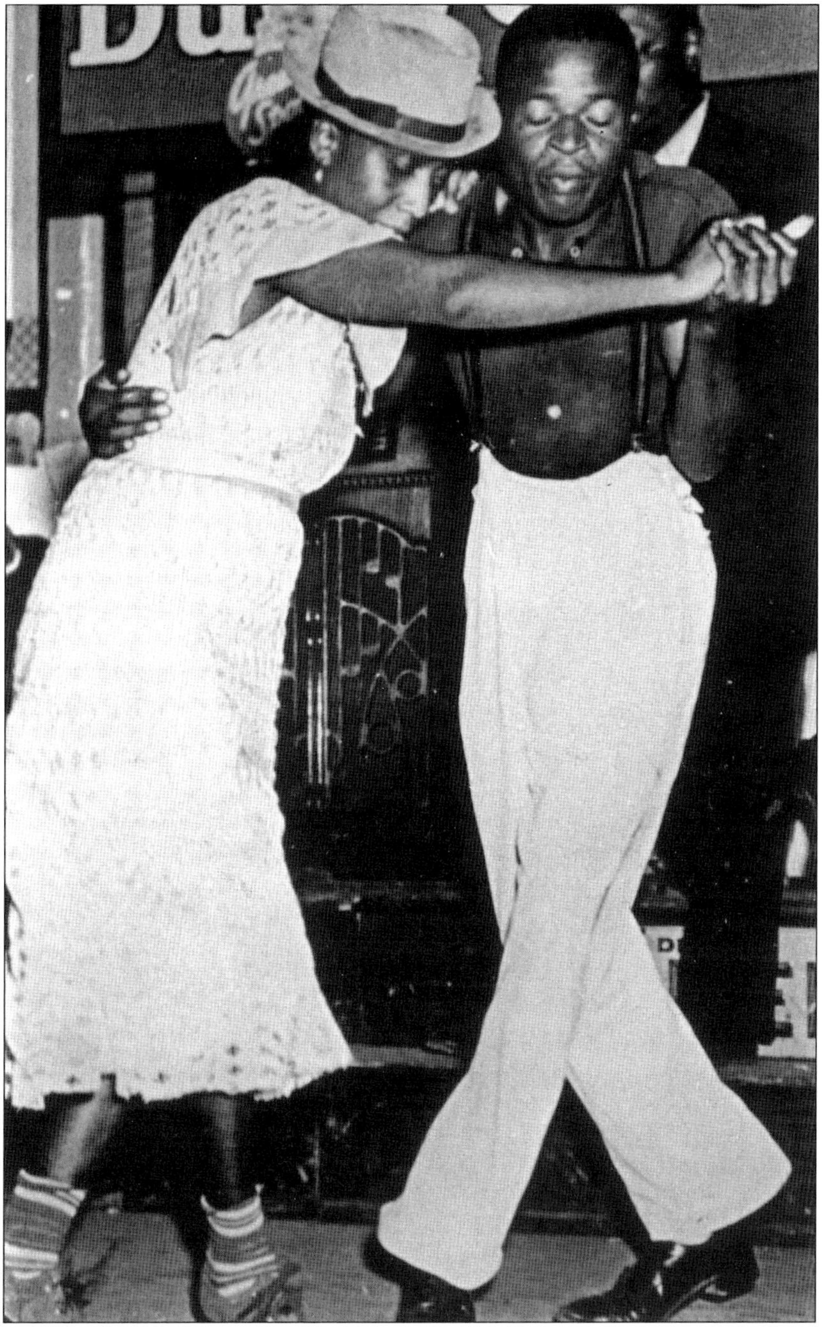

Some students became Big Apple regulars. They watched the dancers and learned the dances that they saw at the popular club. Then, they took the dance form back to campus. They began working with their friends on the dances and adding new steps. Someone would call out the dance steps, and one couple would jump into the middle of the floor and do the steps. Billy Spivey, then 19 years old, composed the tune "Big Apple" and formed a group of spirited students. During April 1938, the group was invited to perform in New York City at the Roxy Theater. (Courtesy of the Richland County Public Library.)

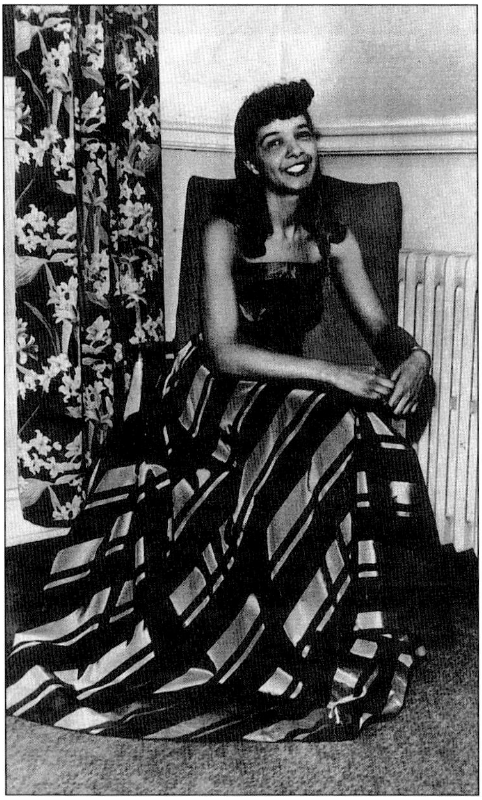

"Most women are fascinated by a display of the latest fashions, but numerous gentlemen were also scattered throughout the audience at the lovely Fashion Show . . . Charming as the models themselves was Mrs. Salle Mae O'Neal, mistress of ceremonies. Mrs. Pauline Williams opened the program with a beautiful rendition of 'Danny Boy' followed with a vocal solo 'The Lord's Prayer.' She also accompanied the narrator throughout the show with appropriate background music." This excerpt appeared in the *Palmetto Times* on October 4, 1962, in a story entitled "Trinity Musical Choir Presents Fashion Show." (Courtesy of the Harriet Titus family.)

Below a baseball game at Allen Field draws a crowd. The date of this picture is unknown. (Courtesy of the South Carolina State Museum.)

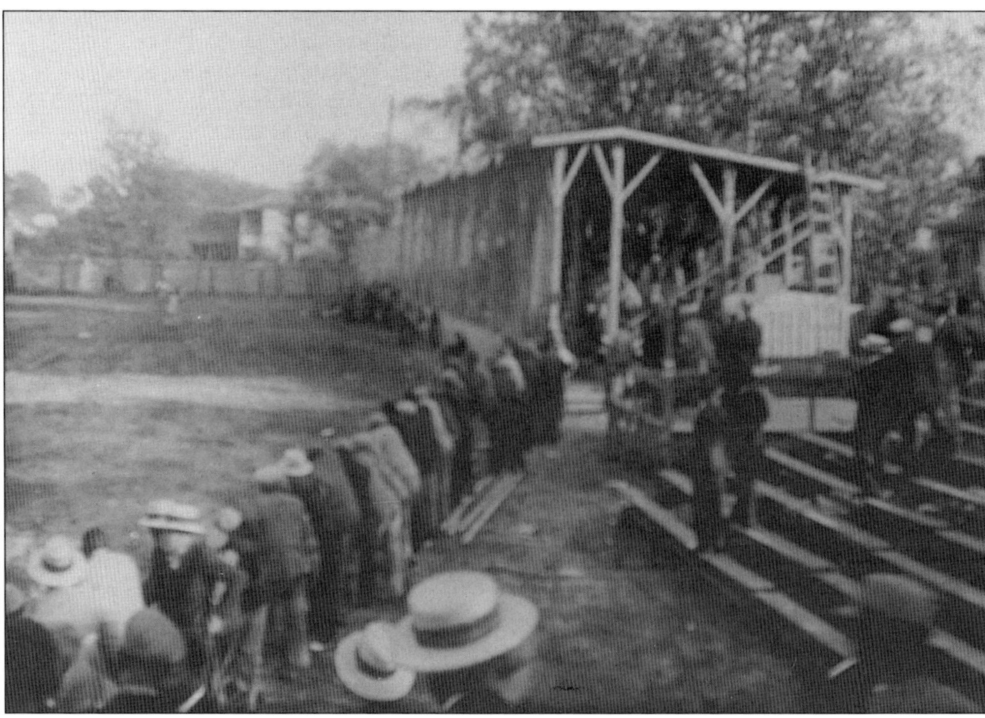

Six

Religious and Educational Life

Among the first acts of the freedmen was to establish churches where they could praise and thank God for deliverance from bondage. Their next thoughts were of schools.

—C.G. Garrett, Reminiscences, MS, Columbia, 1933

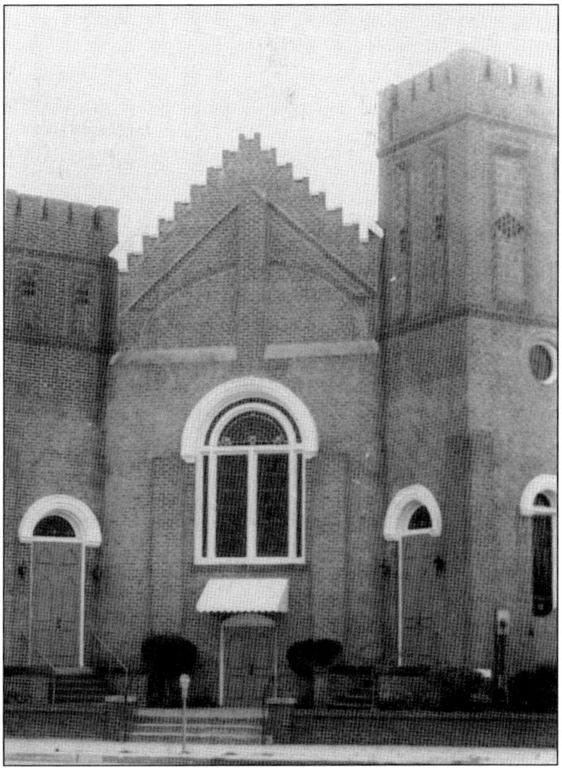

Pictured here in 2000, Ladson Presbyterian Church, the oldest African-American church in the city, began as a mission of the First Presbyterian Church. It was under the leadership of the Reverend Mark G. Johnson from 1876 until 1921.

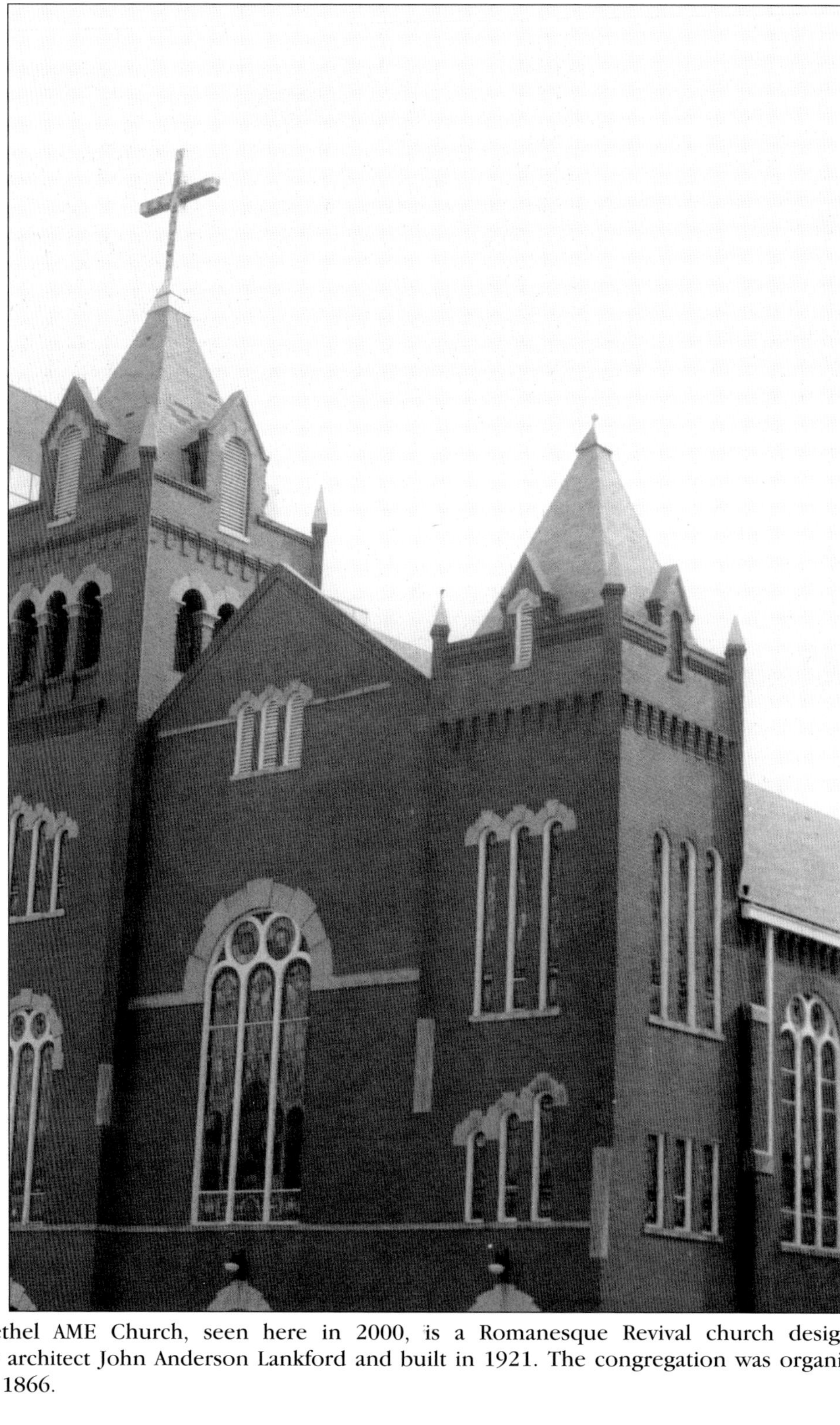

Bethel AME Church, seen here in 2000, is a Romanesque Revival church designed by architect John Anderson Lankford and built in 1921. The congregation was organized in 1866.

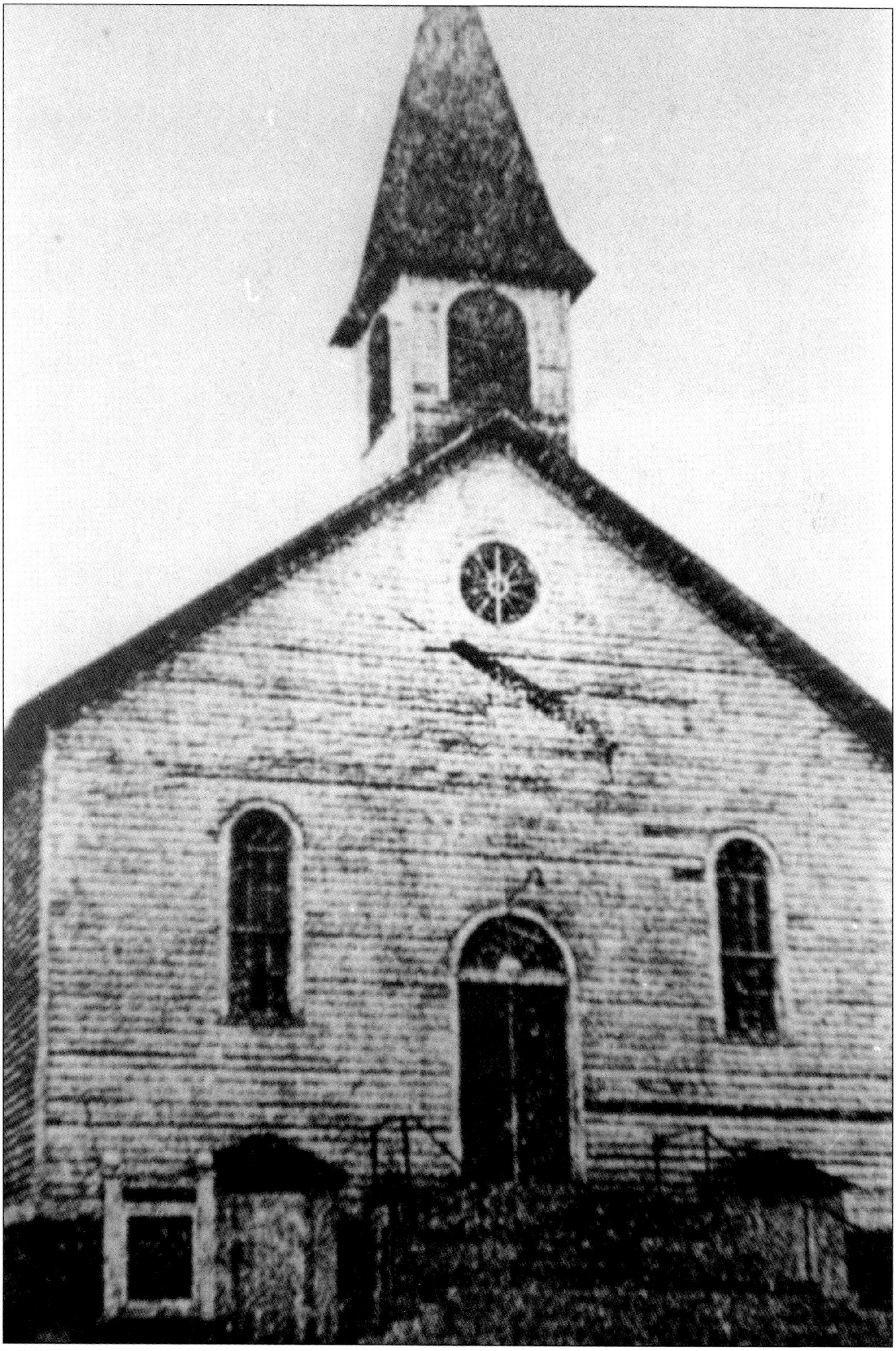

Pictured here is the Second Calvary Baptist Church.

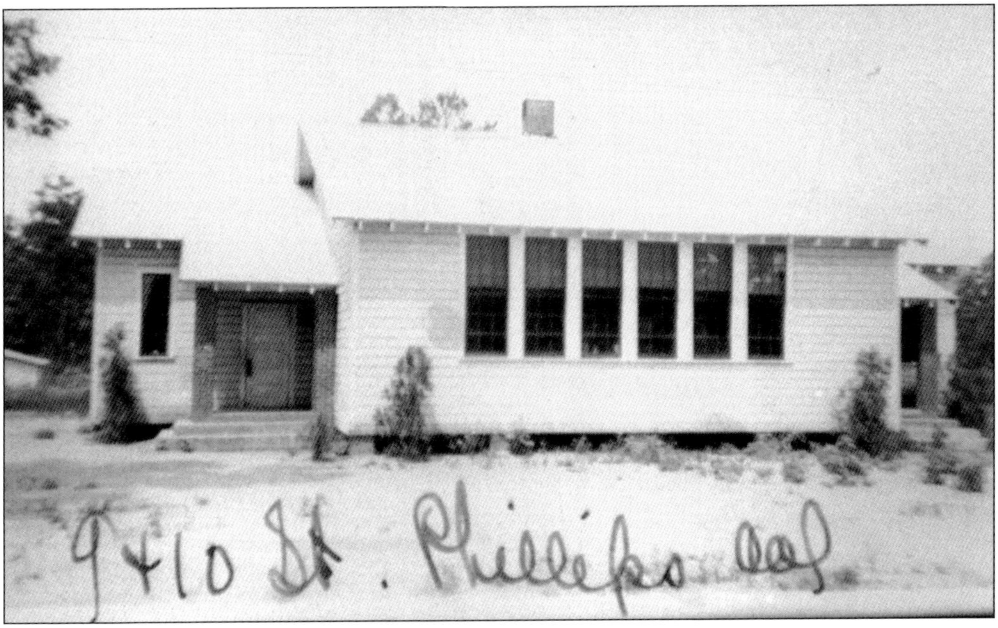

St. Phillip School, pictured here, was a three-teacher school that was in operation between 1938 and 1959. The school was named after the St. Phillip AME Church, which founded the original school probably during the era of Reconstruction. (Courtesy of the South Carolina State Archives.)

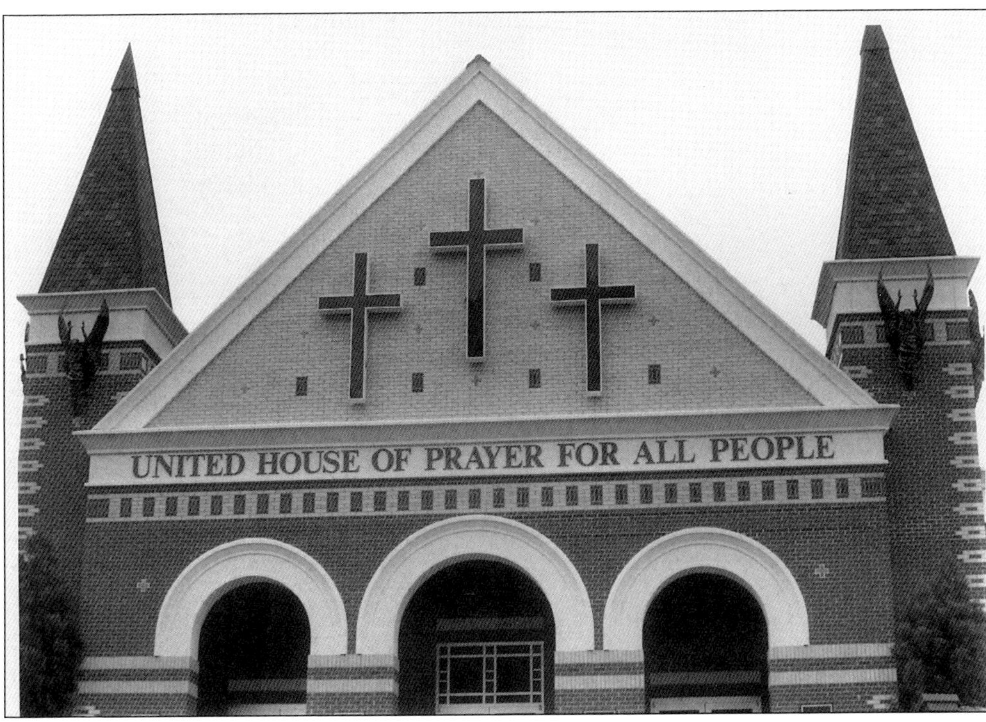

The United House of Prayer for All People is pictured here in the year 2000.

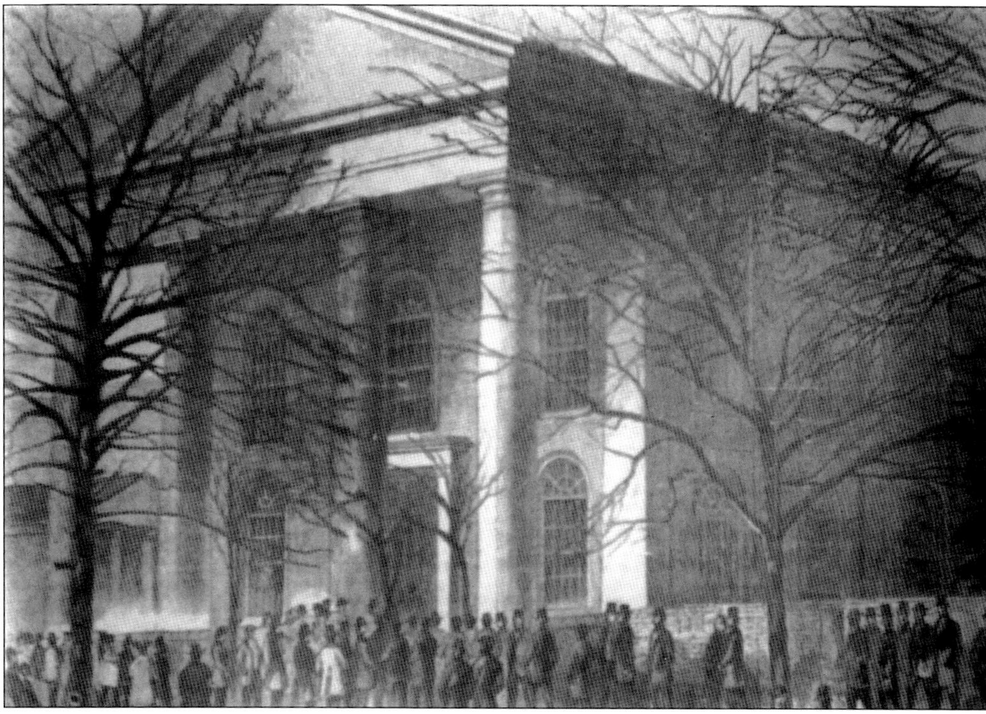

First Baptist Church is pictured above. First Baptist Church's record book, 1809–1840, notes that in 1827 the congregation consisted of 137 black members and 30 white members. Later, First Baptist Church, then a highly conservative white congregation, held the first meeting of the Secession Convention in April 1860. The black church members soon left First Baptist and founded a new church, Calvary Baptist, in 1867, with a membership of 255. It has been said that matriarch Celia Mann, a free person of color, started the church in the basement of her home.

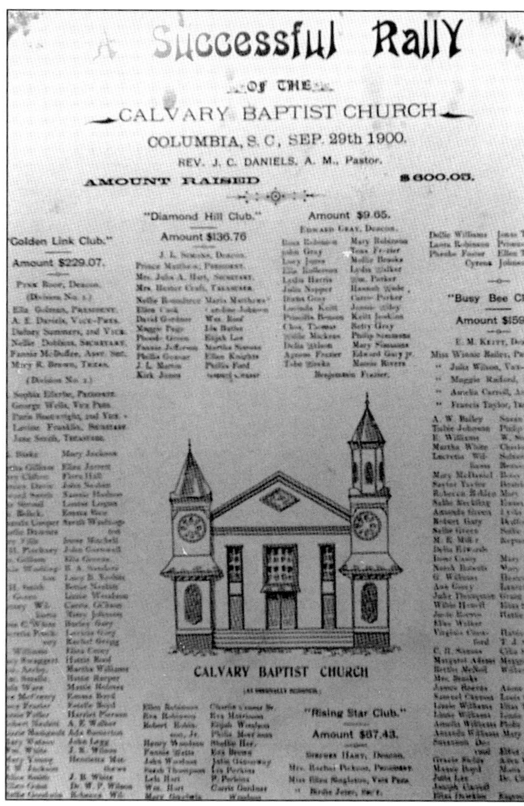

A Successful Rally
of the
CALVARY BAPTIST CHURCH
COLUMBIA, S. C., SEP. 29th 1900.
REV. J. C. DANIELS, A. M., Pastor.
AMOUNT RAISED $600.05.

"Diamond Hill Club." Amount $136.76

Amount $9.65.

"Golden Link Club." Amount $229.07.

"Busy Bee Club" Amount $159.

CALVARY BAPTIST CHURCH

"Rising Star Club." Amount $87.43.

The Calvary Baptist Church held a successful rally as this printed document attests.

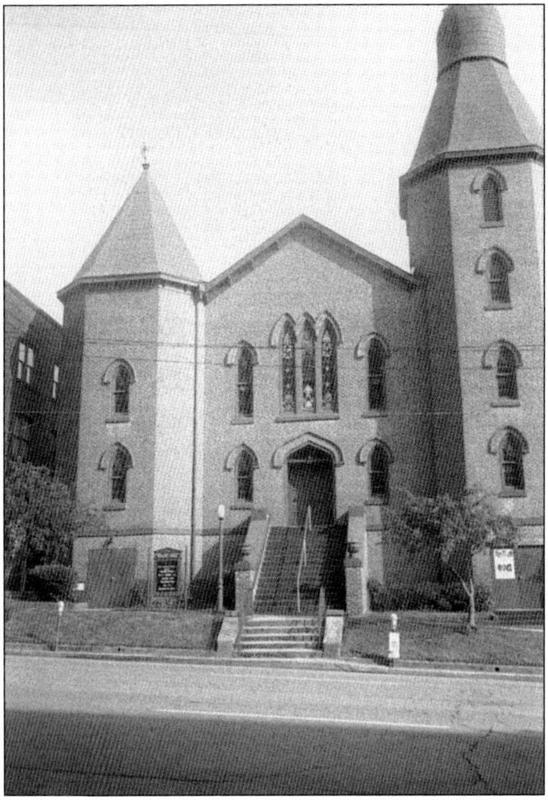

Sidney Park Christian Methodist Episcopal Church is pictured here in the year 2000.

Below is a modern photograph of Jones Memorial AME Zion Church.

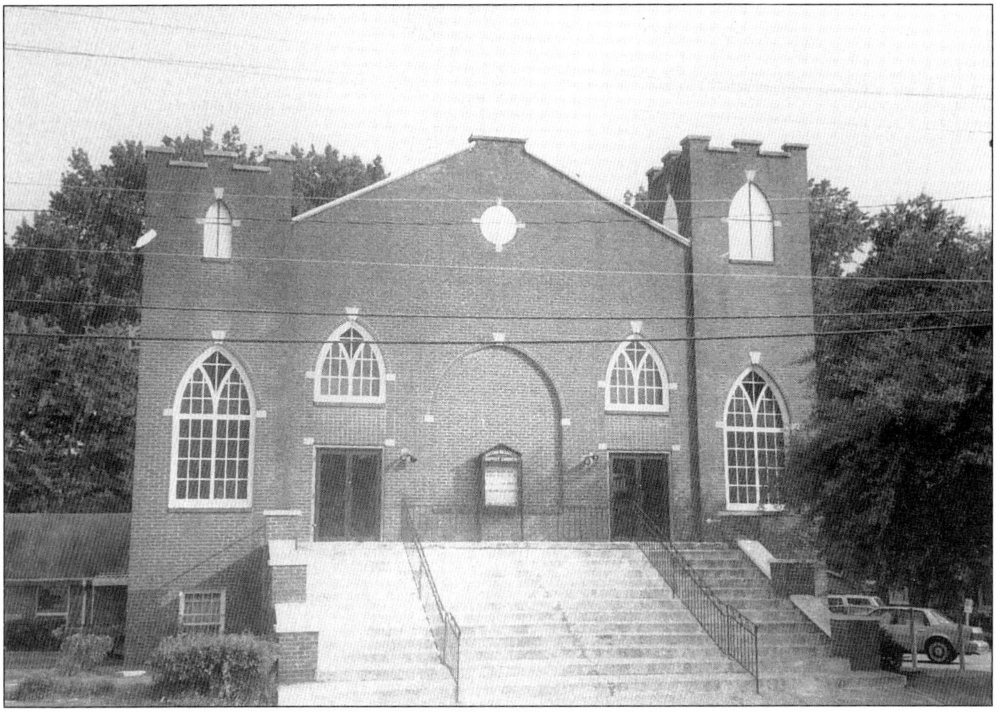

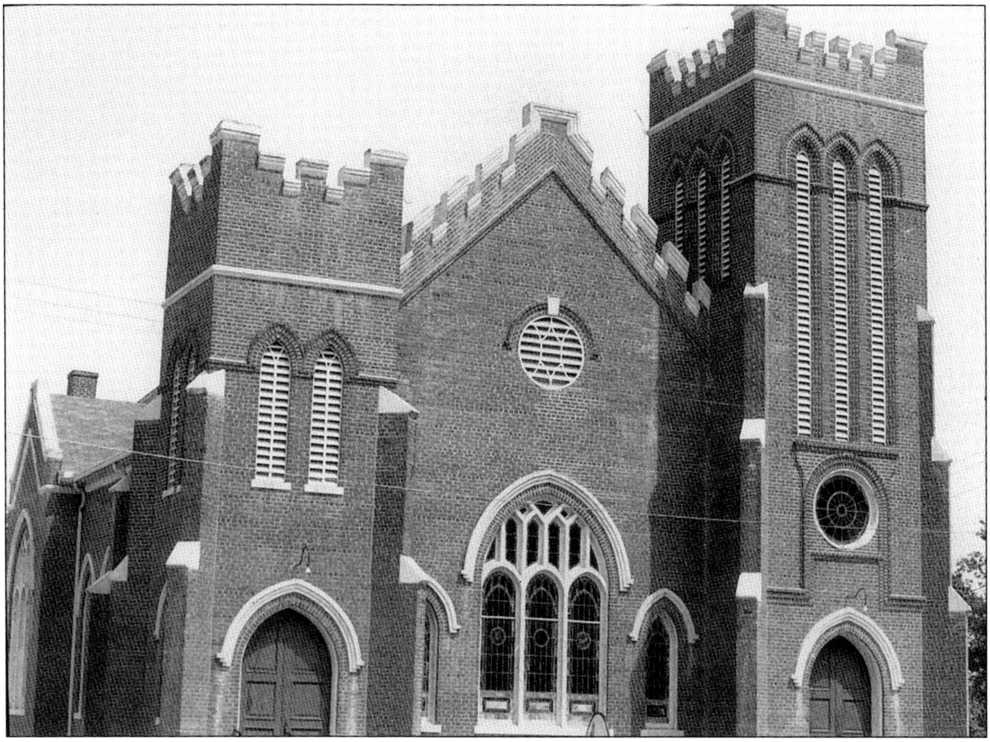

Wesley United Methodist Church appears here in a 2000 photograph.

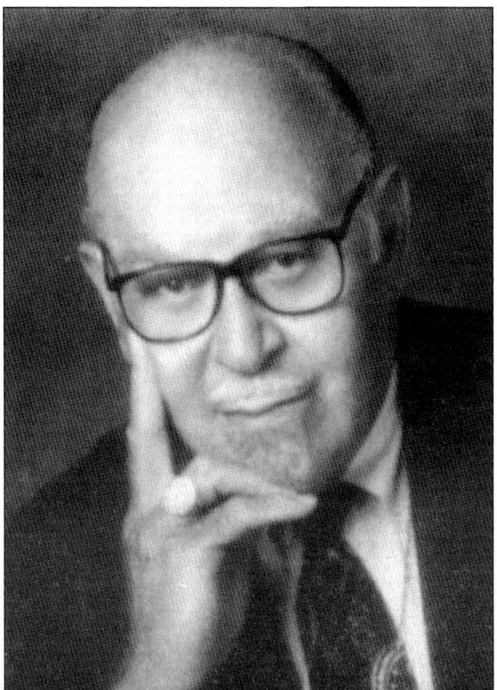

For a half-century, John Hurst Adams has used the pulpit and his influential position as a bishop in the African Methodist Episcopal Church to call for social change in South Carolina and the United States. (Courtesy of Black Media.)

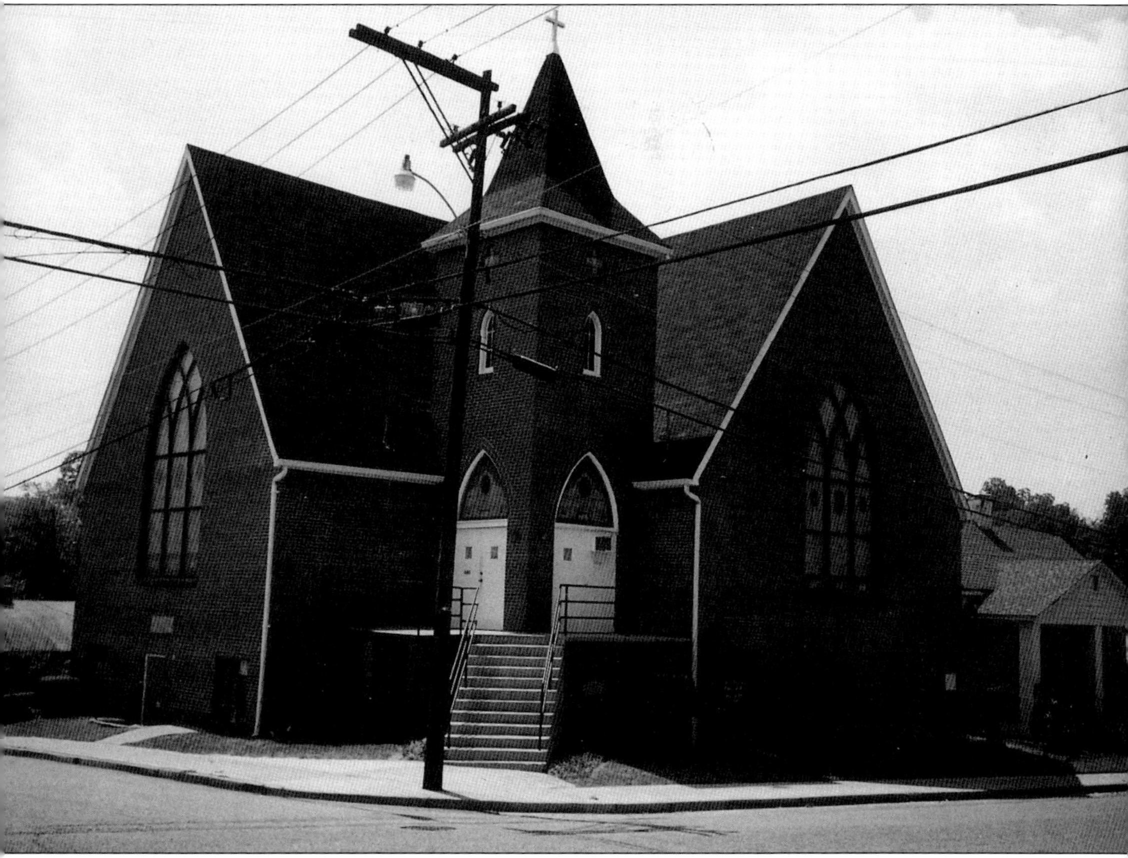

Pictured here is Chappelle Memorial AME Church.

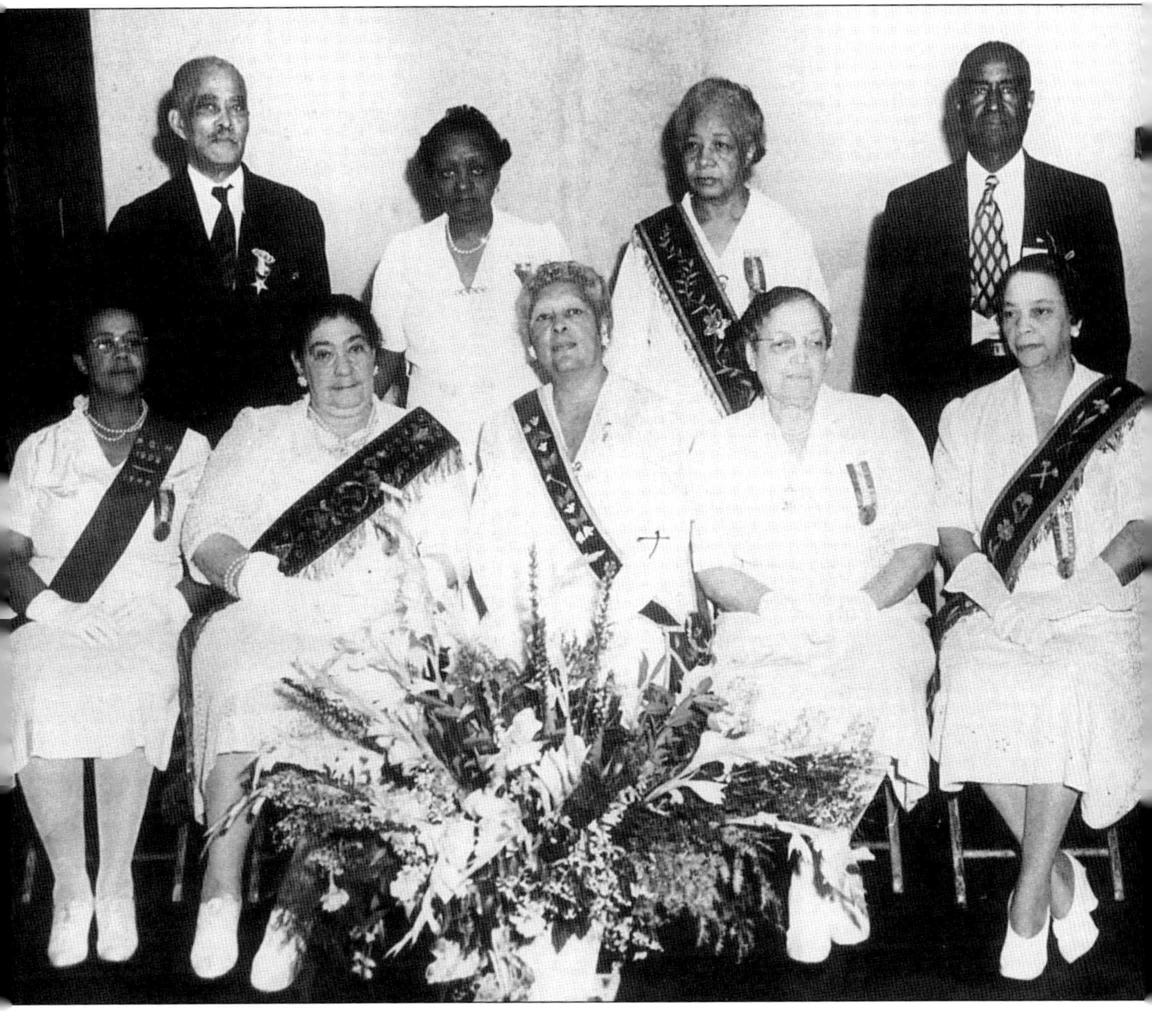

Women of today who wish to become involved in the Masons, a benevolent society, may join the Order of the Eastern Star, an organization created both for the wives of Masons and Masons themselves. Eastern Stars was founded in 1855. Chapters meet in a Lodge hall with whom they are affiliated. In Columbia, the Masonic Temple is located on 2314 Gervais Street. (Courtesy of the McKissick Museum.)

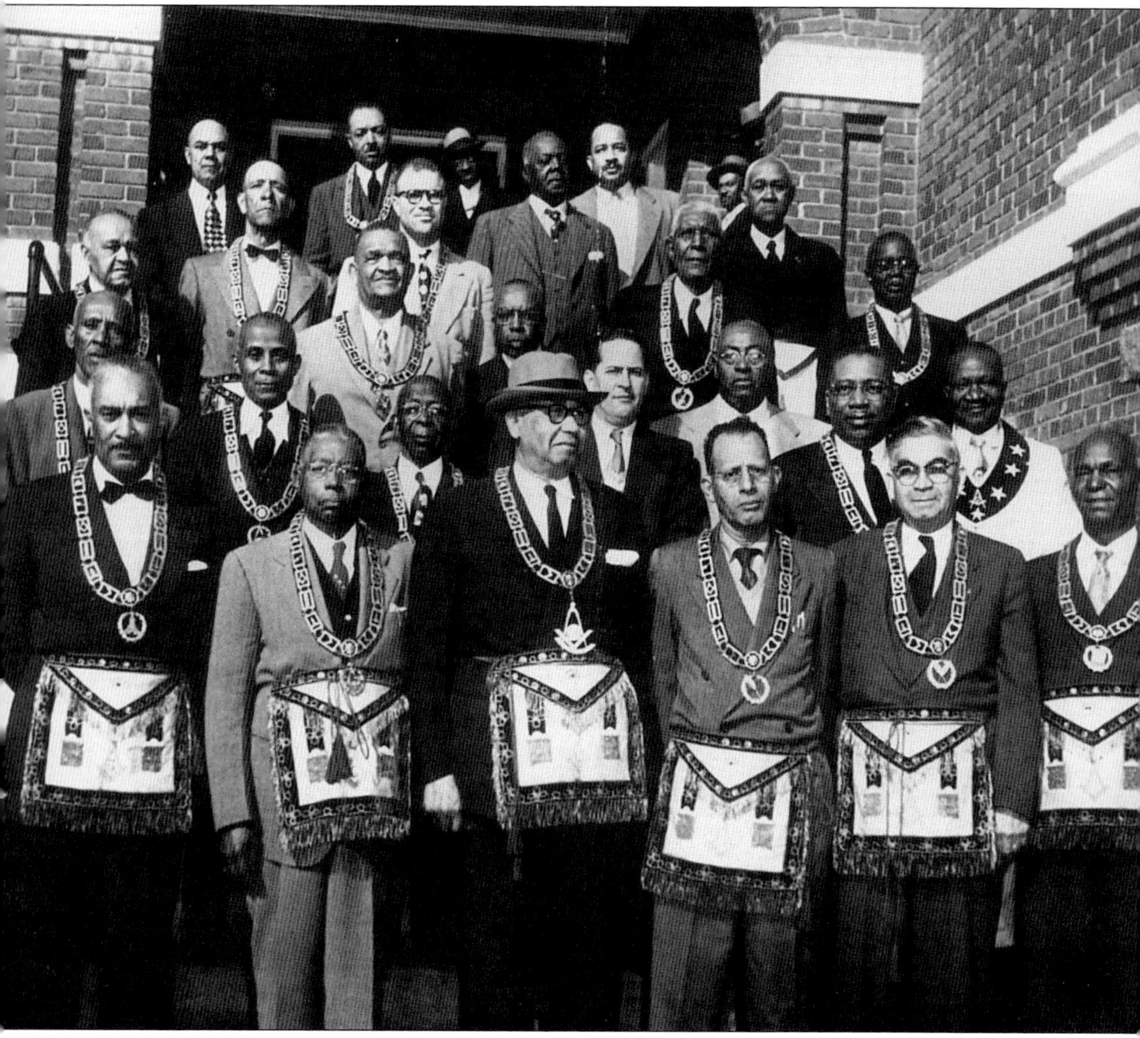

The proud men of the Prince Hall Lodge, wearing their lodge regalia, had this group photograph taken. (Courtesy of the McKissick Museum.)

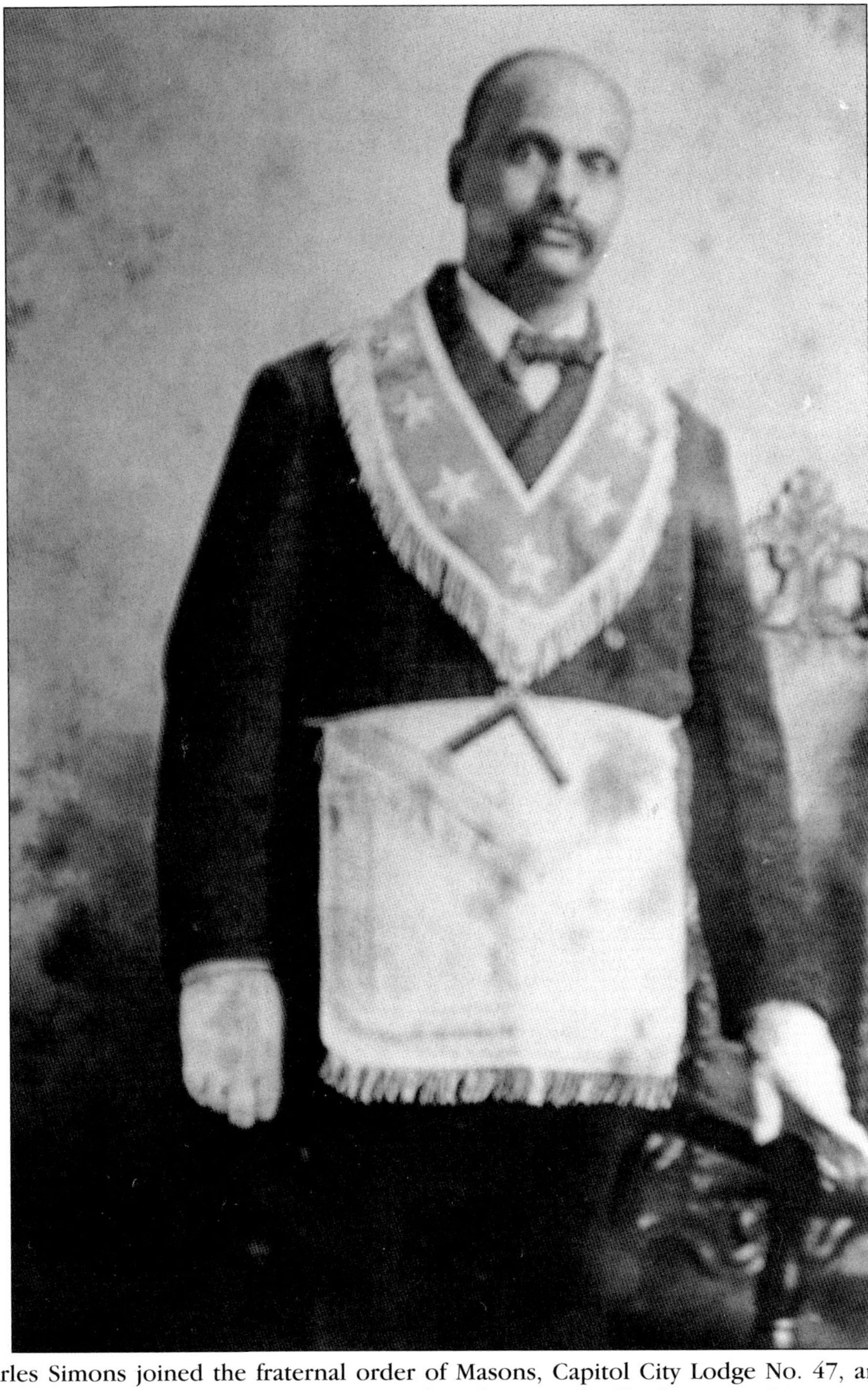

Charles Simons joined the fraternal order of Masons, Capitol City Lodge No. 47, and he became a Worshipful Master in 1912. In this photograph, Charles wears his ceremonial regalia. African-American lodges spread all over the state in the late 1800s and early 1900s, and included such organizations as the Masons, Odd Fellows, Good Templars, Knights of Pythias, and others. (Courtesy of the Historic Columbia Foundation.)

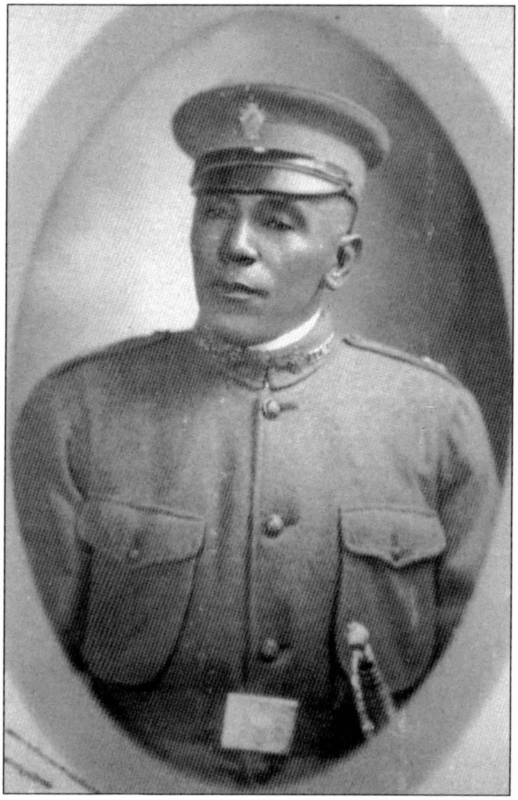

Alonzer Summers, pictured in the early 1900s, was a member of the Knights of Pythias. (Courtesy of Caroline Summers Floyd.)

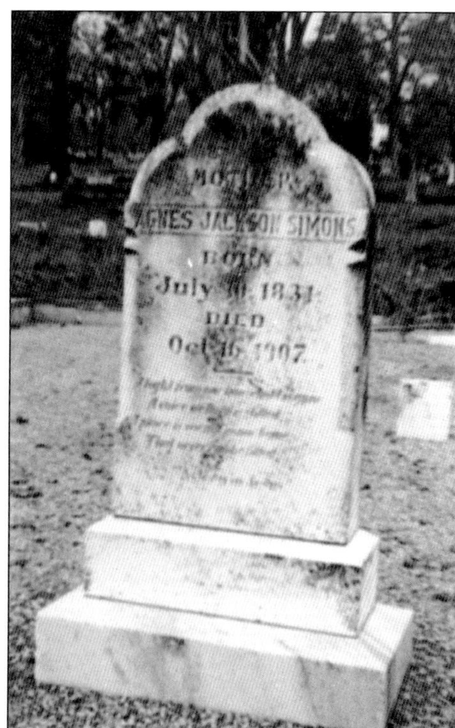

Randolph Cemetery is a memorial to Benjamin J. Randolph, a delegate to the South Carolina General Assembly during Reconstruction. When Randolph was assassinated in 1868, his colleagues established this cemetery in his honor. Some of South Carolina's most prominent black leaders are buried here. (Courtesy of the Historic Columbia Foundation.)

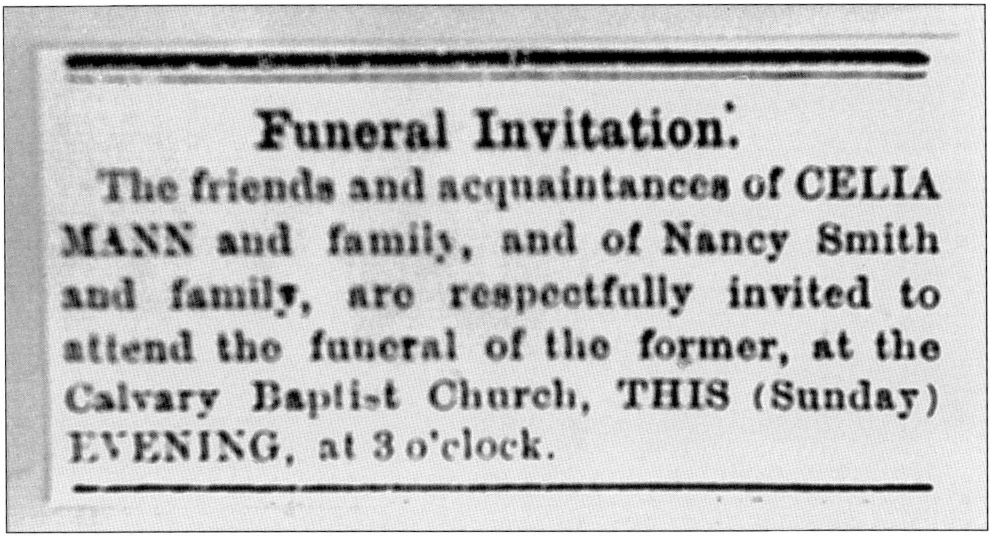

Funeral Invitation.

The friends and acquaintances of CELIA MANN and family, and of Nancy Smith and family, are respectfully invited to attend the funeral of the former, at the Calvary Baptist Church, THIS (Sunday) EVENING, at 3 o'clock.

This is an invitation to the funeral of Celia Mann. (Courtesy of the Historic Columbia Foundation.)

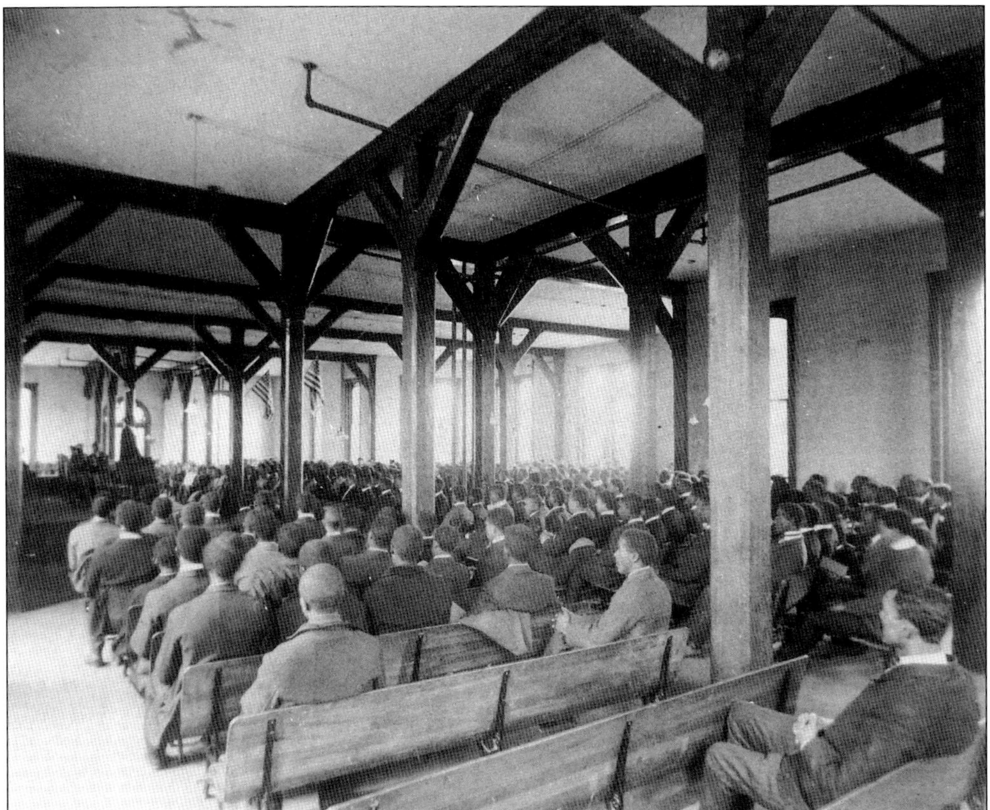

A Benedict University graduation ceremony is shown here in 1920. Benedict University was founded *c.* 1870 by the American Baptist Mission Society to educate freed men and their descendants. (Courtesy of the McKissick Museum.)

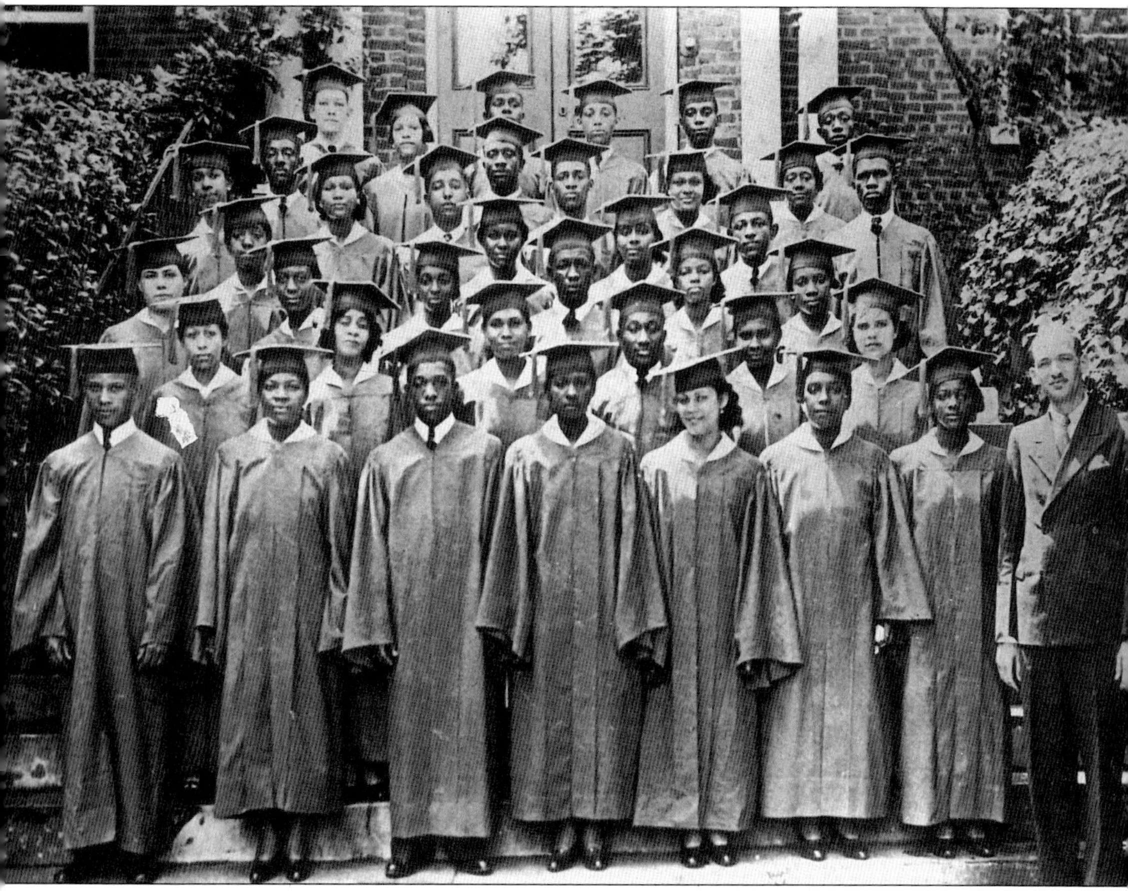

Allen University was founded in 1881. Operated by the African Methodist Episcopal Church, the institution was established to educate clergy for AME churches. Allen also offered law and vocational degrees. Pictured here is Allen University's Class of 1935. (Courtesy of the McKissick Museum.)

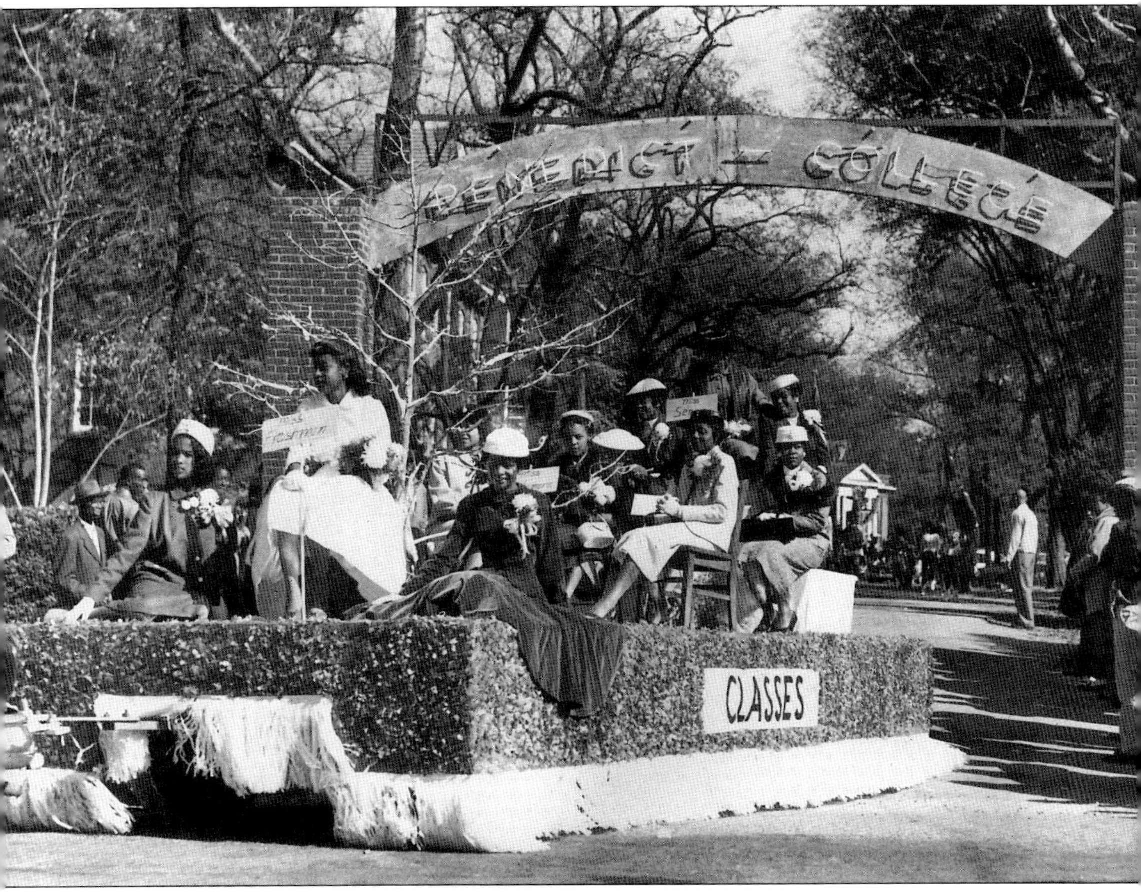

A Benedict College parade is shown here at the campus's entrance. (Courtesy of the McKissick Museum.)

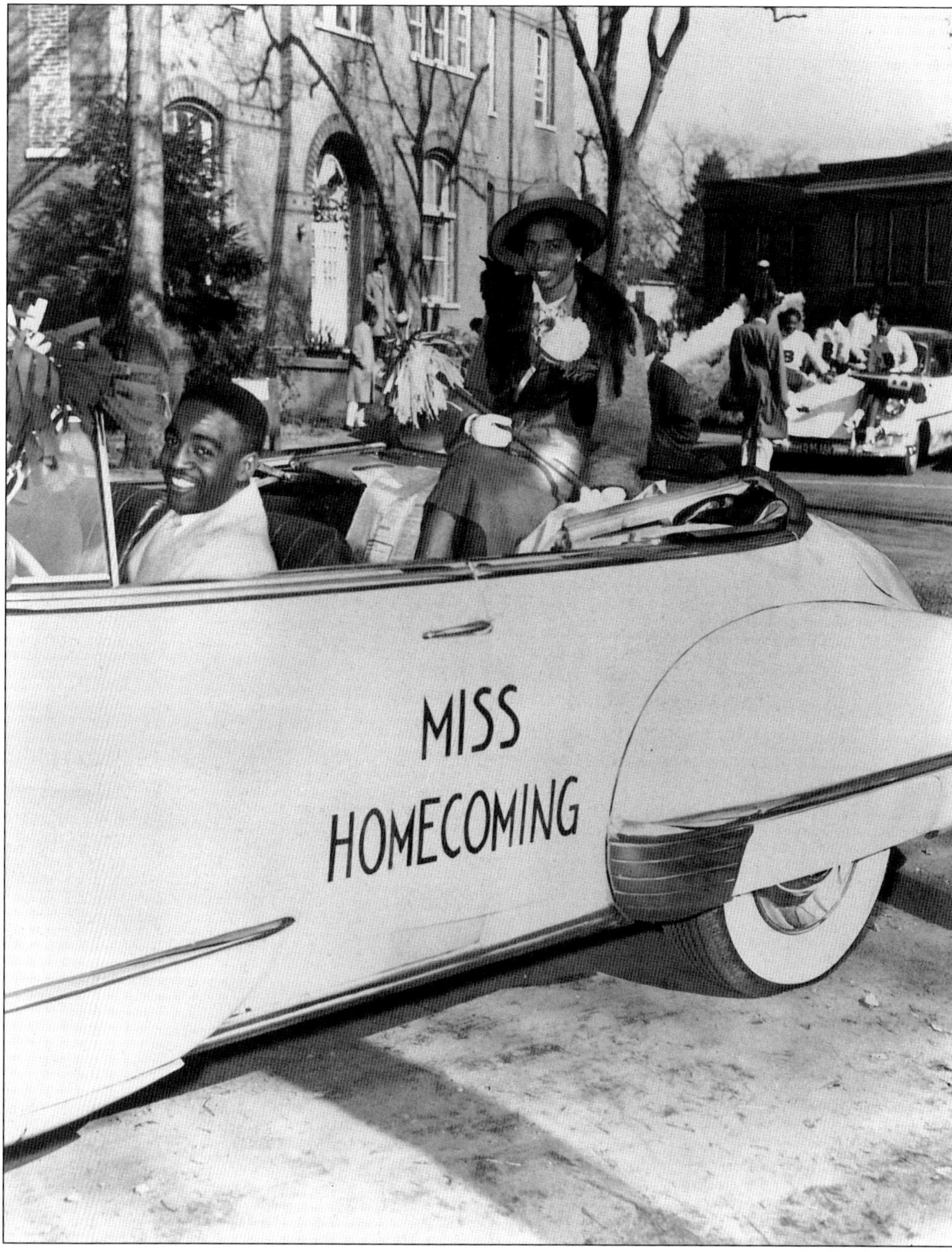

Miss Homecoming travels in style in this Benedict College parade. (Courtesy of the McKissick Museum.)

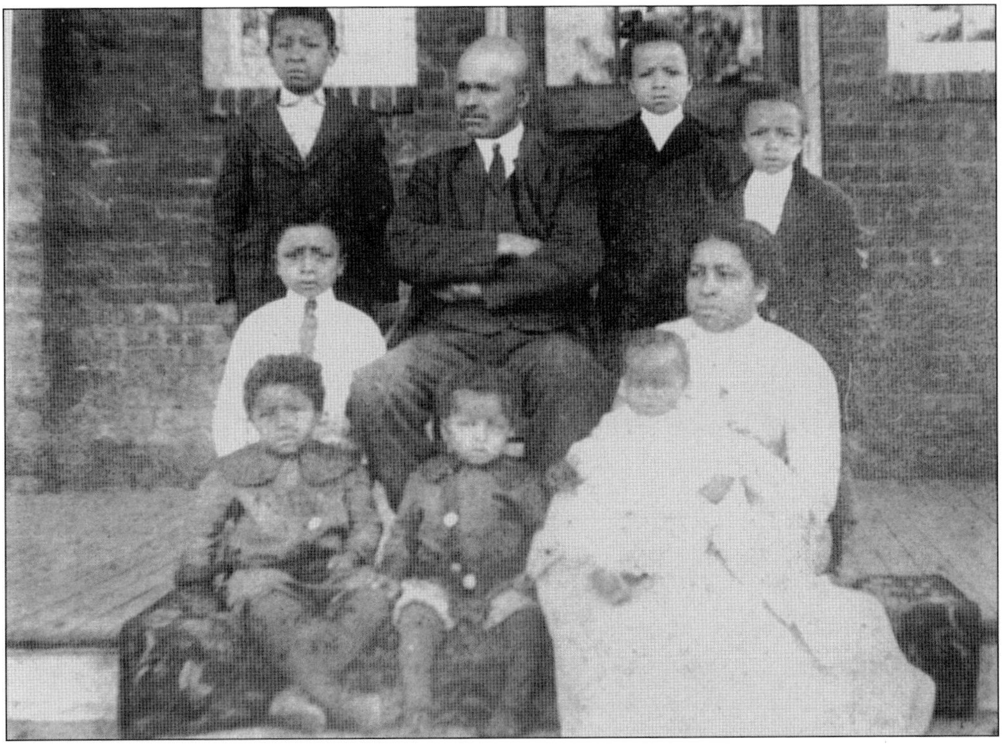

Above is a group photograph of the Harper family. (Courtesy of the Harper family.)

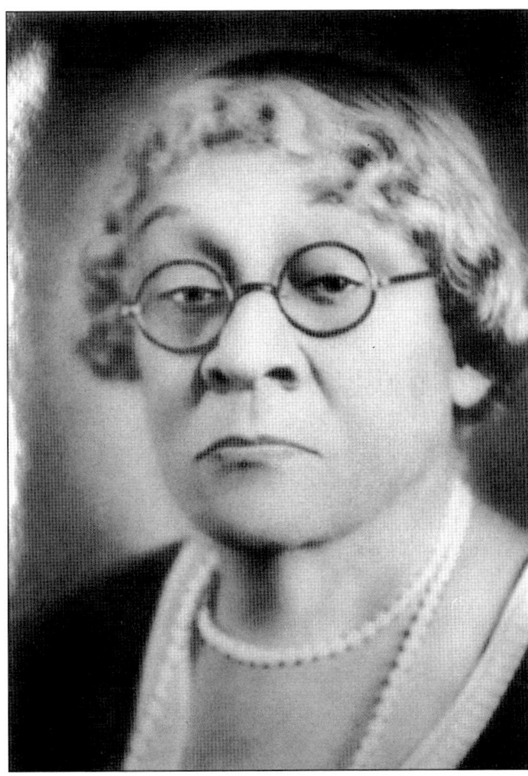

Celia Dial Saxon, raised in Columbia, was born in 1857 during the time of slavery. She earned a degree from the Normal School for teachers on the USC campus during Reconstruction. Saxon entered the classroom as a teacher at age 20 and, for 55 years, she taught in the schools of Columbia. She taught in secondary schools, including Booker T. Washington High School, and was an active member of the Federation of Negro Women, a group whose members helped establish the Fairwold Home for Girls (later known as the Wilkinson Home). (Courtesy of the United Black Fund.)

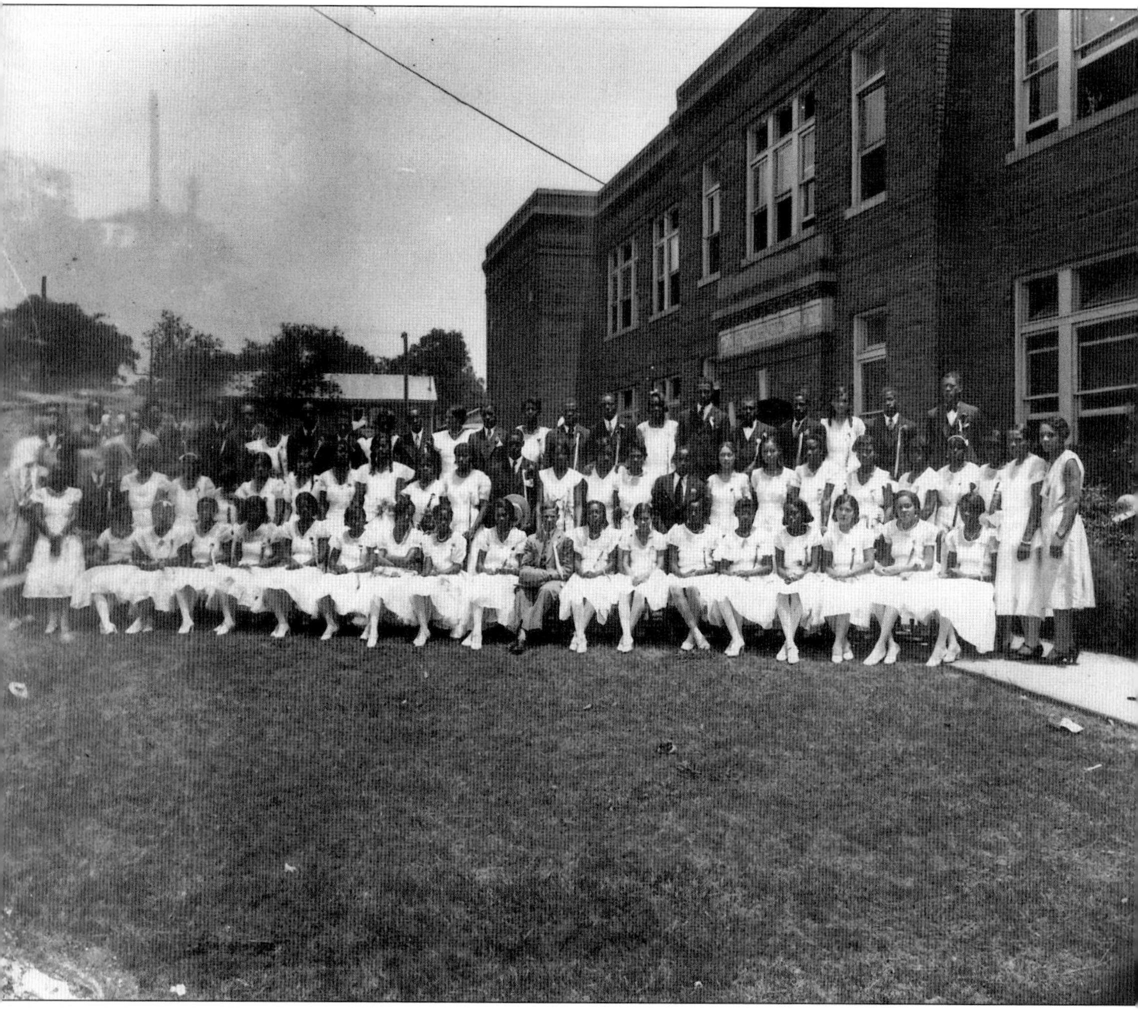

Students at Booker T. Washington High School are pictured here in 1933. In 1916, Booker T. Washington became the second public school for blacks in Columbia. Howard Elementary, founded in 1883 in the Arsenal Hill neighborhood, was the first. Booker T. Washington served grades one through ten in the earlier years, and from 1916 until 1948 it was the only public high school for blacks in Columbia. It was accredited by the Southern Association of Colleges and Schools at that time. (Courtesy of the McKissick Museum.)

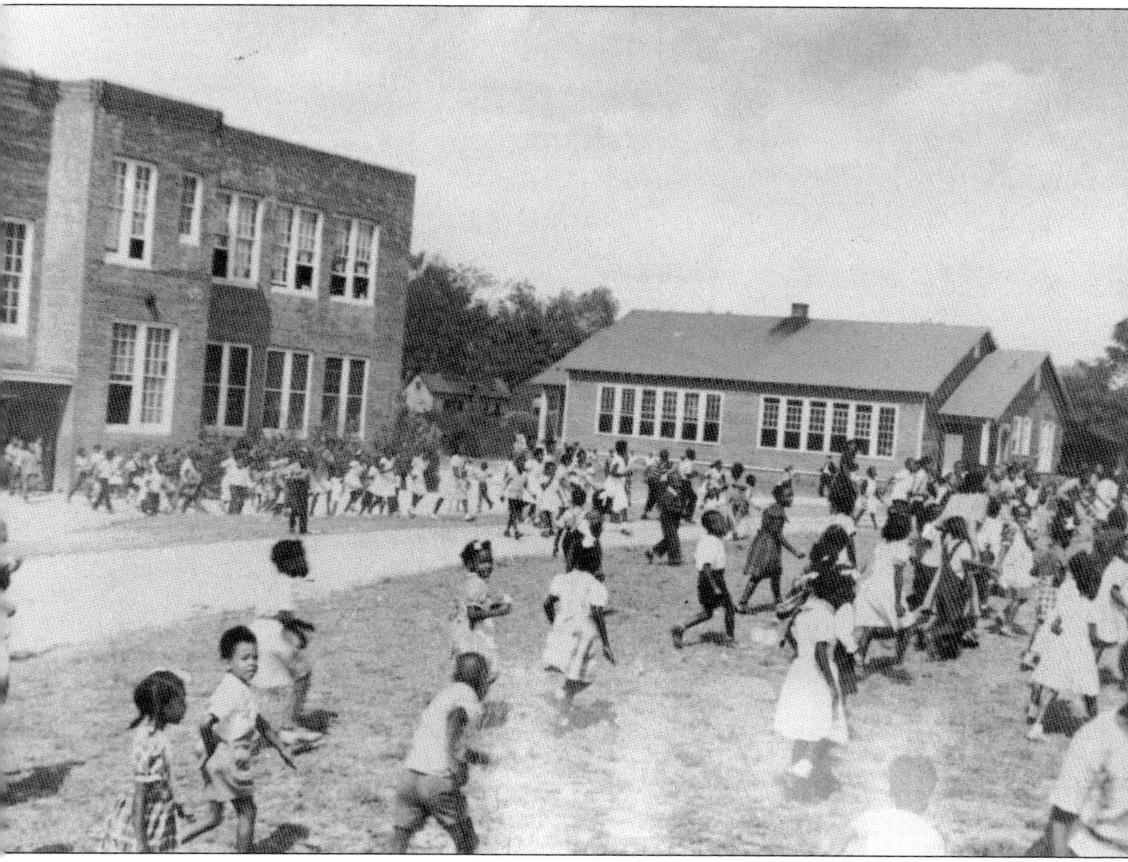

Children at Carver Elementary School are pictured here. (Courtesy of the Columbia Fire Dept.)

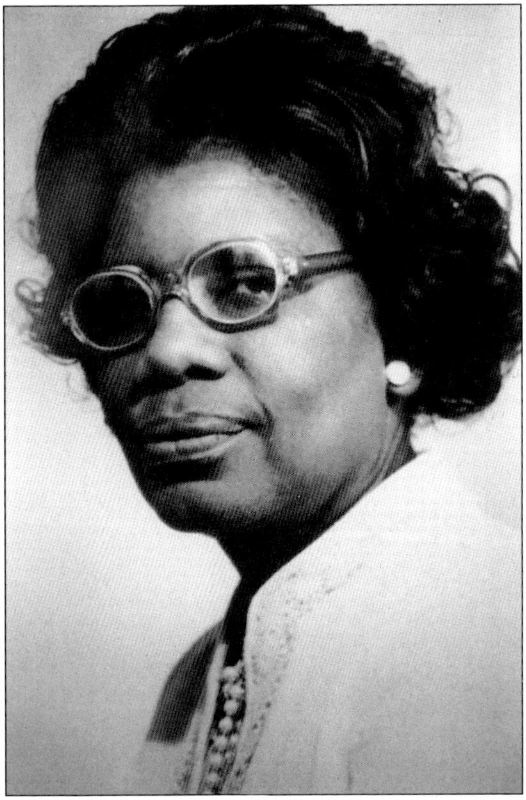

Fannie Phelps Adams was a longtime teacher at Booker T. Washington and won the prestigious National Teacher of the Year award. (Courtesy of the United Black Fund.)

Pictured below is the backyard of Howard Elementary School. (Courtesy of the Columbia Fire Dept.)

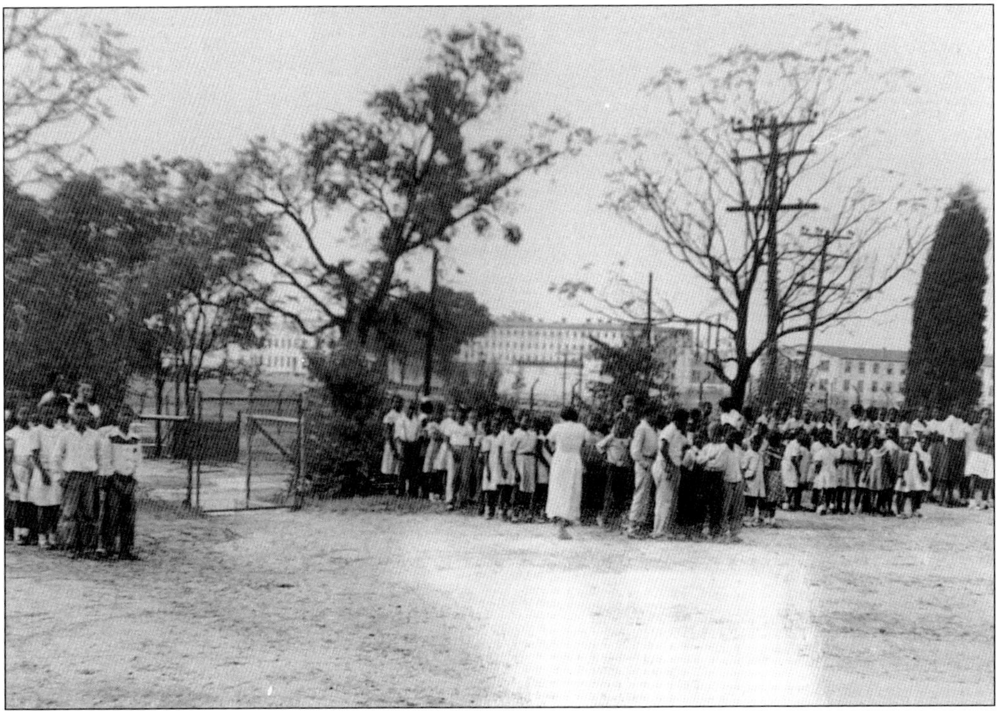

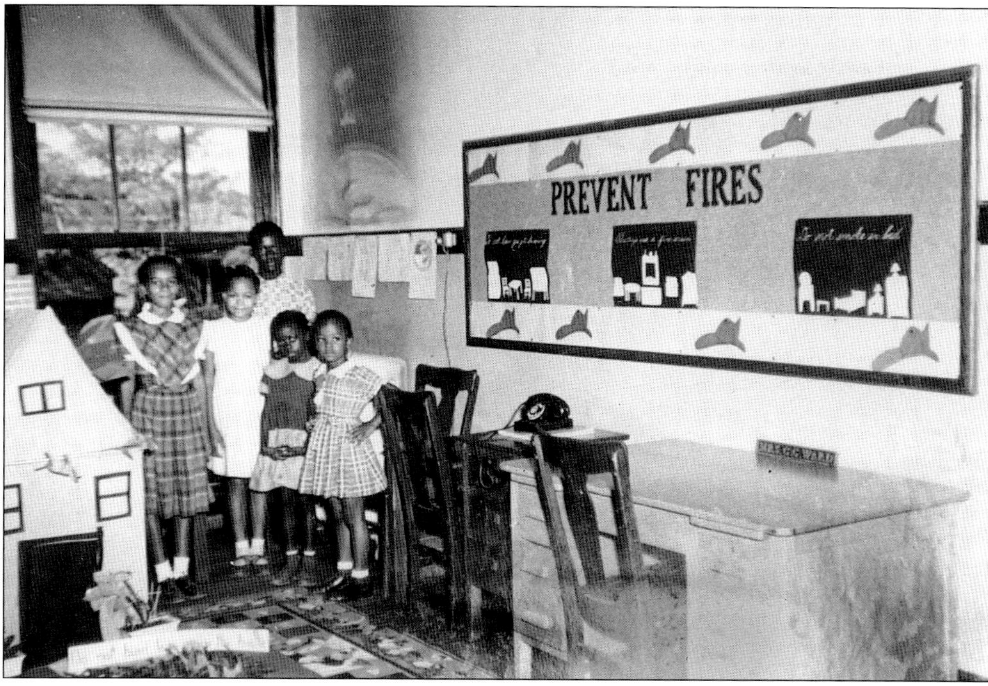

Pictured here is a scene from Howard Elementary School, Columbia's first public school for African-American children. In 1866, newly emancipated followers of African Methodists in Columbia organized the Bethel Society. The church first met in a former sword factory on Wayne Street and, later, gave its property at Lincoln and Hampton Streets to Columbia for the site of Old Howard School. (Courtesy of the Columbia Fire Dept.)

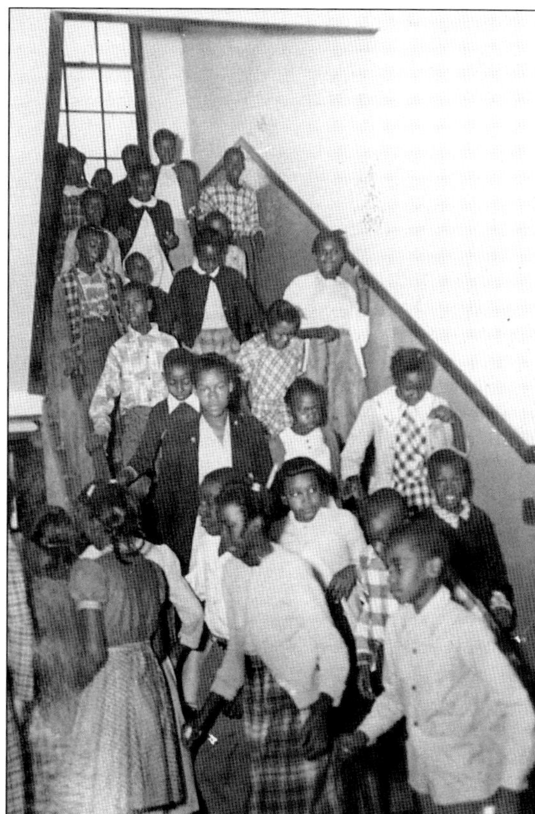

Students climb the stairs at Saxon Elementary School. (Courtesy of the Columbia Fire Dept.)

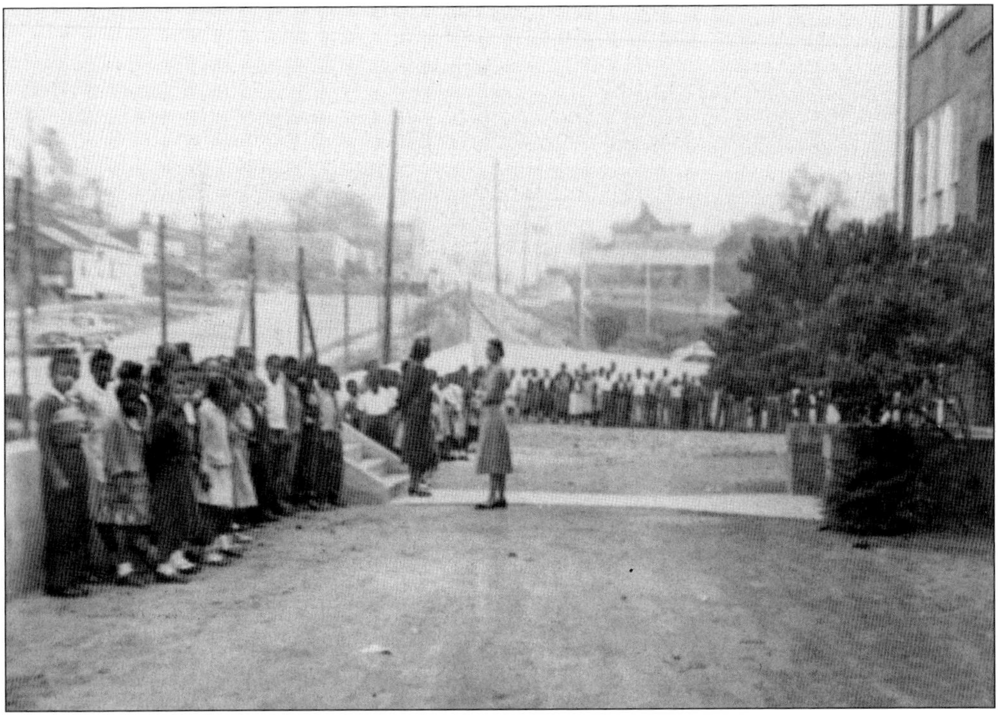

Here is another view of students at Saxon Elementary School. (Courtesy of the Columbia Fire Dept.)

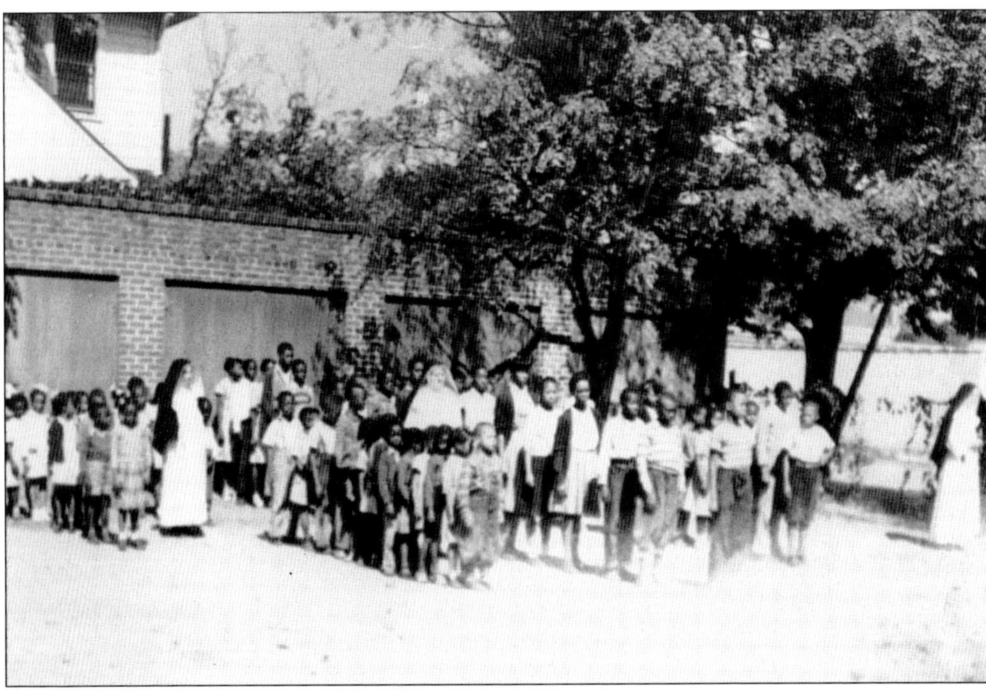

These children attended Blessed Martin Parochial School. (Courtesy of the Columbia Fire Dept.)

Ferguson Academy began in 1886 in Abbeville. Later renamed for Samuel P. Harbison, this institution moved to Columbia in 1910 following a disastrous fire on the Abbeville campus and remained in operation until 1958. Pictured at right is J.W. Harper, who taught on the Harbison campus for many years. (Courtesy of the Harper family.)

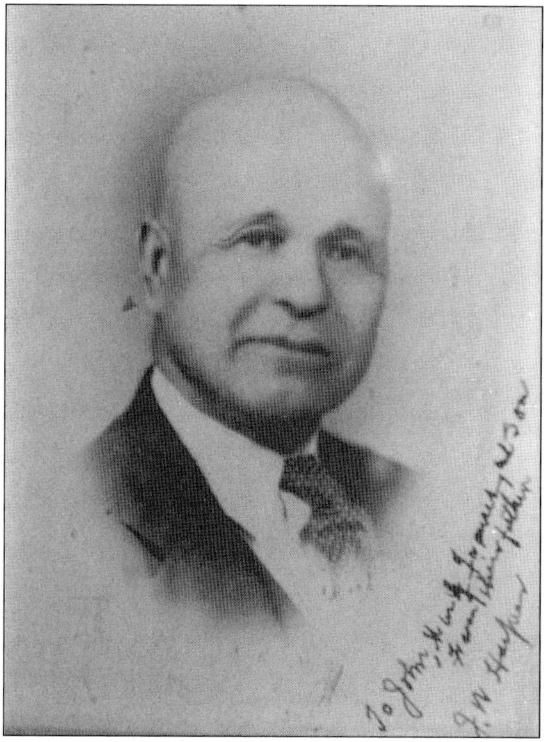

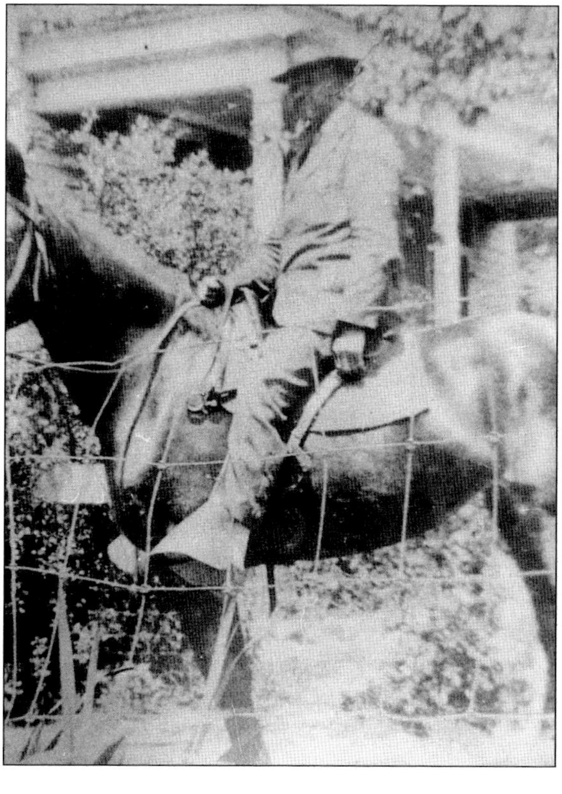

J.W. Harper rides a horse in this view. (Courtesy of the Harper family.)

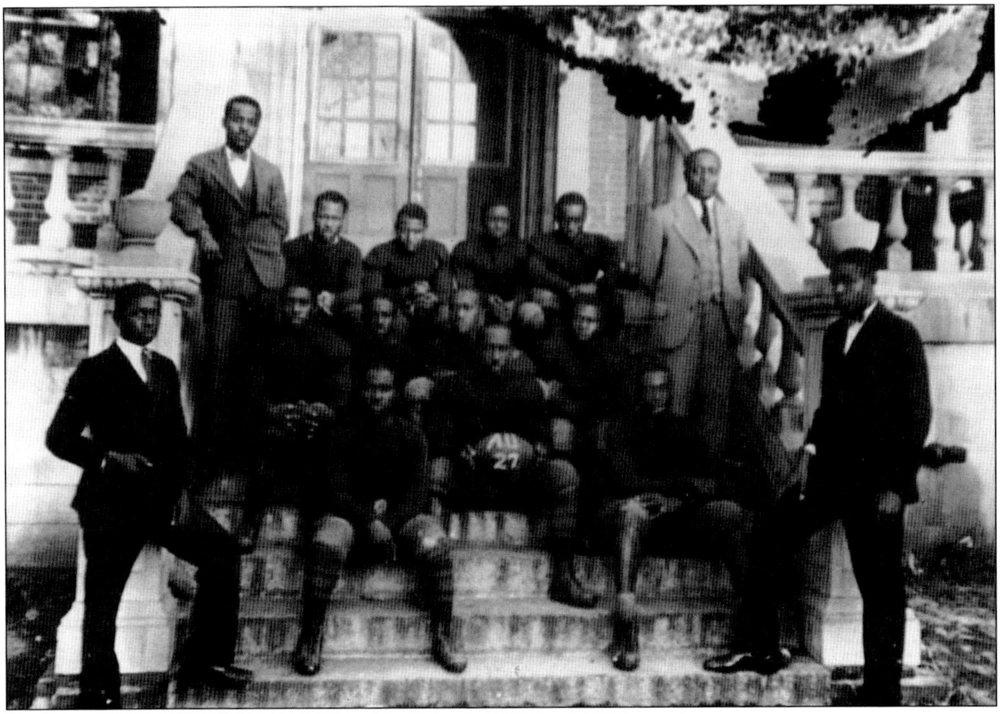

The Allen University football team gathered for the above photograph in 1927. (Courtesy of the South Carolina State Museum.)

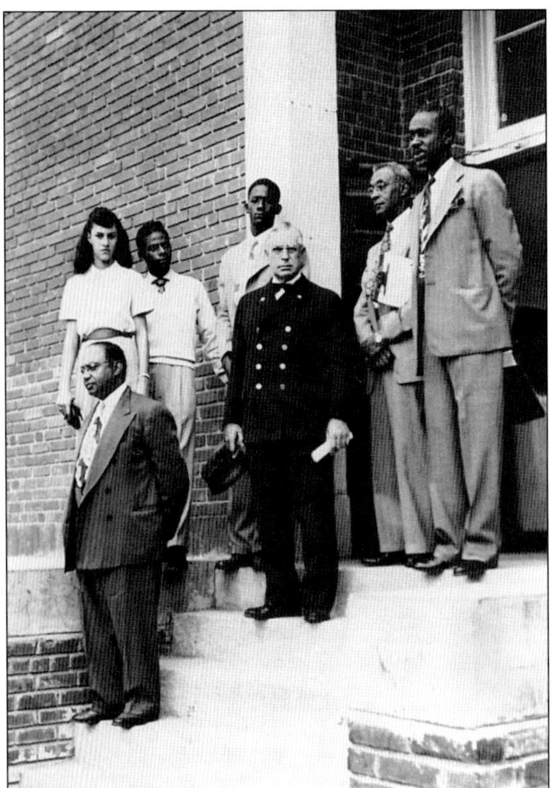

Standing outside after a fire drill at Howard School are, from left to right, Principal Madden, three students from Booker T. Washington High School, Chief Marsh, W.C. Johnson, and Windfred Mundle. (Courtesy of the Columbia Fire Dept.)

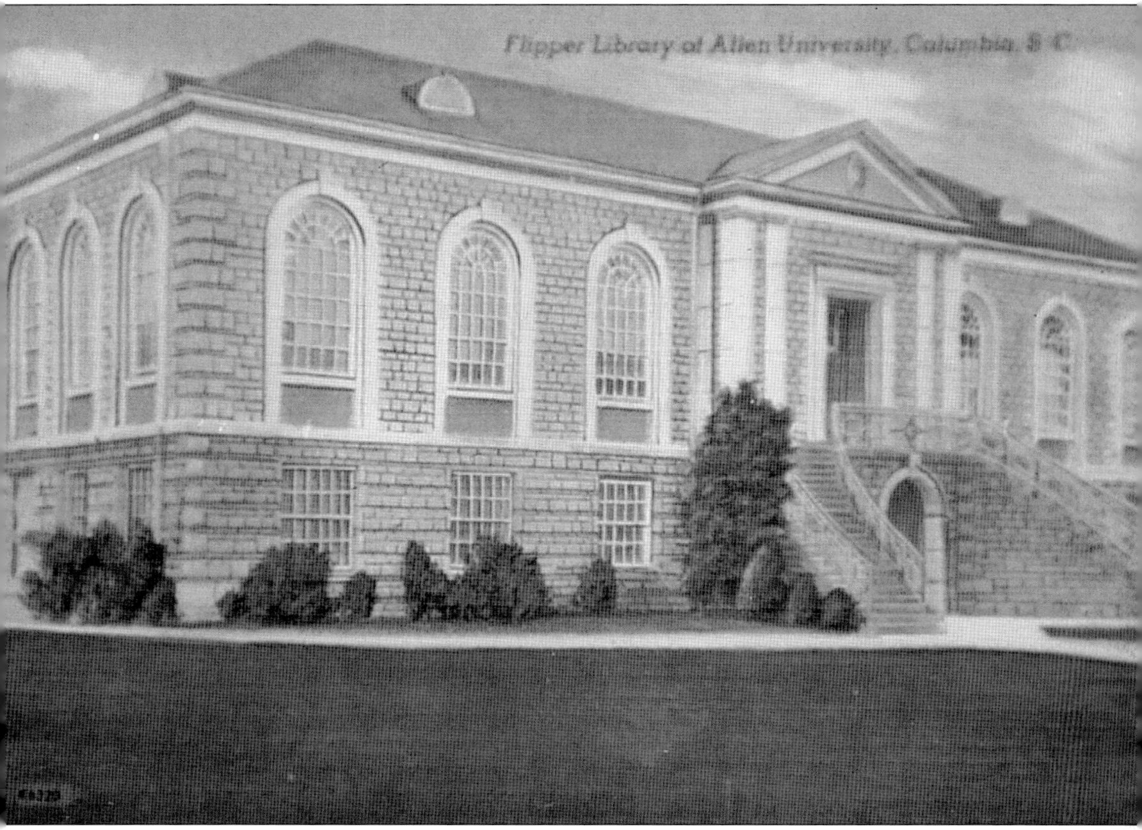

The subject of this postcard is the Flipper Library of Allen University. (Courtesy of Five Points Book Shop.)

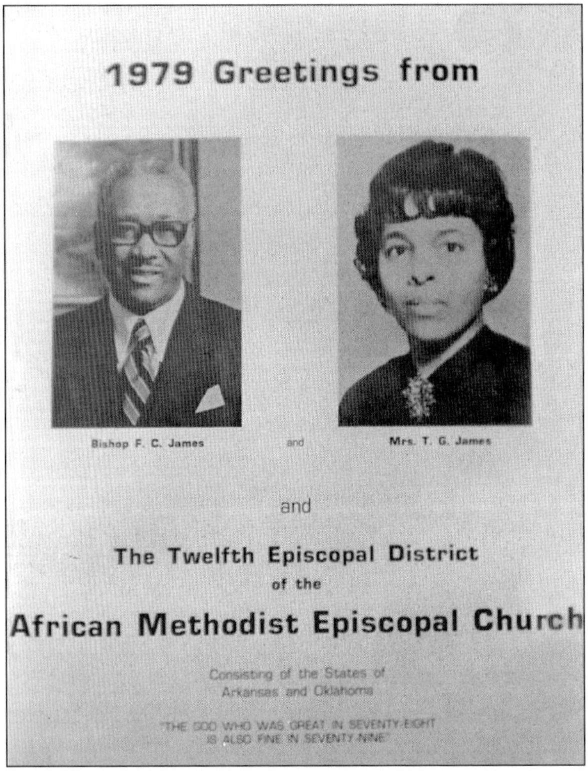

Bishop Frederick C. James led the 7th Episcopal District (comprising the state of South Carolina) of the AME Church. During his ministry, James served as a pastor in the United States and in southern Africa. He also served as the board chairman of Allen University.

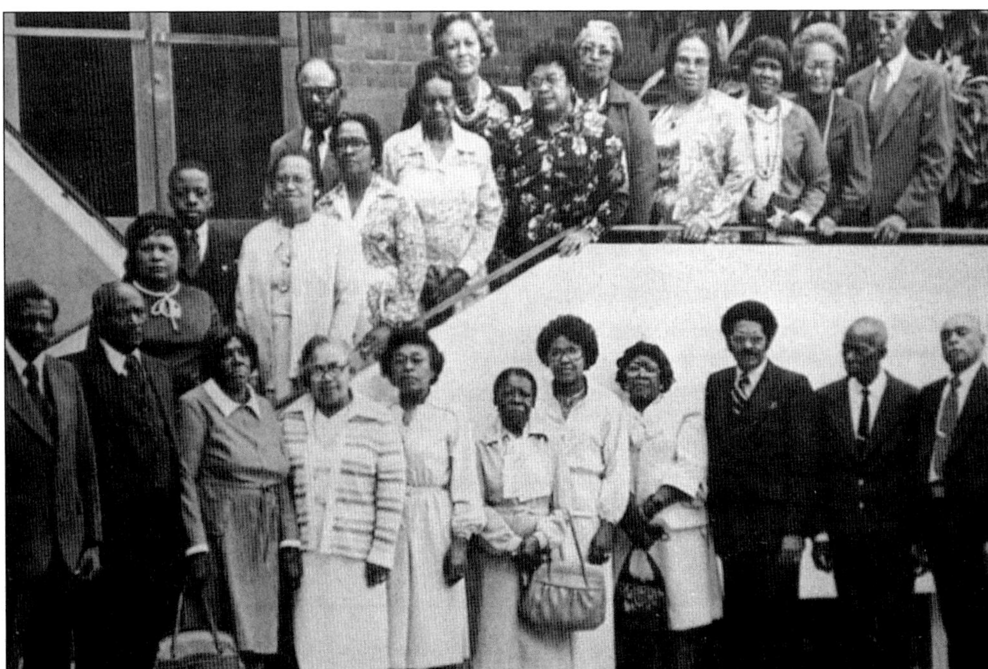

Pictured above is the Columbia Conference Laymen Organization of the 7th Episcopal District.

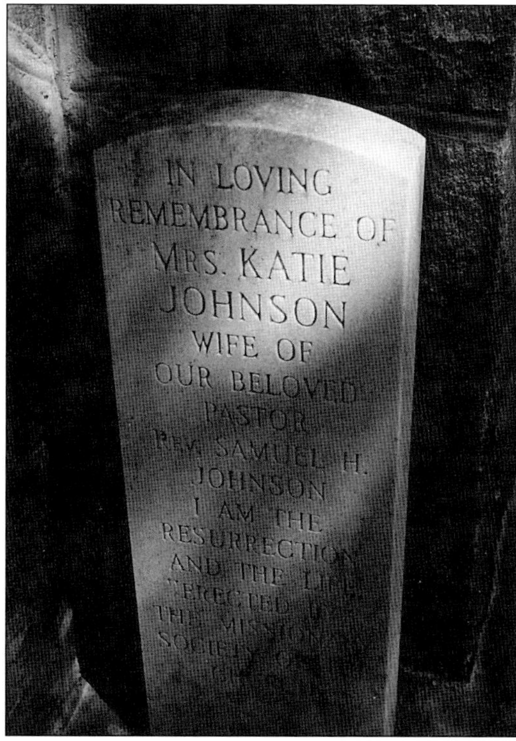

The congregation of First Calvary Baptist Church organized under a brush arbor in 1865 and then moved to the basement of the Mann-Simons Cottage, the home of Celia Mann. The original grave markers of the Reverend Samuel Johnson and his wife, Katherine Johnson,were placed in front of the new church building in 1950, although their graves remain at the site of first church. First Calvary has incorporated the original cornerstone in the façade of their new building.

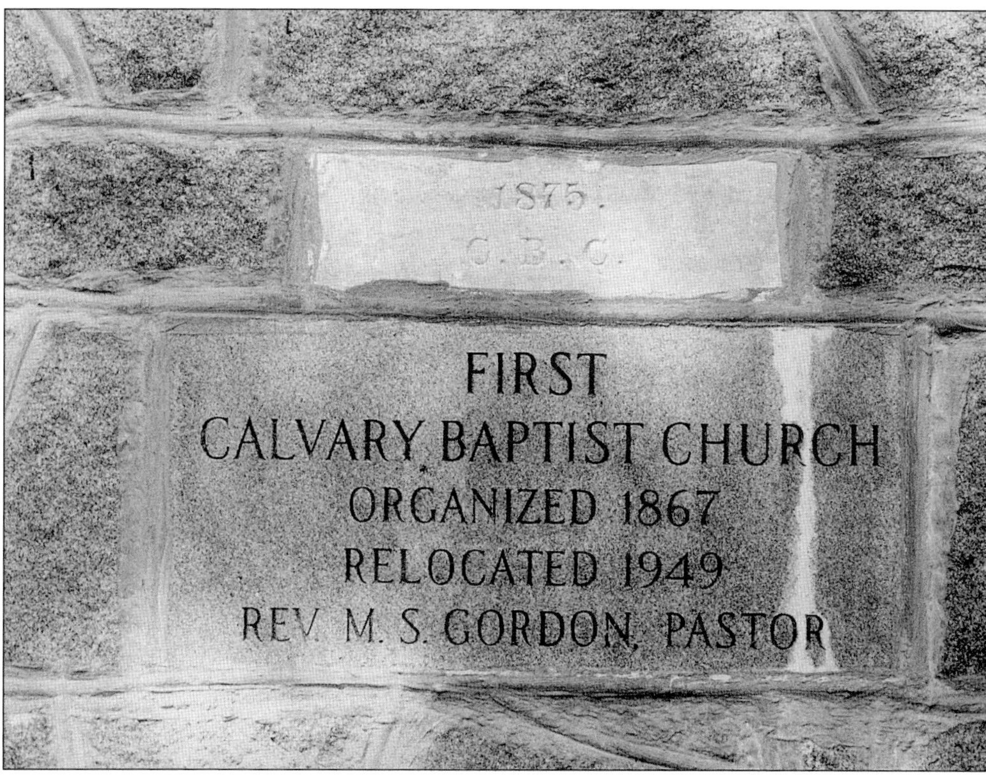

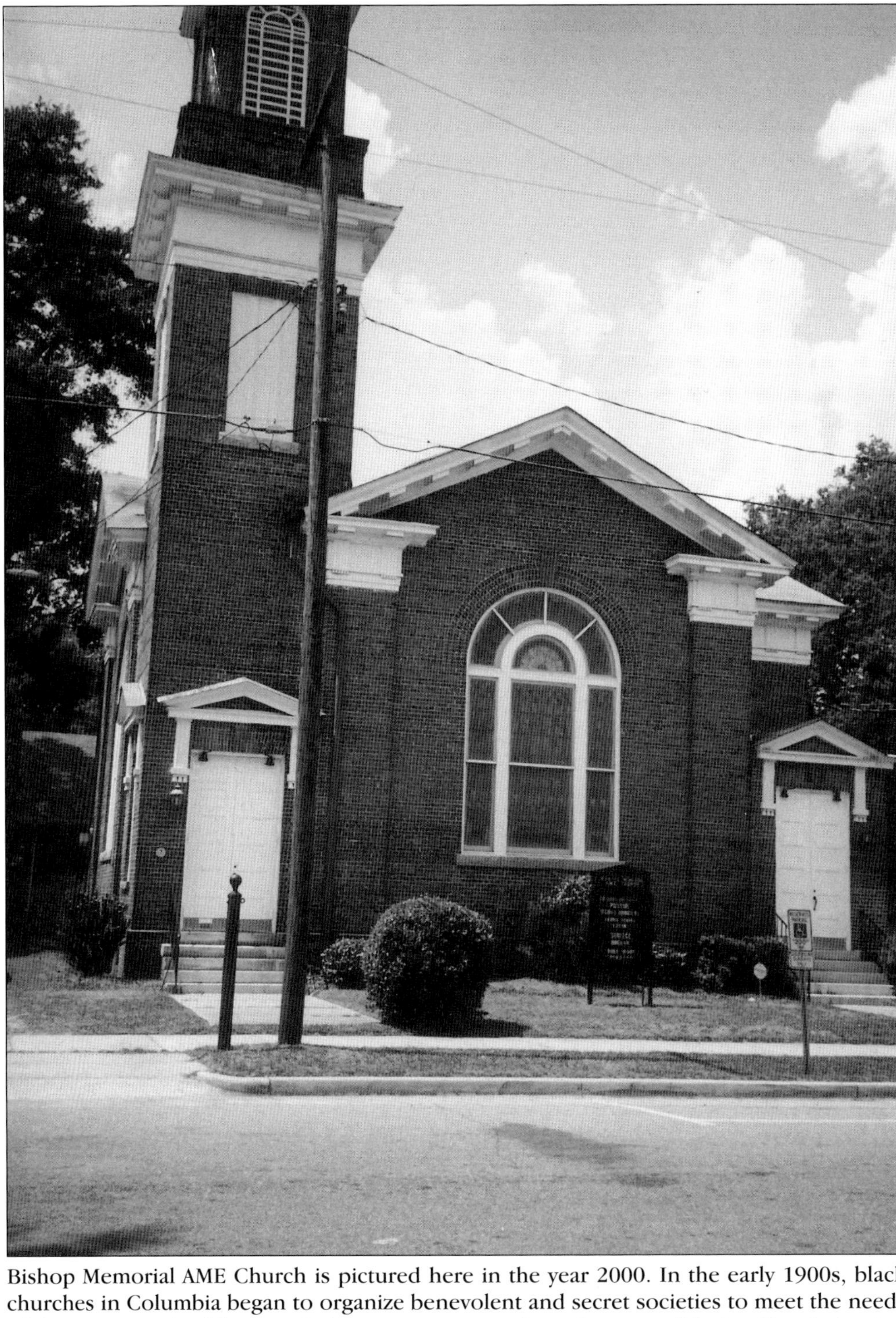

Bishop Memorial AME Church is pictured here in the year 2000. In the early 1900s, black churches in Columbia began to organize benevolent and secret societies to meet the needs of their community. These societies were an expression of group solidarity. They helped to take care of the sick and bury the dead. They also initiated the formation of black-owned banks and insurance companies.

Seven

New Era Politics

A.V. Huff once said, "South Carolina Politics: The more things change the more they stay the same." At the end of the 20th century, African Americans returned to the steps of the State Capitol. They came this time not to raise the American flag out of the burning ruins of Sherman's fiery march but to bring down the Confederate flag above the dome of capitol. The Confederate battle flag was placed on the capitol dome during the heat of the Civil Rights Movement of the 1960s to celebrate the centennial of the Civil War.

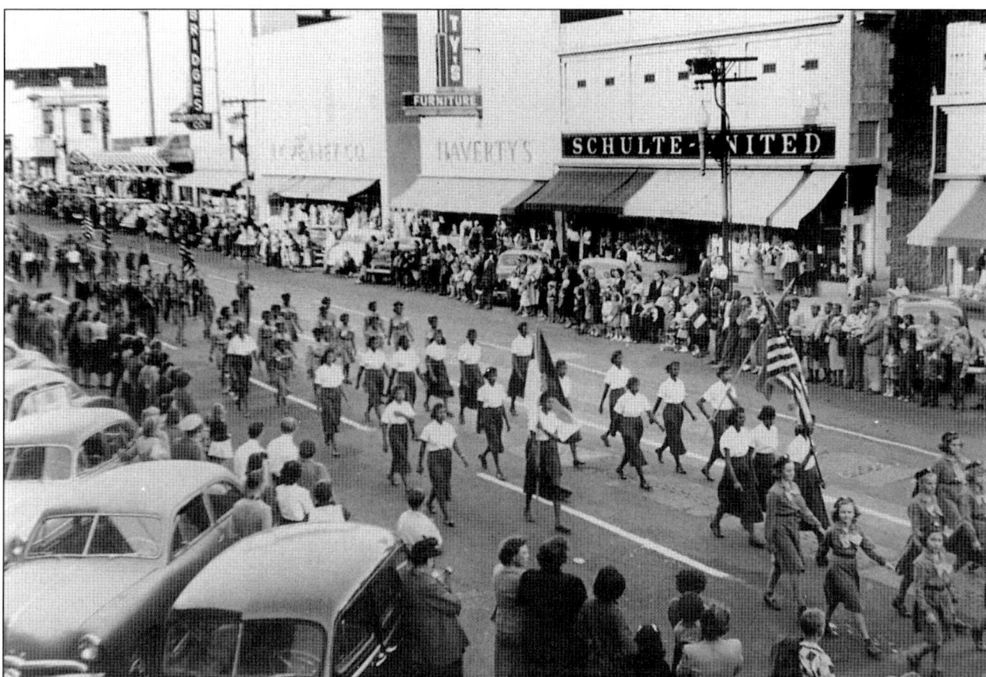

Here a parade marches down Columbia's Main Street. (Courtesy of the Columbia Fire Dept.)

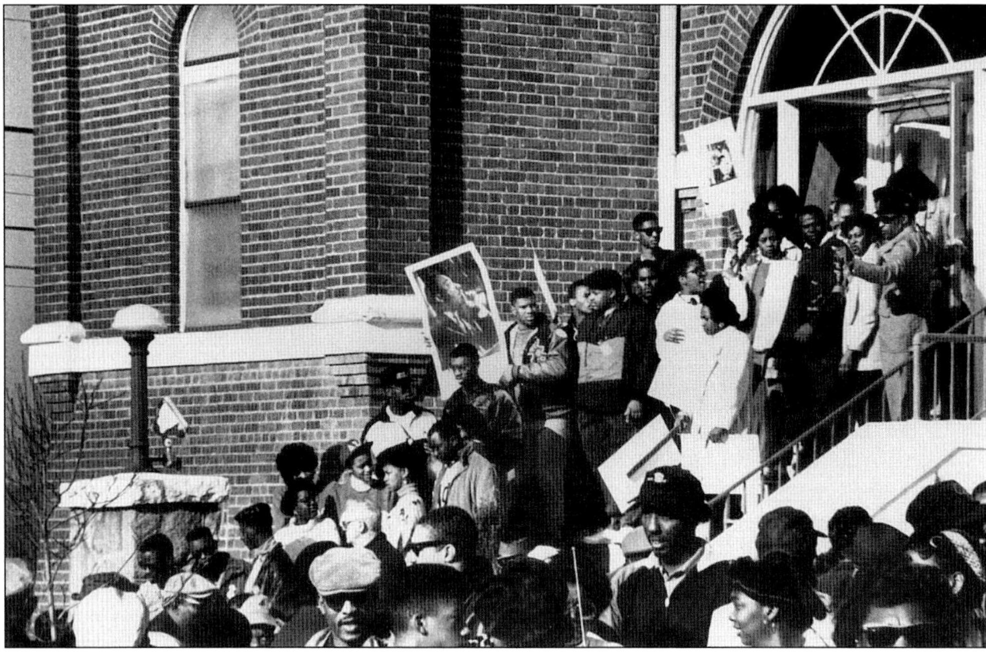

This is a picture of a Martin Luther King Day march in front of Zion Baptist Church in the late 1980s. (Courtesy of the McKissick Museum.)

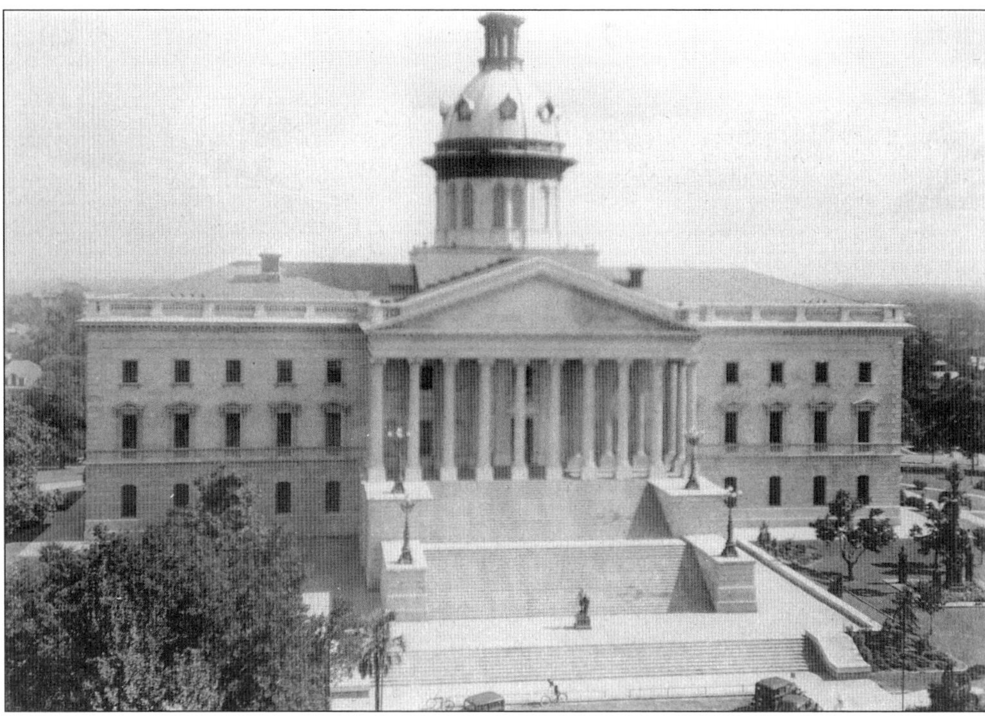

In Columbia, parades provided an avenue for public visibility. Speeches were given on the steps of public buildings, such as the State House, seen here, and parades were held downtown on Main Street. (Courtesy of the South Carolina State Archives.)

Rev. James M. Hinton was the state president of the NACCP. He served the state for over 20 years. Hinton battled to equalize the salaries of black teachers with those of white teachers. He also assisted attorney Thurgood Marshall when he came to South Carolina to represent the National NAACP. (Courtesy of the United Black Fund.)

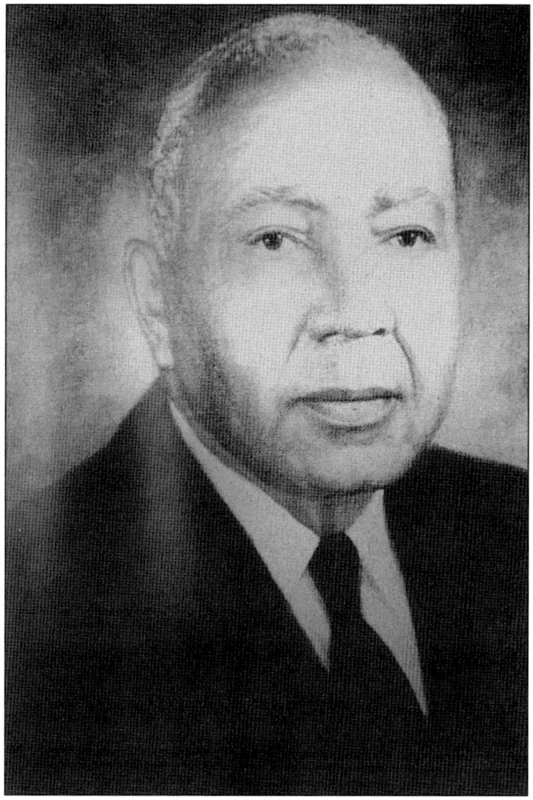

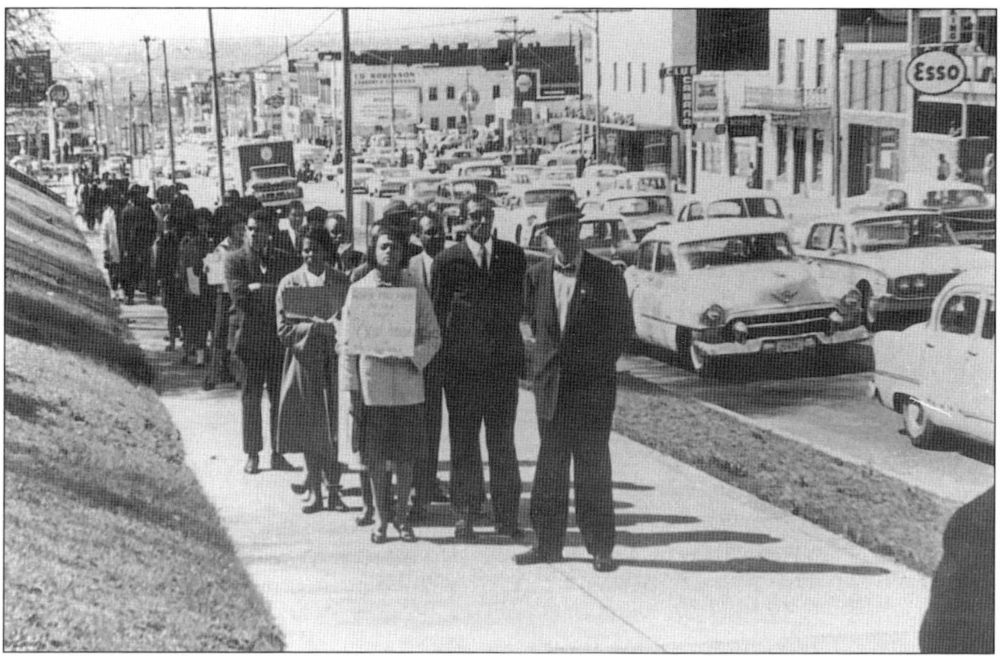

Pictured here is a march to the Capitol on Gervais Street. (Courtesy of the Richland County Public Library.)

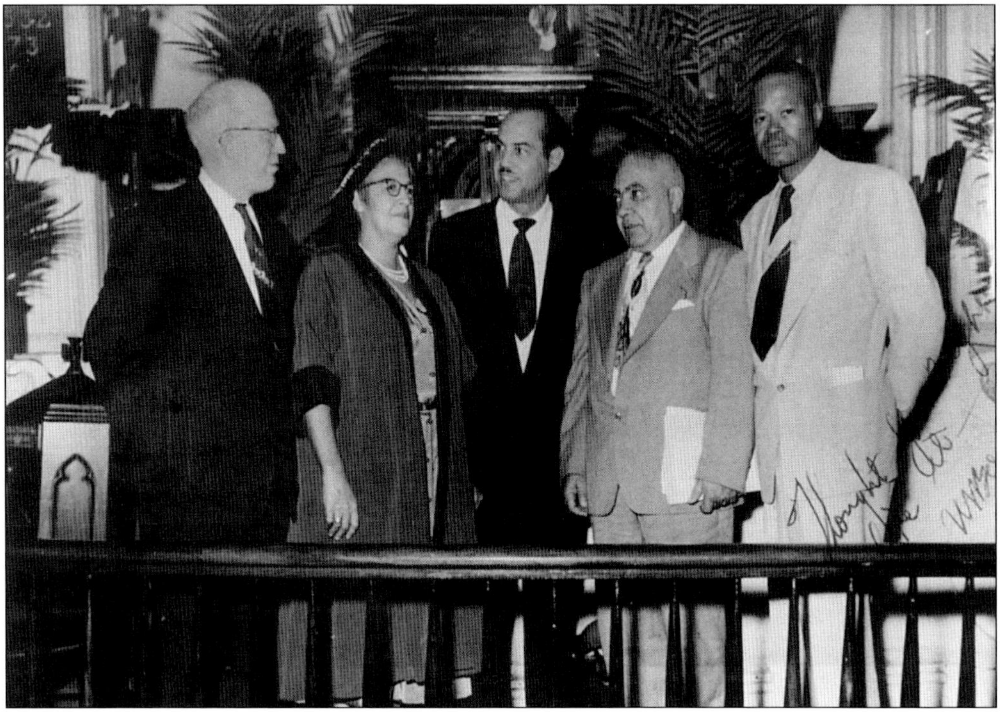

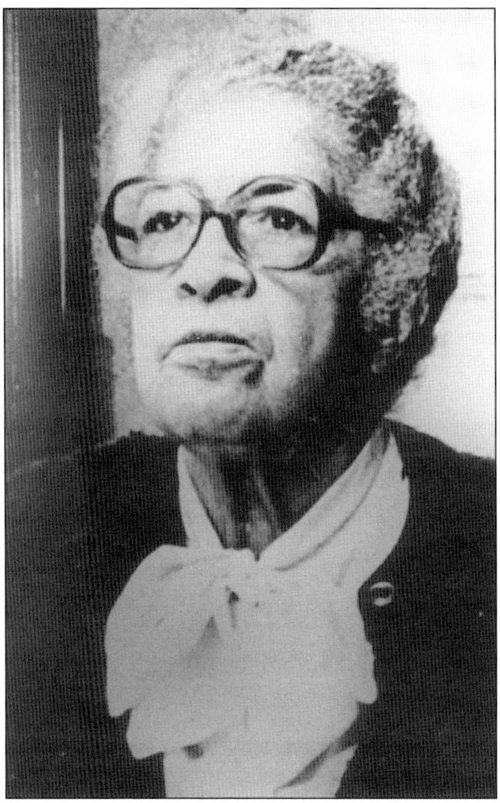

Members of the NAACP are pictured above. The day of emancipation would not be considered the beginning of freedom, nor the Civil Rights Movement the end of the struggle. Through the NAACP, Modjesta Simkins, James H. Hinton, and Harold Bouleware fanned the flames of change during the 1940s and into 1960s in South Carolina. (Courtesy of the South Caroliniana Library, USC.)

From 1931 until her death in 1992, Modjesta Monteith Simkins made significant contributions to African-American public heath reform, as well as to the national Civil Rights Movement. For years, Simkins's home served as a meeting place for dignitaries, including Thurgood Marshall, who litigated *Briggs v. Elliot* in 1954 and a part of the famous Supreme Court case, *Brown v. Board of Education*. (Courtesy of the United Black Fund.)

George Elmore courageously brought legal action involving racial discrimination against the South Carolina Democratic Party. His actions resulted in the 1948 landmark case of *Elmore v. Rice* and gained African Americans the right to participate in primary elections nationwide. (Courtesy of the United Black Fund.)

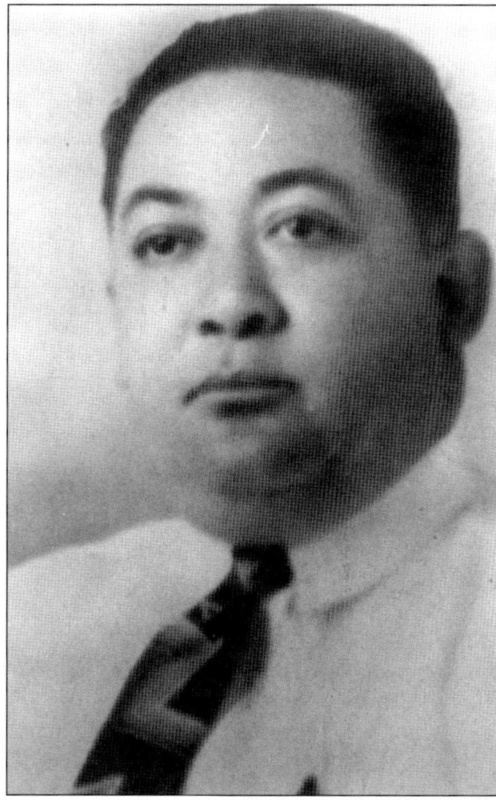

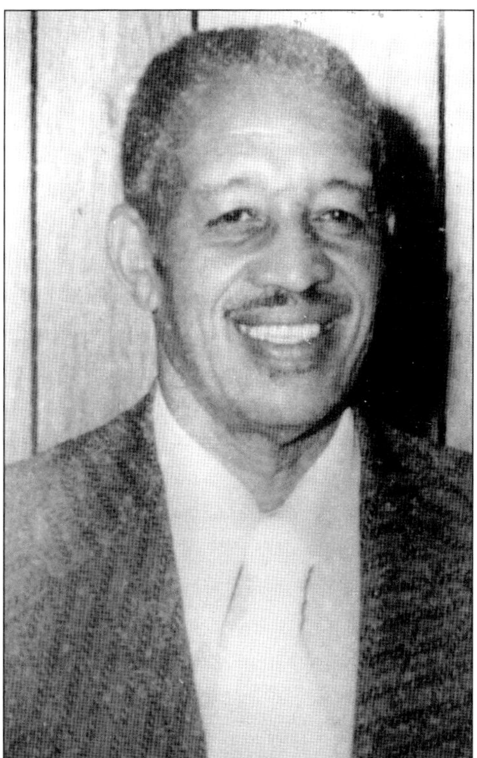

The Honorable Harold R. Boulware Sr. was a judge in the Family Court of the Fifth Judicial Circuit of South Carolina. He became the first chief counsel for the South Carolina Conference of NAACP in 1941 and had a national impact on the Civil Rights Movement as an attorney in *Elmore v. Rice*. Boulware also worked closely with Thurgood Marshall on *Brown v. Board of Education*. (Courtesy of the United Black Fund.)

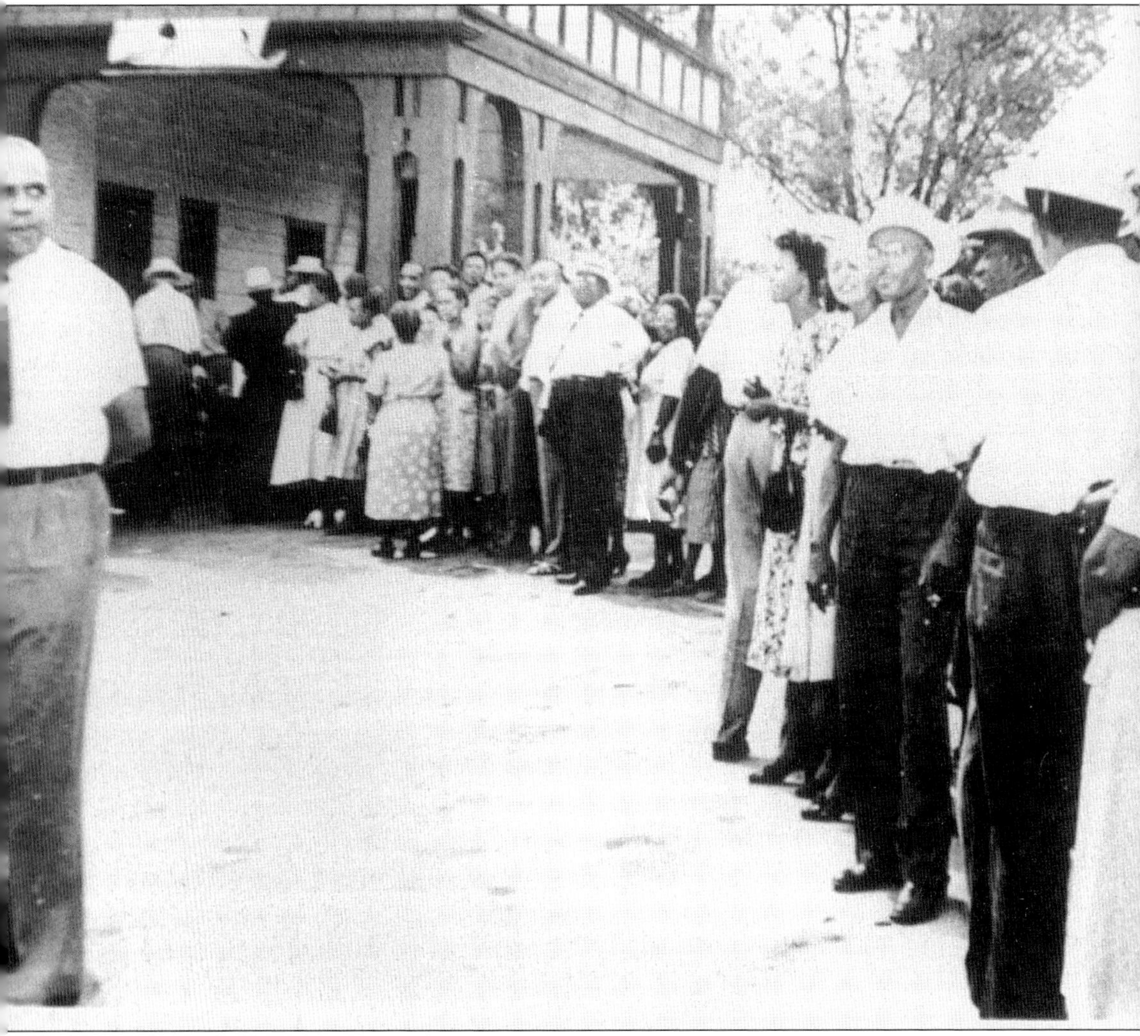

John McCray and Harold Bouleware, leaders of Progressive Democrats, wait in line with other black Columbians to exercise their right to vote in the 1948 Democratic primary. (Courtesy of the South Caroliniana Library, USC.)

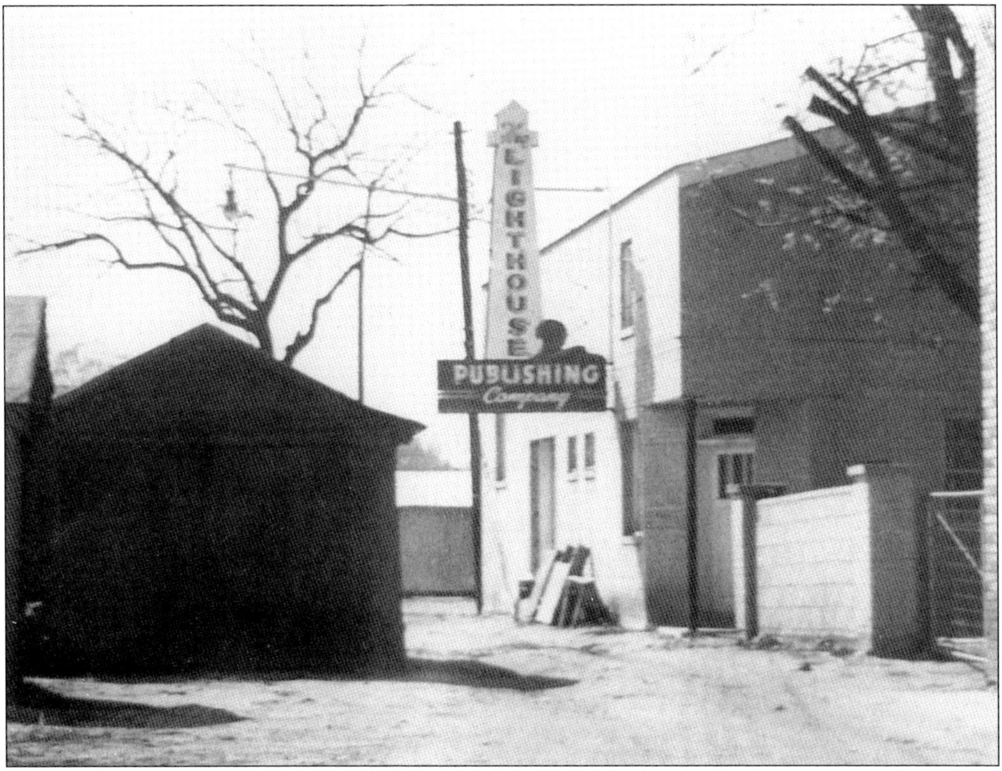

John H. McCray was the founder and editor of the *Lighthouse and Informer* newspaper, created by merging *Charleston Lighthouse* and *People's Informer, c.* 1941. As a journalist, McCray exposed the racial climate and horrid injustice in the state. (Courtesy of the South Caroliniana Library, USC.)

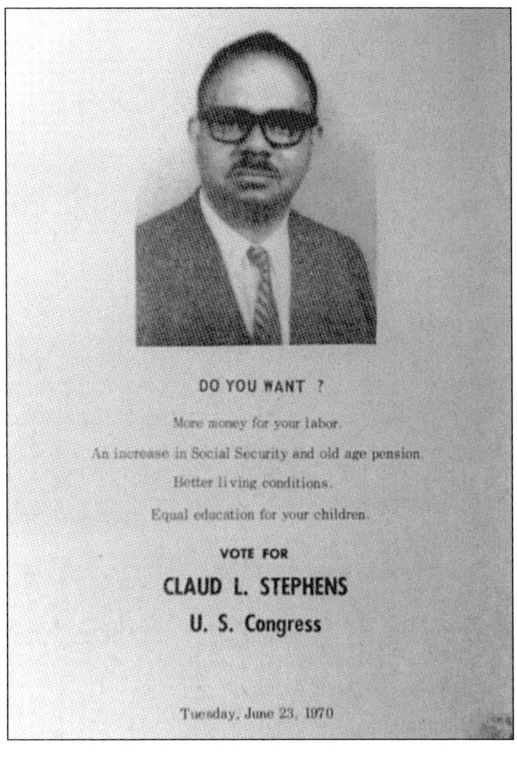

This flyer urges citizens to "Vote For Claud L. Stephens, U.S. Congress" in the 1970s. (Courtesy of the Harper family.)

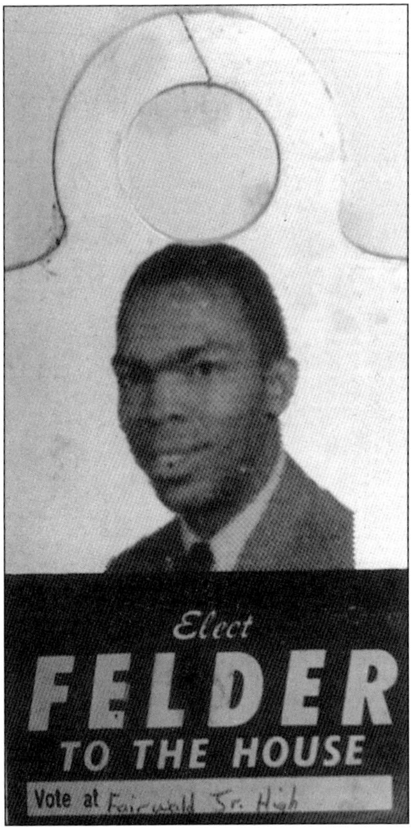

In 1970, James L. Felder won the Democratic election to the South Carolina State House of Representatives. This door hanger encourages voters to "Elect Felder to the House." (Courtesy of the Harper family.)

Below is a picture of a State Capitol session. Gov. Carroll Campbell is at the podium. (Courtesy of the South Carolina State Archives.)

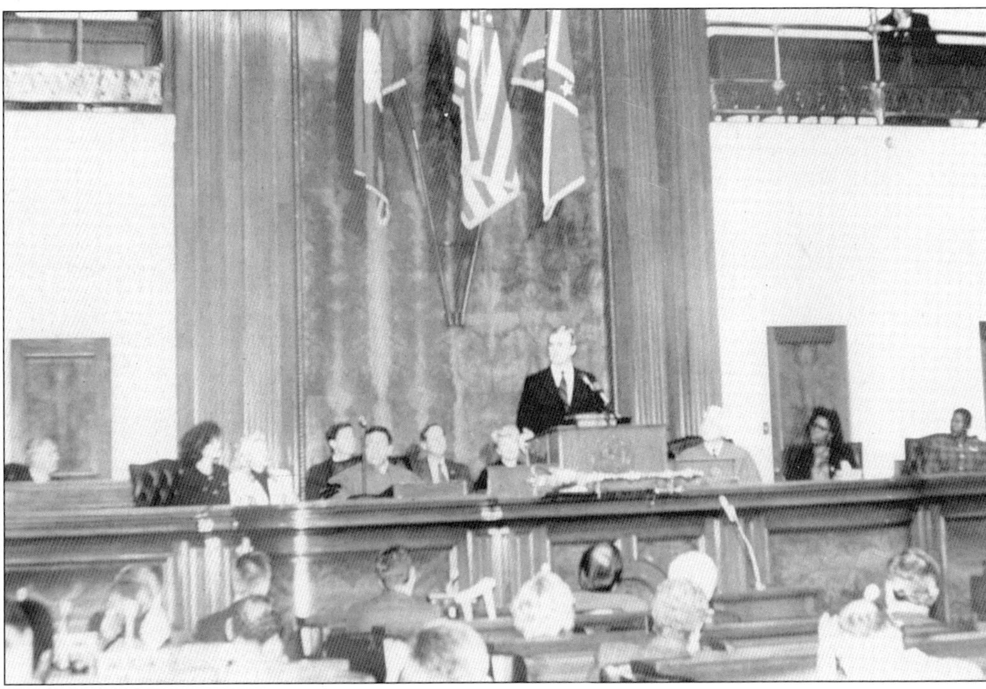

The United Citizens Party was launched in 1969 when blacks and whites from 20 South Carolina counties met in Columbia to express the group's dissatisfaction with the political status of black and poor people in the state. The group initiated a statewide drive to secure the signature of 10,000 registered voters on a petition to the secretary of state for the formation of a fourth political party. (Courtesy of the Harper family.)

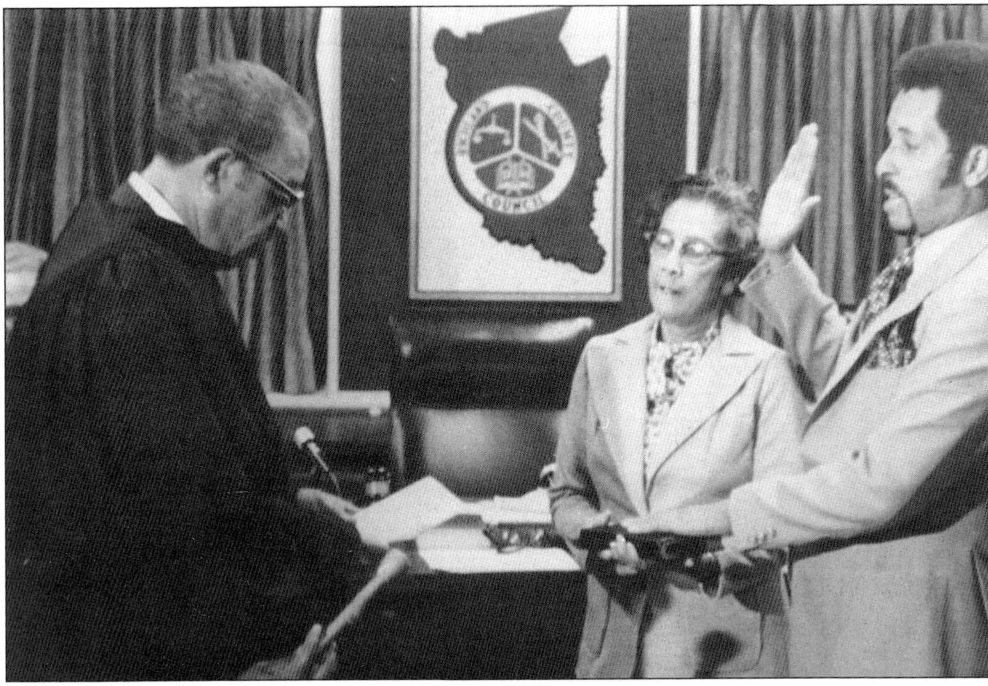

John Harper, right, is being sworn into the Richland County Council in January 1977 by Harold Boulware, left. Watching the ceremony is Frances Harper, John Harper's mother. (Courtesy of the Harper family.)

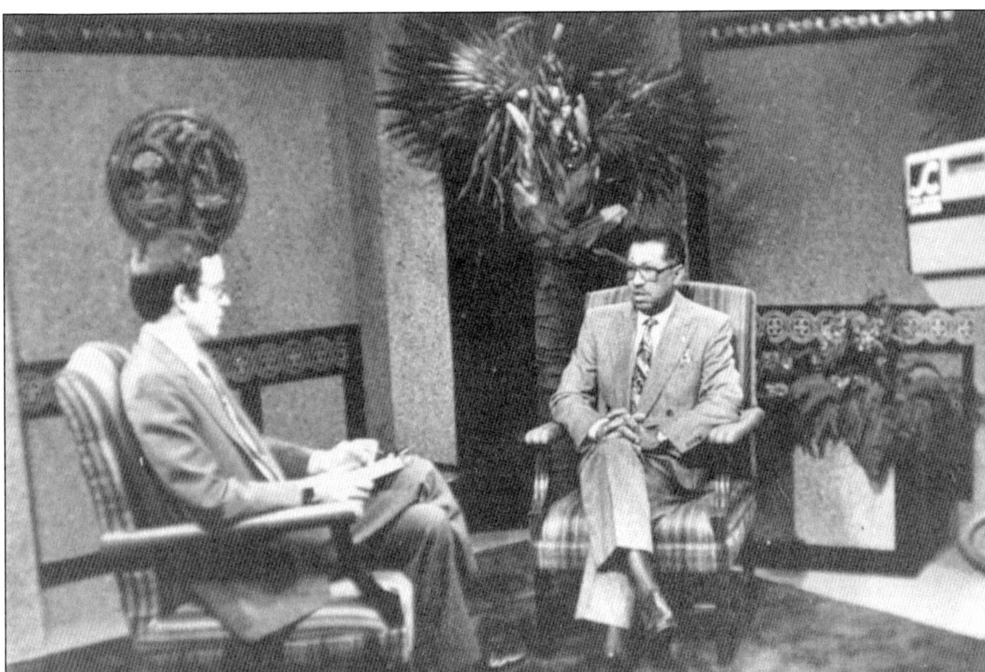

State Senator Kay Patterson is pictured here being interviewed by Tom Fowler for the SCETV program *Capitol View*. (Courtesy of Black Media.)

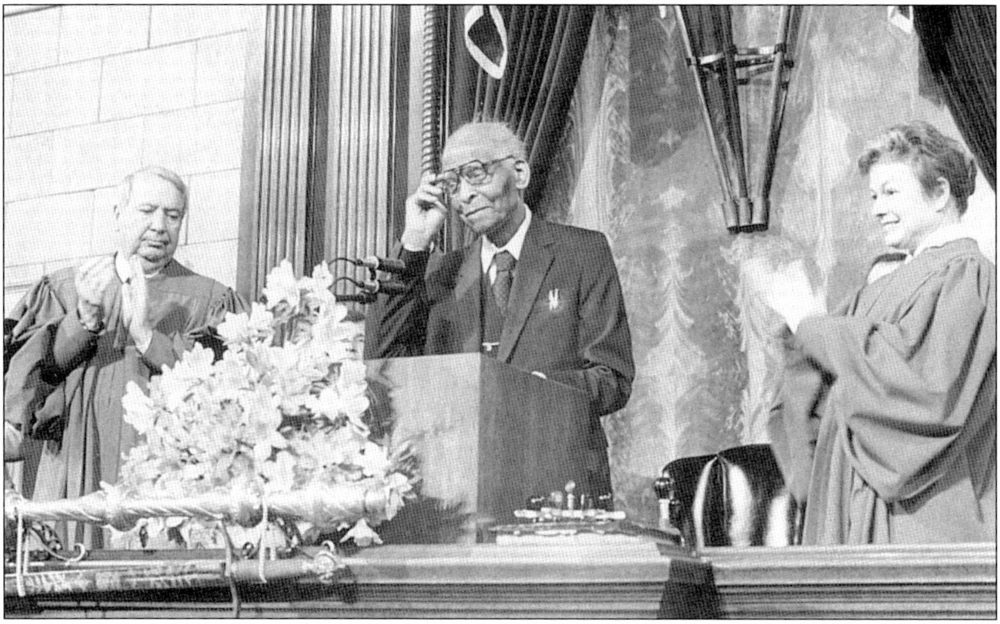

Nancy Stevenson applauds Dr. Benjamin E. Mays (middle), a noted African-American educator, following his address to a joint session of the South Carolina General Assembly on April 14, 1981. Ramon Schwartz Jr., speaker of the South Carolina House of Representatives, standing on the left.

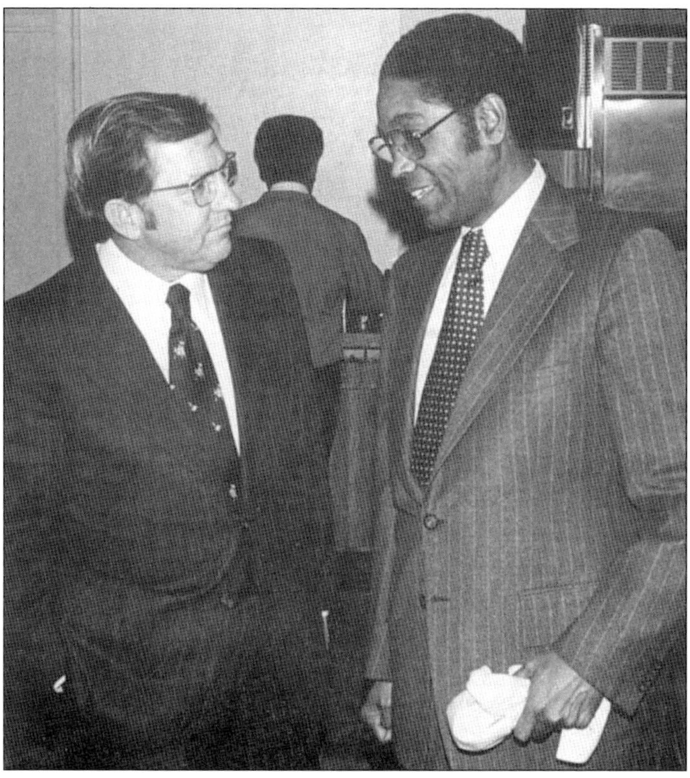

James B. Edwards (left), who was elected governor in 1974 and was the first Republican to hold the office since Reconstruction, greets Judge Matthew Perry, the first African American to serve as a federal judge in South Carolina.

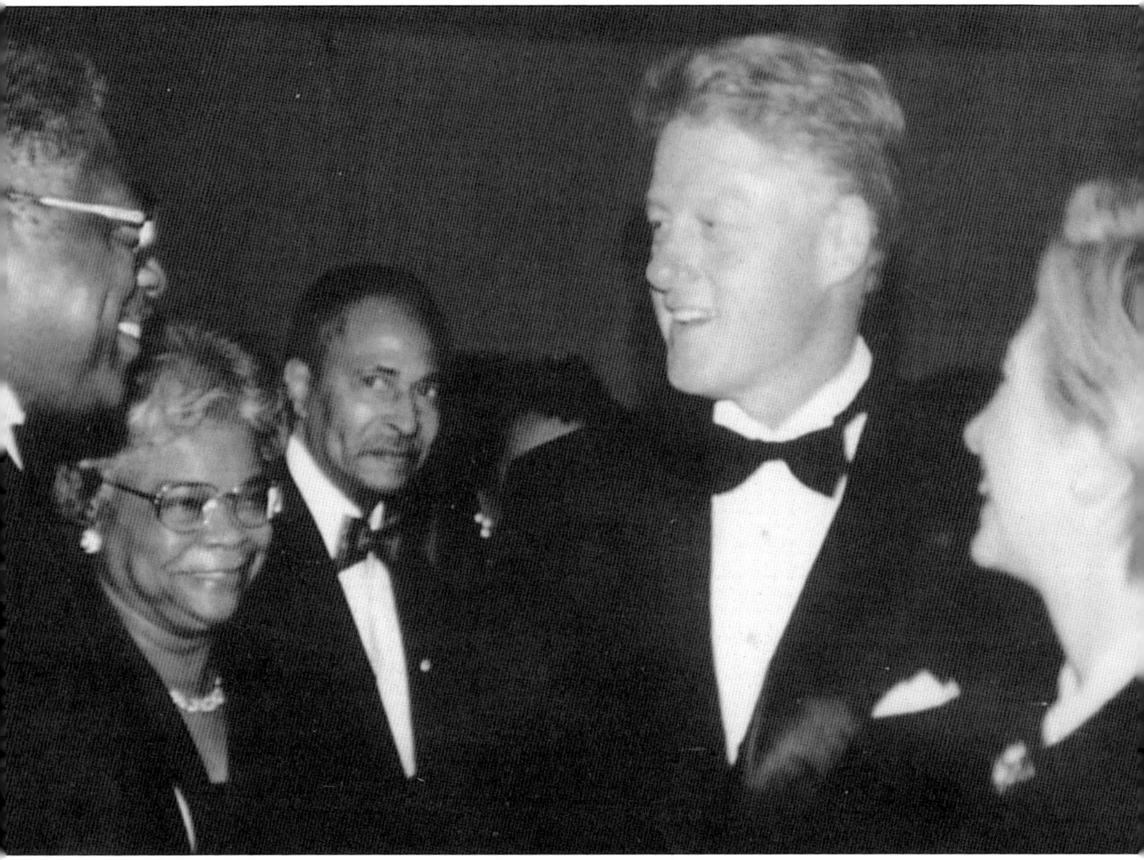

Congressman James Clyburn has lived in Columbia since 1972. He was elected to the 103rd Congress of the United States on November 3, 1992, and has served as the whip of Zone 12, which encompasses South Carolina, North Carolina, and Tennessee. Prior to Clyburn's election it had been nearly 100 years since an African American from South Carolina had occupied a congressional seat. Congressman Clyburn is pictured here on the far left; President and Mrs. Bill Clinton appear on the right.

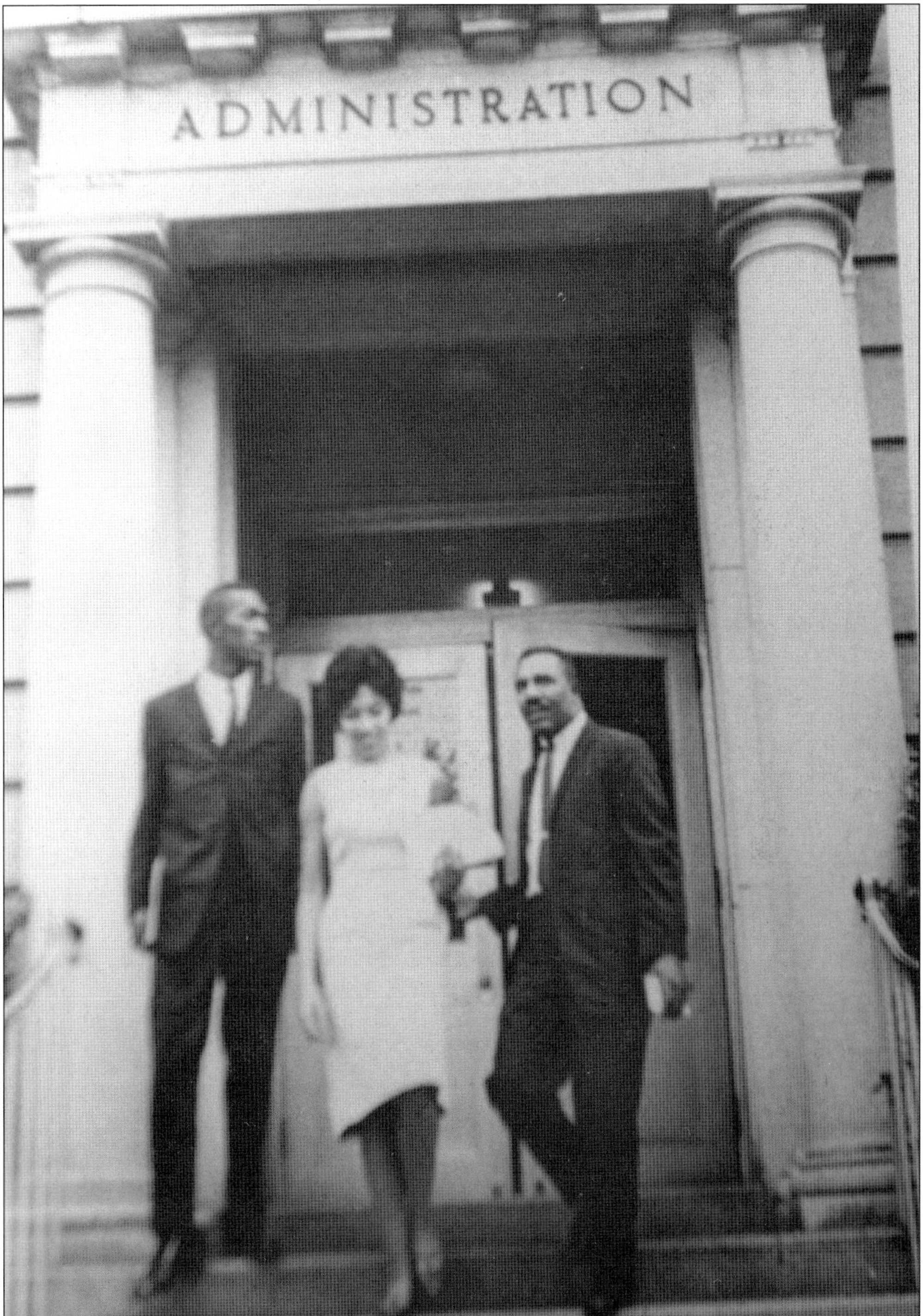

Robert Anderson, Henri Monteith, and James Solomon walked through the doors of the administration building on September 11, 1963. African-American students returned to campus of the University of South Carolina in 1963. (Courtesy of the USC Collection.)

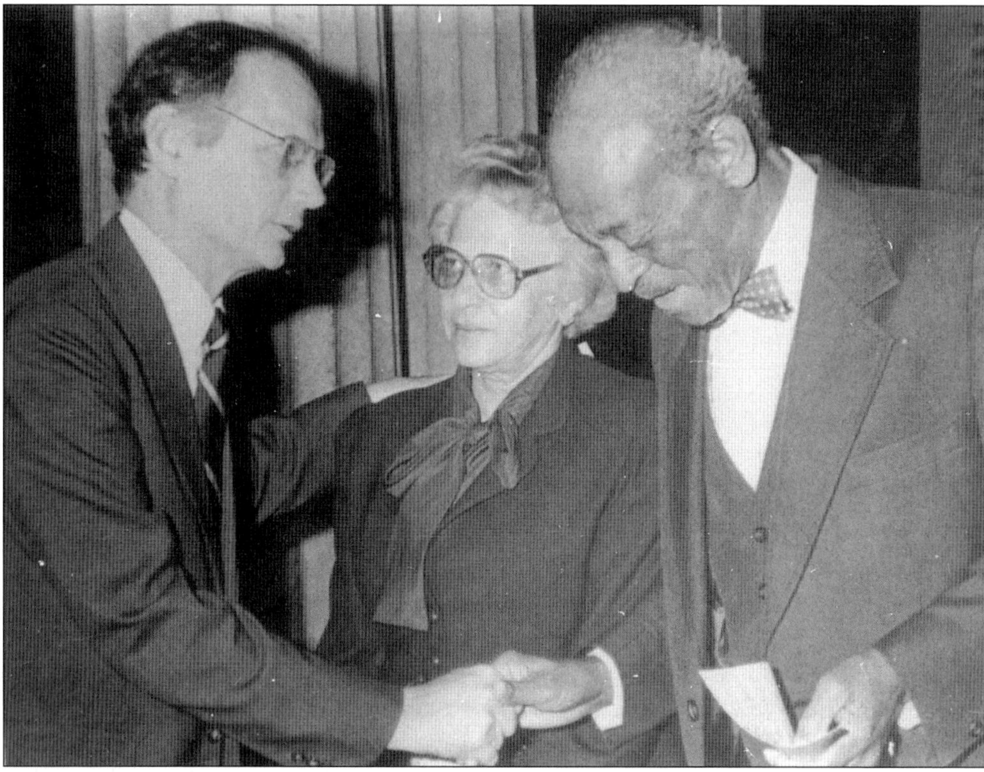

In 1983, the Reverend Isaiah DeQuincey Newman, right, became the first African American to serve in the South Carolina Senate since Reconstruction. An advocate of civil rights, this Methodist minister assisted the state and its citizens in adjusting to integration. In this picture, Gov. Richard W. Riley Jr greets the Senator and Mrs. I. DeQuincey Newman. (Courtesy of the South Carolina State Archives.)

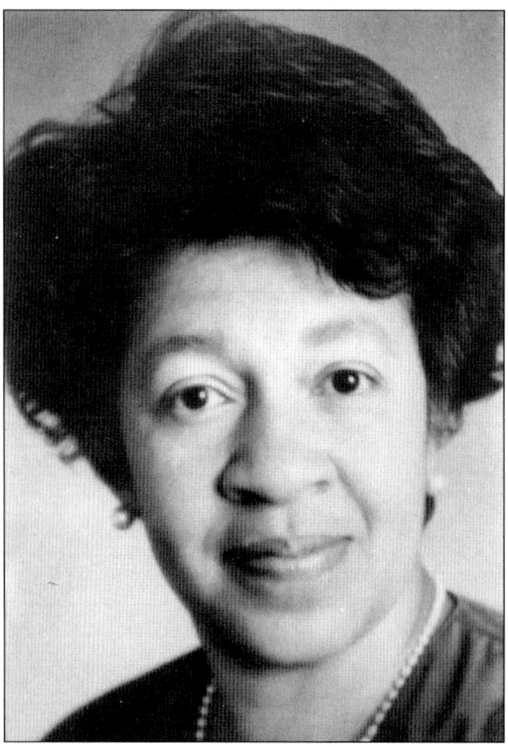

When the University of South Carolina was desegregated in the 1960s, Henri Monteith Treadwell was among the first of three black student to enroll since the Reconstruction era. Treadwell became a biochemist with an impressive list of accomplishments, recognized both nationally and internationally. (Courtesy of the USC Collection.)

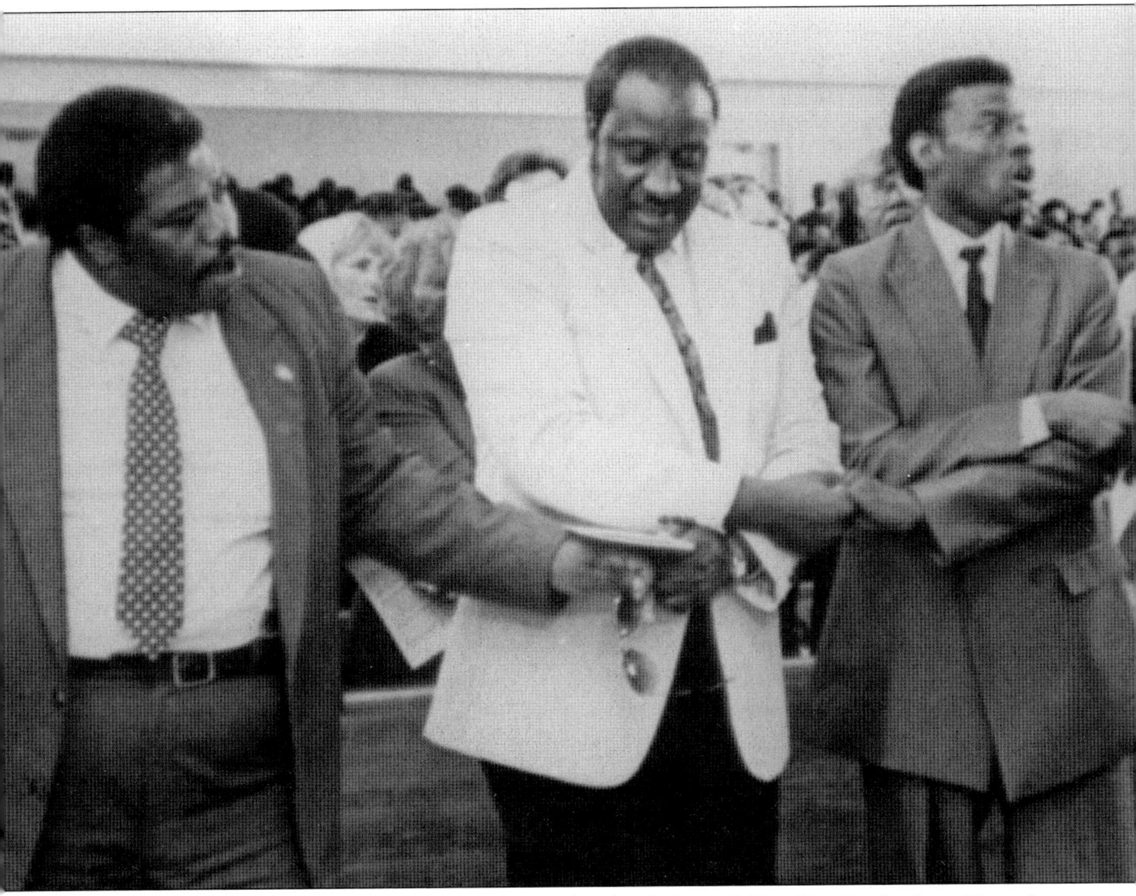

At Benedict College, on January 17, 1989, the birthday of Dr. Martin Luther King Jr. was observed at a public assembly. Joining in the singing of the African-American anthem "Lift Ev'ry Voice and Sing" are, from left to right, Booker Counts, director of housing; James F. Davis, vice president for student affairs; and David Kinley, assistant professor of business administration.

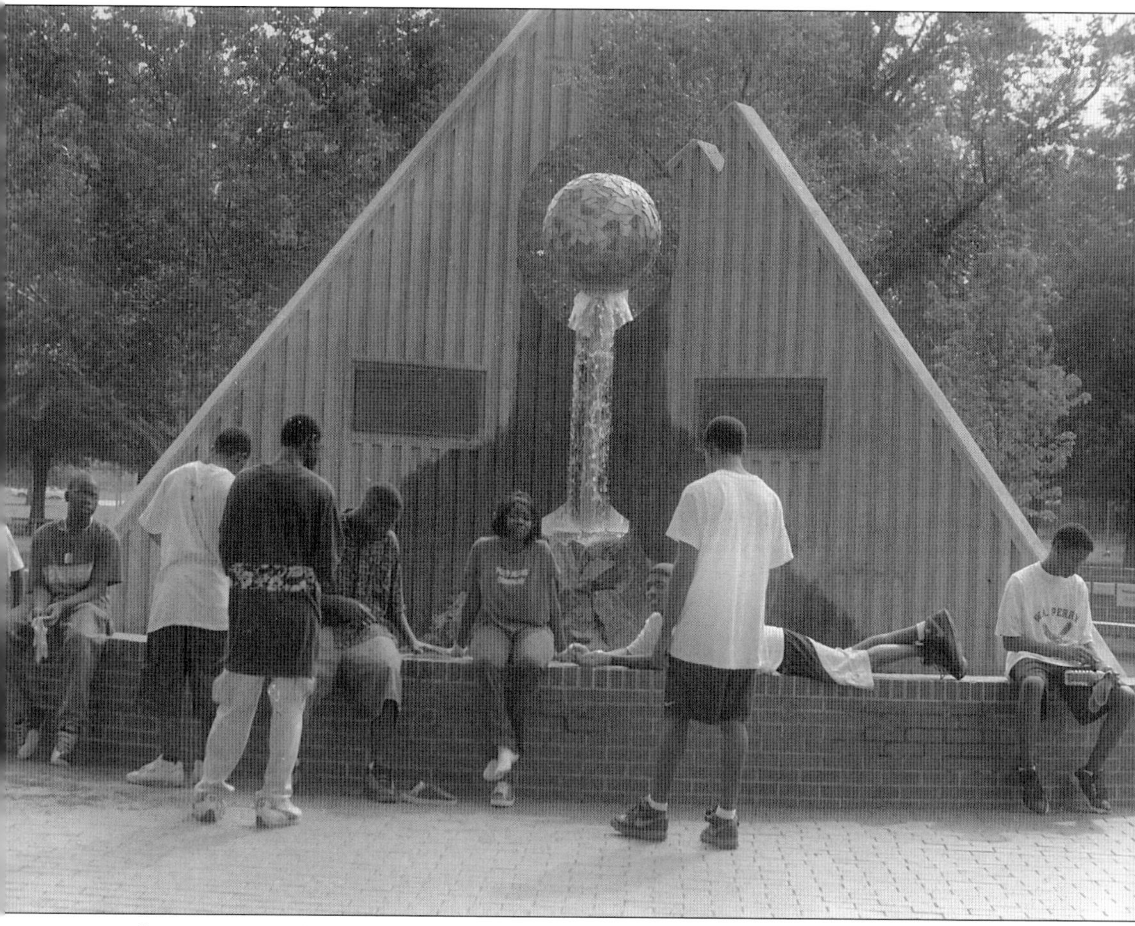

Local teenagers gather around the Stone of Hope monument at the Martin Luther King Recreation Park in Columbia.

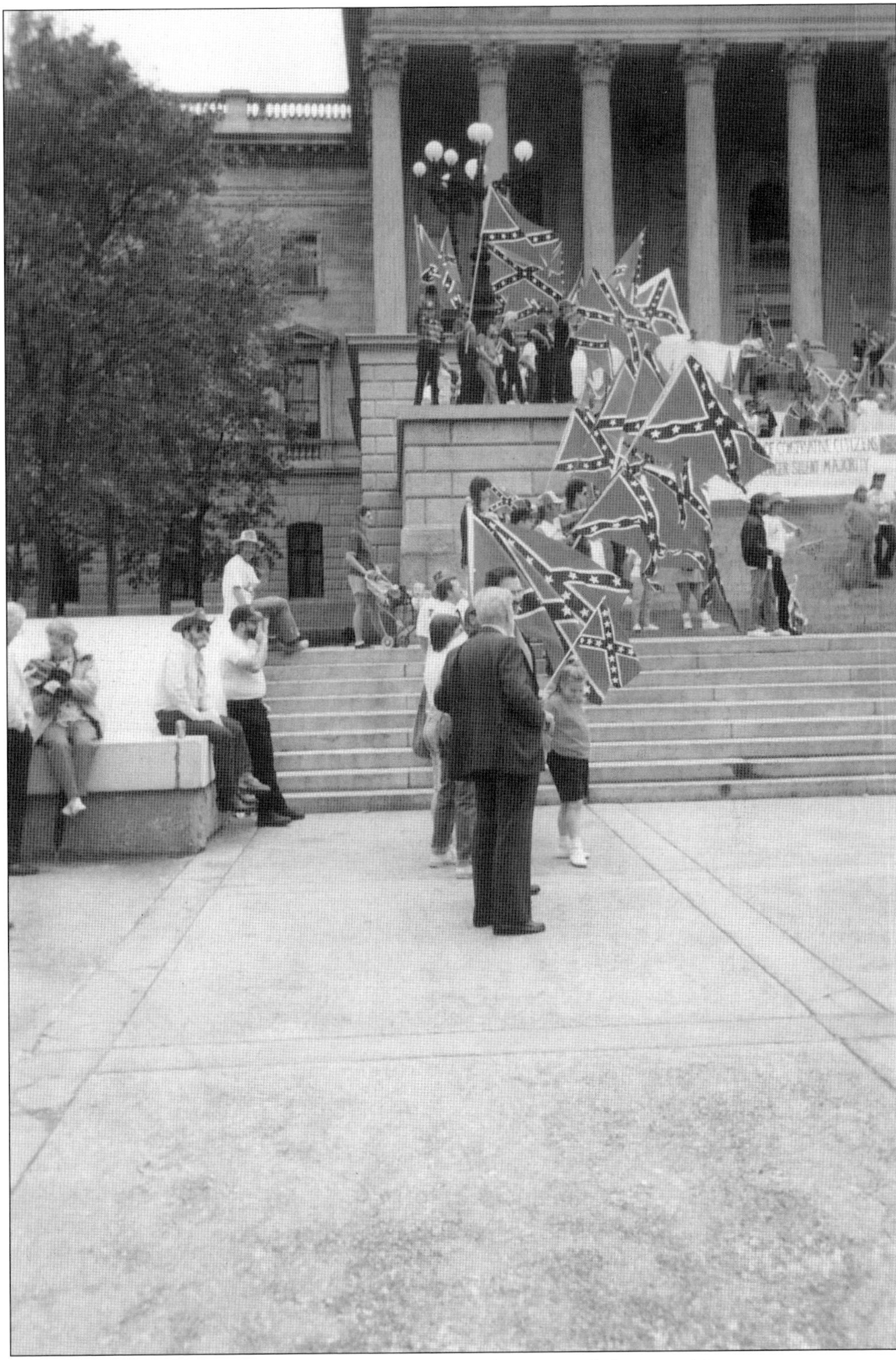

Confederate flag supporters also held rallies on the steps of the State House.

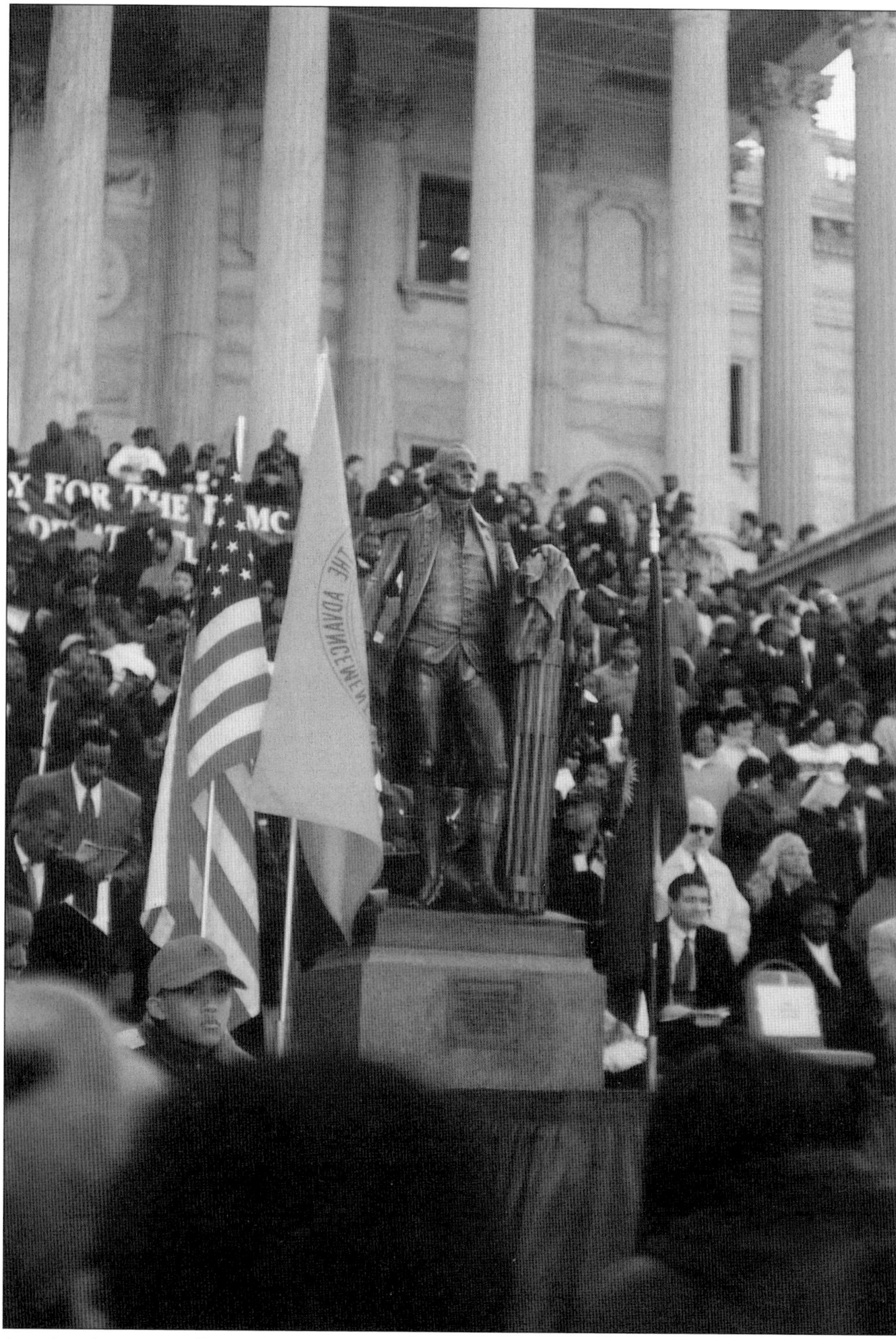

A national NAACP rally was held in the year 2000 to appeal for the removal of the Confederate flag from the State House dome.

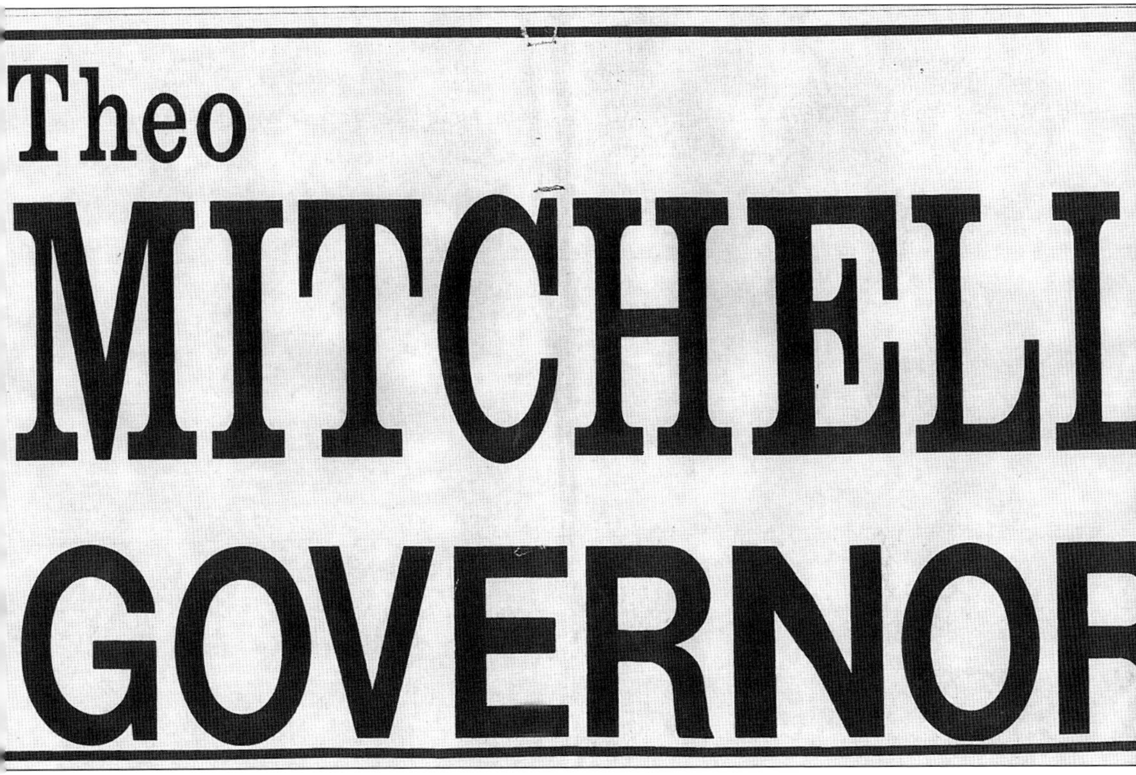

In 1990, Sen. Theo Mitchell won the Democratic nomination for governor. He was the first African American in South Carolina nominated for governor by the Democrats. He lost the election to Republican incumbent Gov. Carroll Campbell.

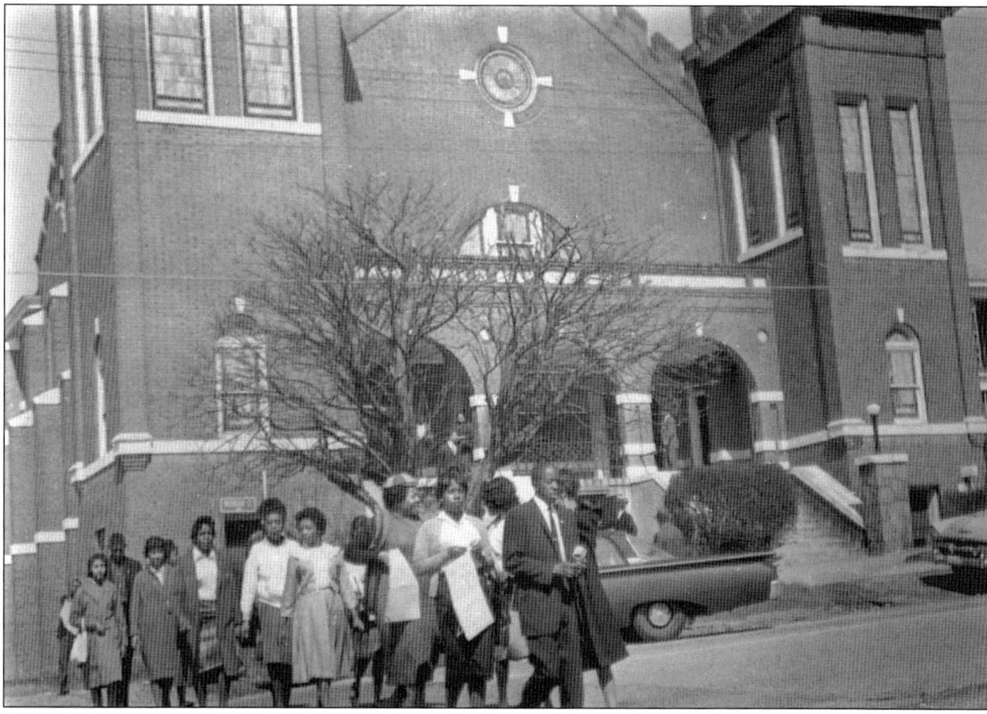

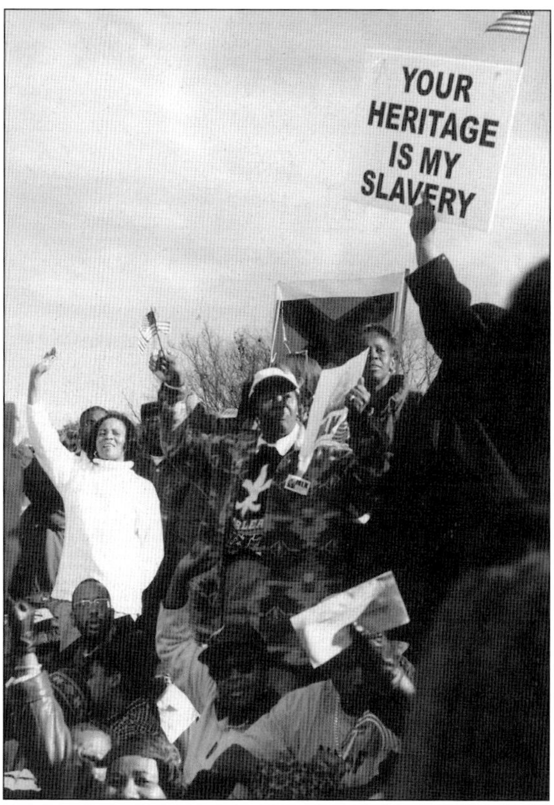

These marchers in the 1950s begin their journey at the Zion Baptist Church, seen in the background. (Courtesy of the Richland County Public Library.)

On Martin Luther King Day, these protesters rallied for the removal of the Confederate flag from the State House dome.

Eight

PEOPLE

Times have changed, but the aggressive nature of African-American Columbians remains the same in education, political activities, social justice, and business. Not only do they have a great impact on the state level, but they also contribute significantly on a national scale. These contributions include the areas of science, politics, and entertainment.

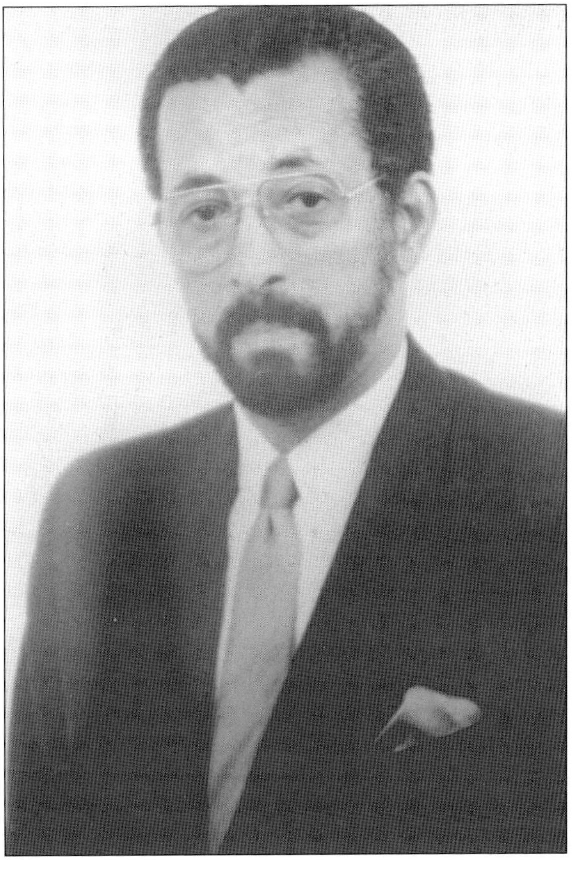

John Roy Harper II has practiced law in Columbia, focusing on civil rights, constitutional law, and voting law. During much of his career, Harper has been engaged in complex federal litigation in the U.S. District Court for the District of South Carolina, the Fourth Circuit Court of Appeals, and the United States Supreme Court.

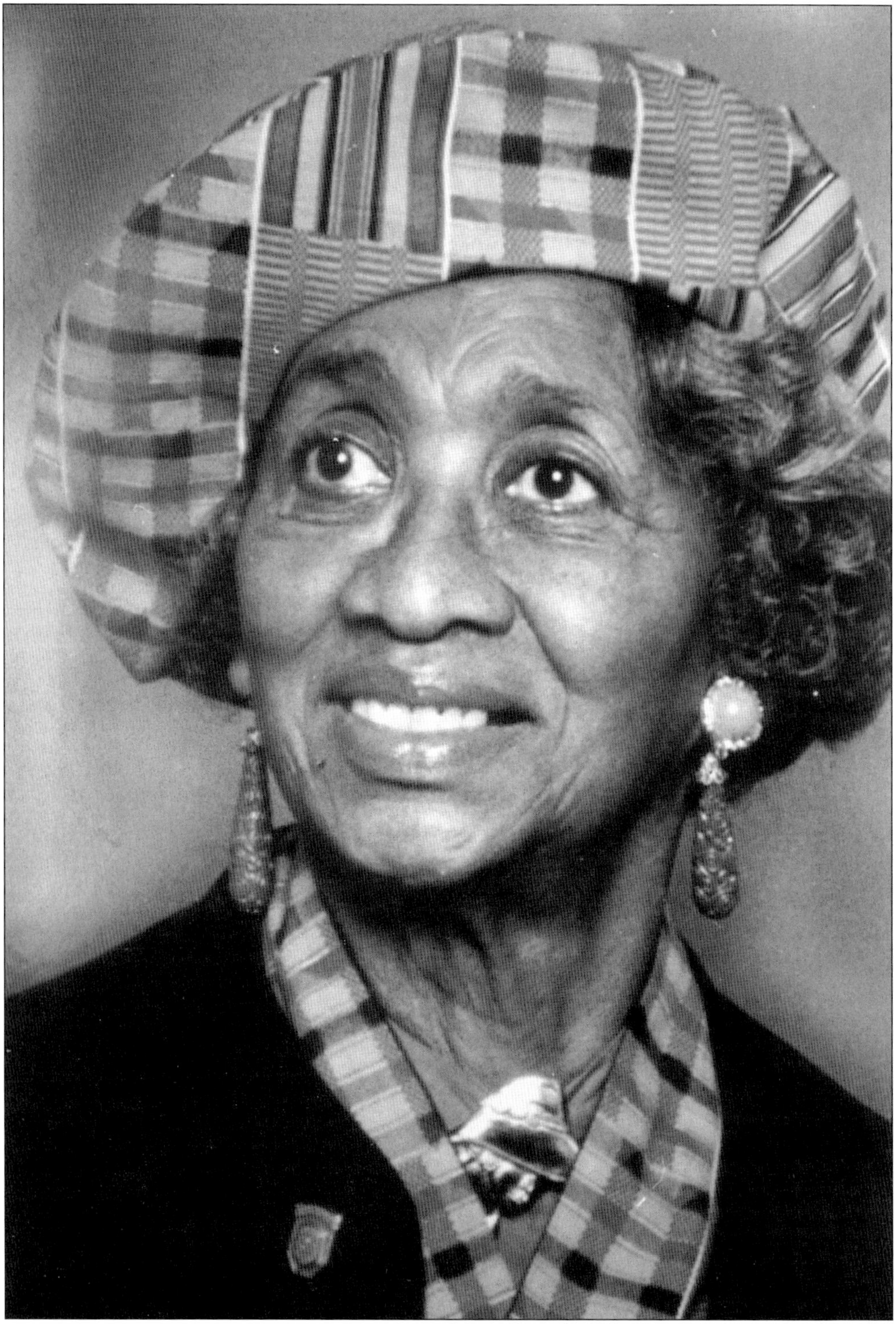

Amy Surginer Ligon Northrop is an entrepreneur and a successful cosmetologist. She assisted in organizing the Citywide Cosmetology Association in 1938.

Charity Edna Adams served in the Women's Auxiliary Corps (WAAC) during World War II. She rose to the rank of lieutenant colonel, becoming the highest-ranking black woman in the military. (Courtesy of the South Carolina Black Hall of Fame.)

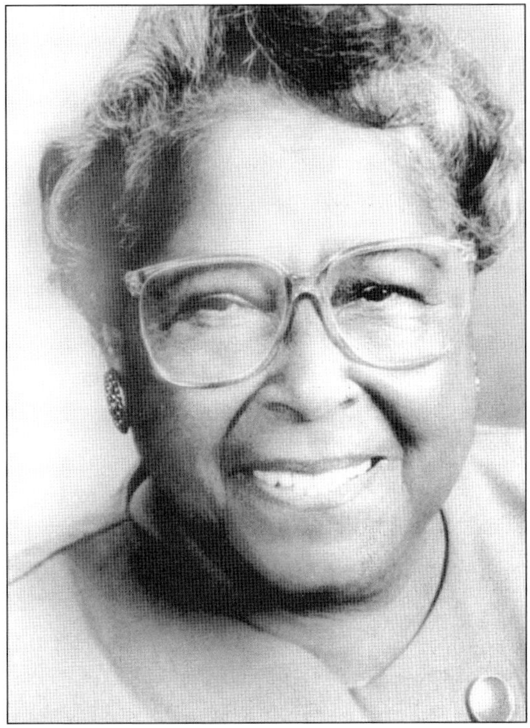

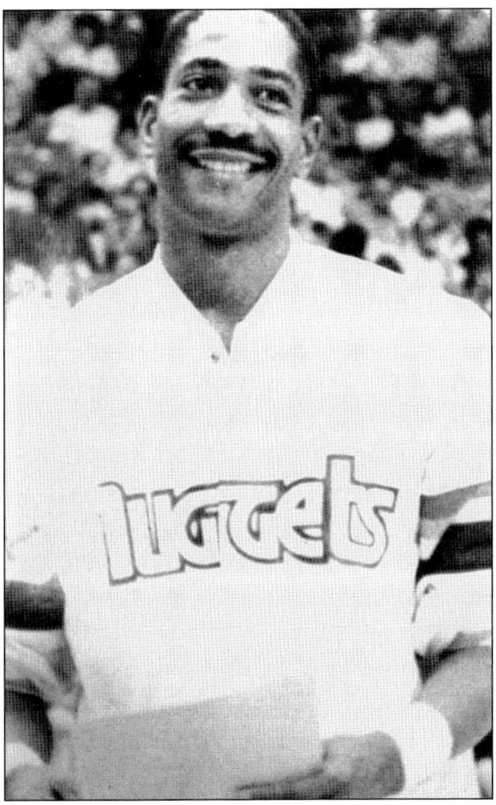

Alexander English was the NBA's leading scorer in the 1980s and the Denver Nuggets all-time leading scorer. English made the NBA All-Star team for eight consecutive years. (Courtesy of the South Carolina Black Hall of Fame.)

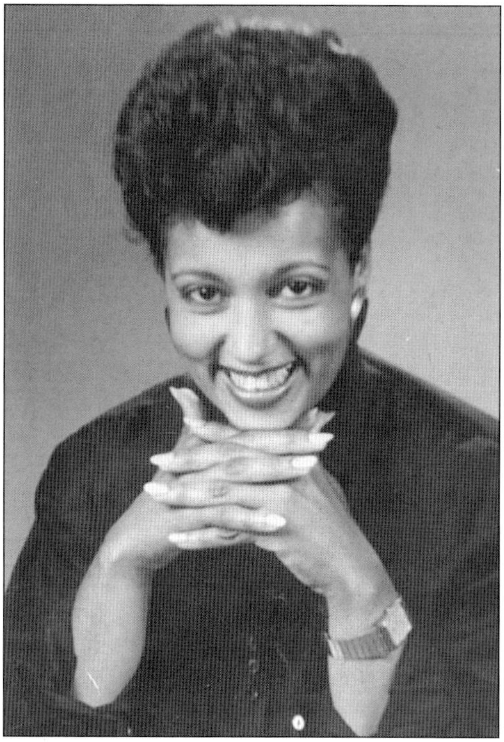

Shelia Johnson Chaney hosted the SCETV talk show *CrossTalk* in the 1990s. (Courtesy of Black Media.)

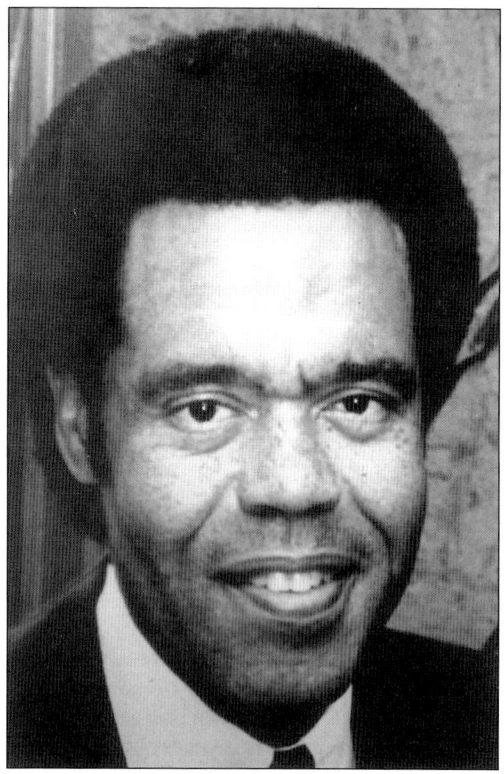

Gilroye A. Griffin Jr., a lawyer and labor relations expert, was vice president of the Bristol-Myers Squibb company in New York City. (Courtesy of Black Media.)

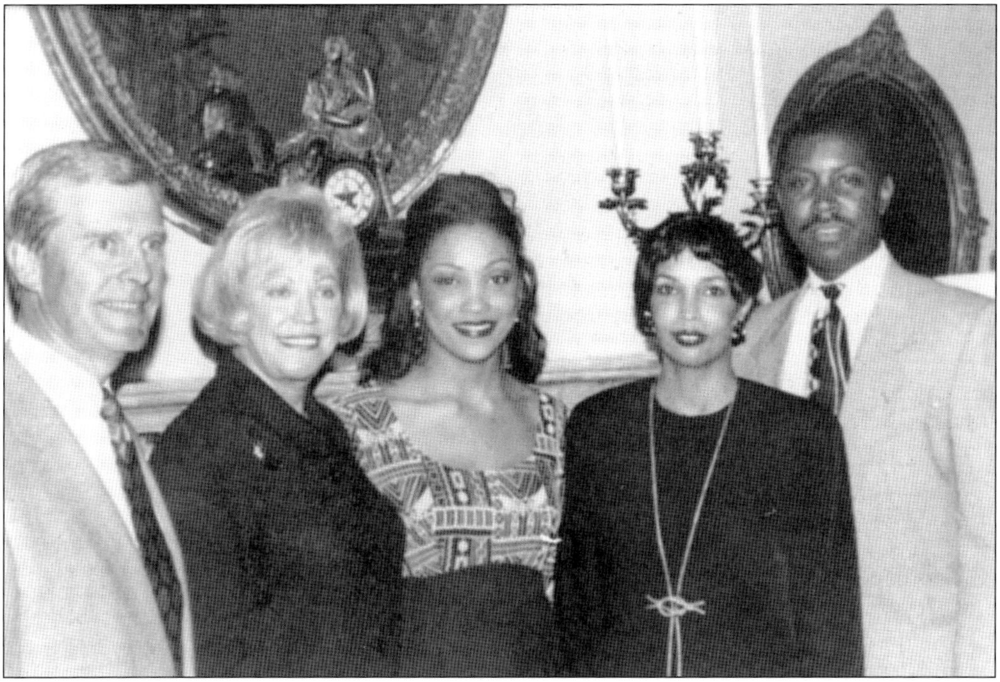

The winner of the title of Miss America 1994, Kimberly Clarice Aiken (center) was born on October 11, 1974, to Charles and Valerie Aiken. Kimberly graduated from Columbia High School in 1992 and is pictured here with Gov. and Mrs. Carroll Campbell and her parents. (Courtesy of Black Media.)

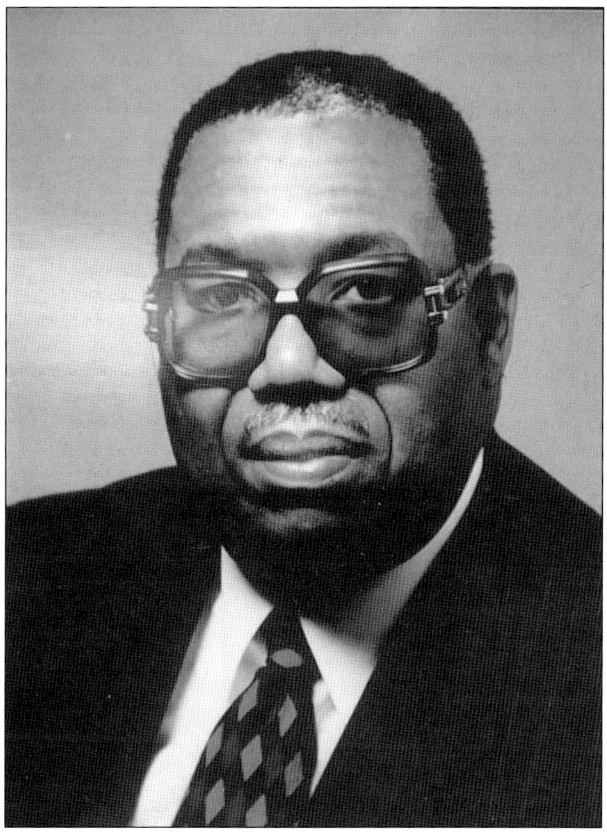

Attorney E.W. Cromartie II is a member of the Columbia City Council. His law firm, Cromartie and Williams, is located across from Benedict College on Harden Street.

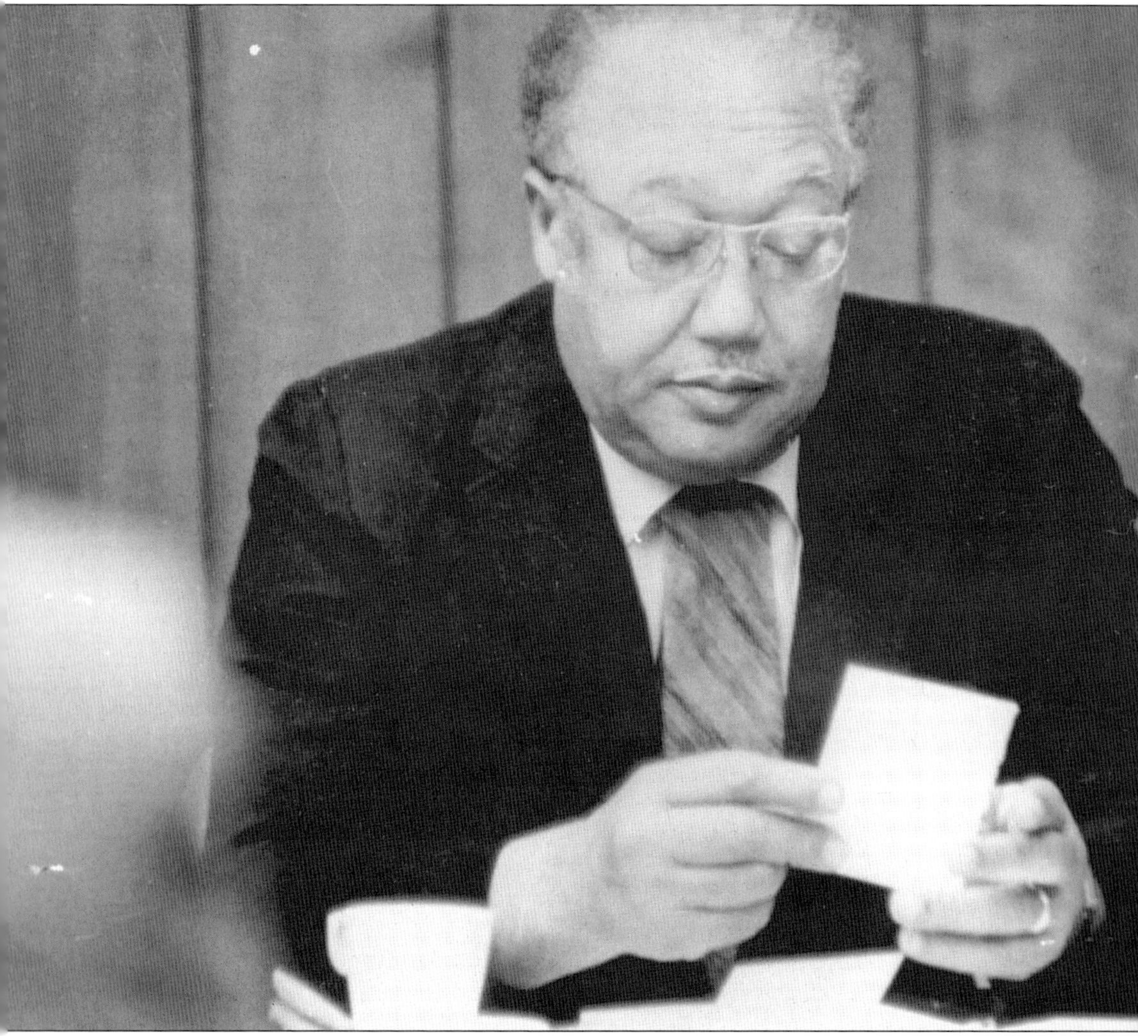

Dr. J.C. Bull, a Spartanburg physician, was appointed to the South Carolina Mental Health Commission by Gov. Robert E. McNair in 1967, thus becoming the first black to be appointed to a major state board in modern times.

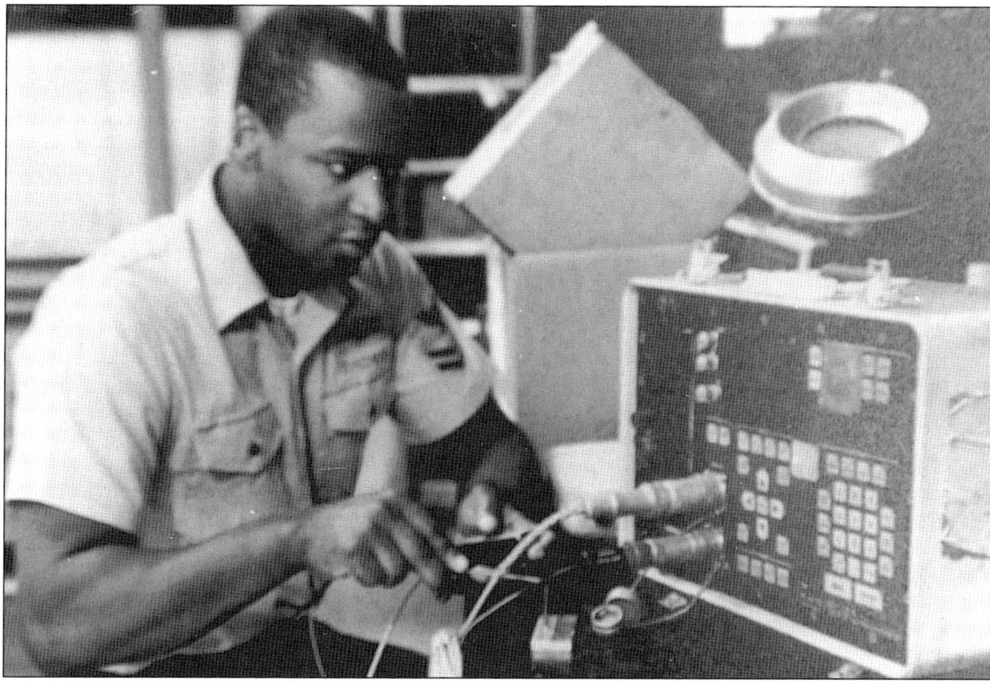

Navy petty officer second class Vernon K. Brown, the son of Albert and Janie Brown of Columbia, has seen much of Europe and other far-away locales since joining the Navy in 1984.

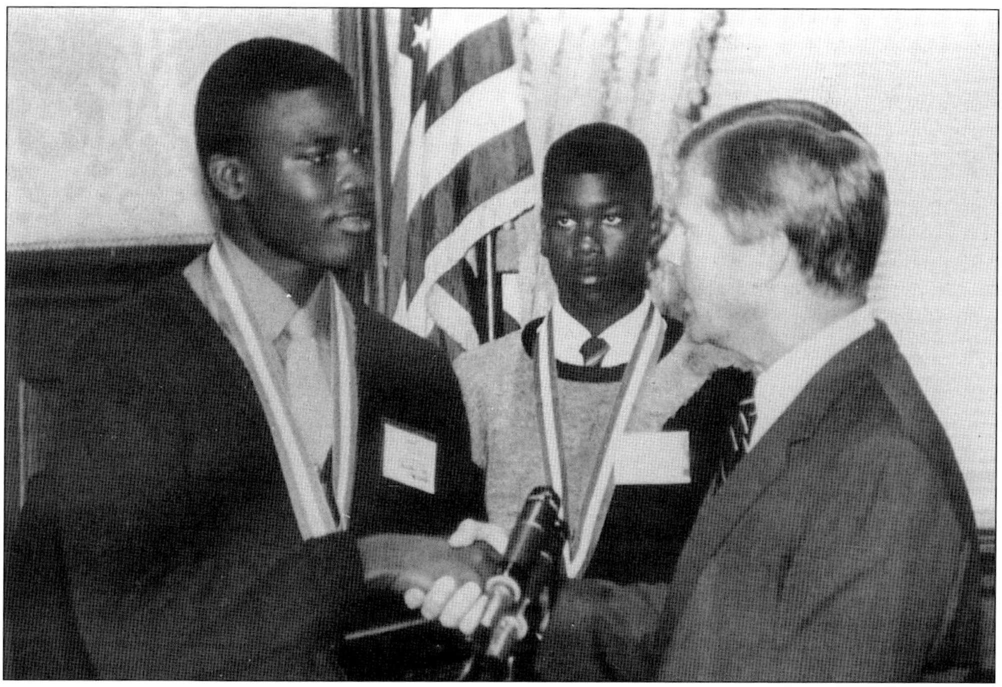

Members of the Boys' Club meet with Gov. Carroll Campbell in this picture. (Courtesy of the South Carolina State Archives.)

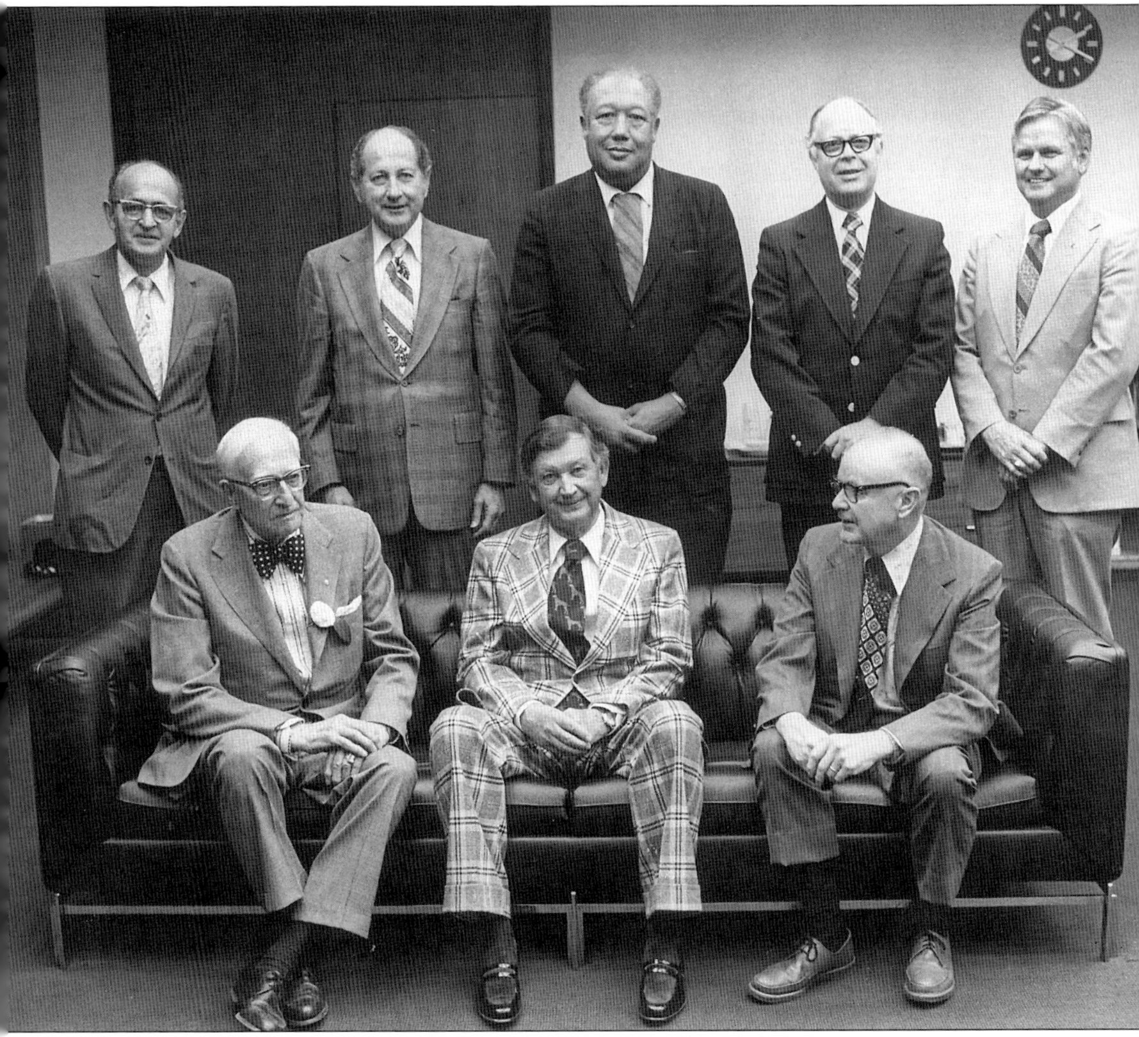

The members of the Mental Health Board pose for this picture, and Dr. J.C. Bull, the first black member of the board, is in the back row, center. Bull served on this board from 1968 to 1982.

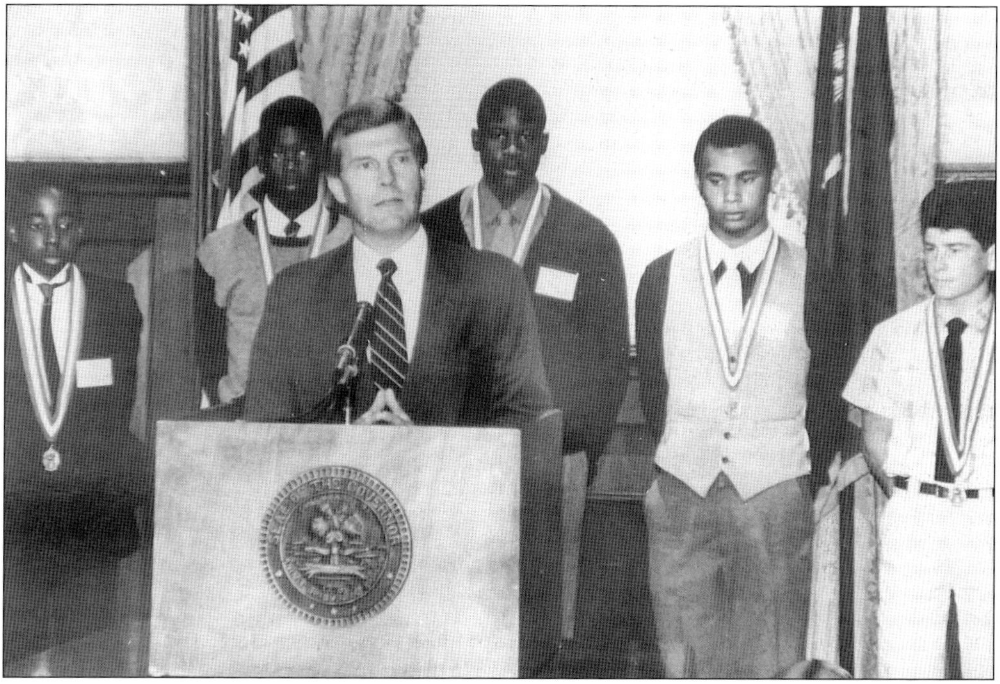

Members of the Boys' Club appear behind Governor Campbell. (Courtesy of the South Carolina State Archives .)

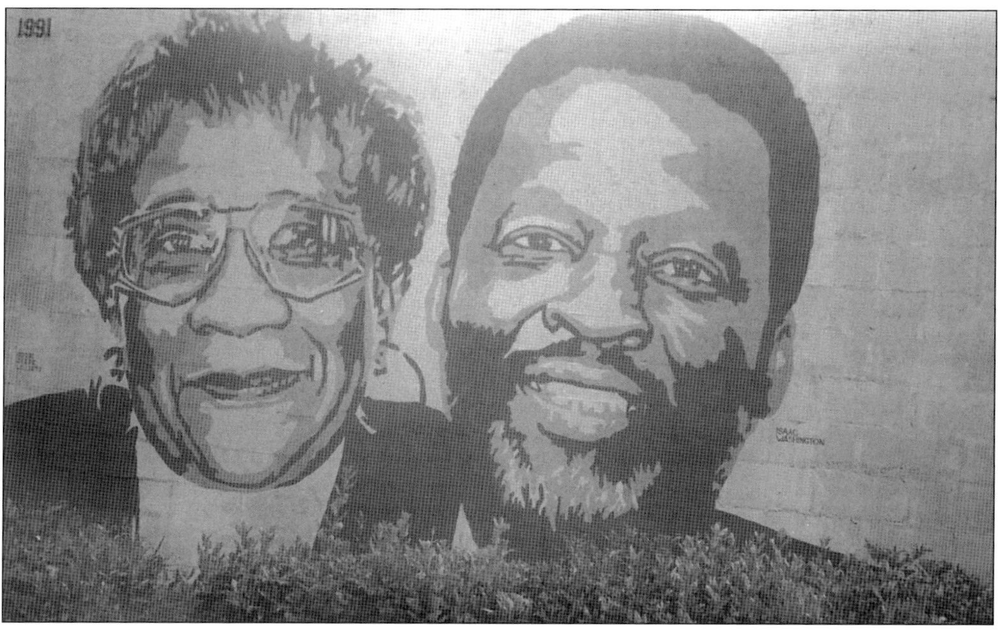

The "Wall of Fame" honors former residents of the Columbia Housing Authority communities who have made outstanding contributions in the areas of education, government, business, and civic affairs. Pictured here are Bessie Pauline Williams, formerly of Saxon Homes 1954–1963, for achievements in education; and Issac Washington, formerly of Allen-Benedict Court 1942–1964, for achievements in business.

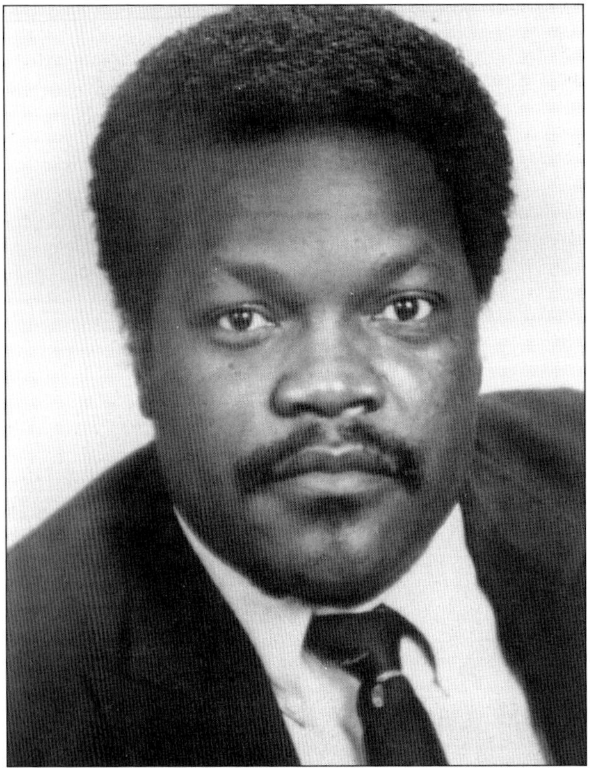

Listervelt Middleton produced and hosted the award-winning SCETV program *For The People*, which was aired nationally. Middleton was a forerunner in the movement to unlock the true history and identity of the African people. (Courtesy of the United Black Fund.)

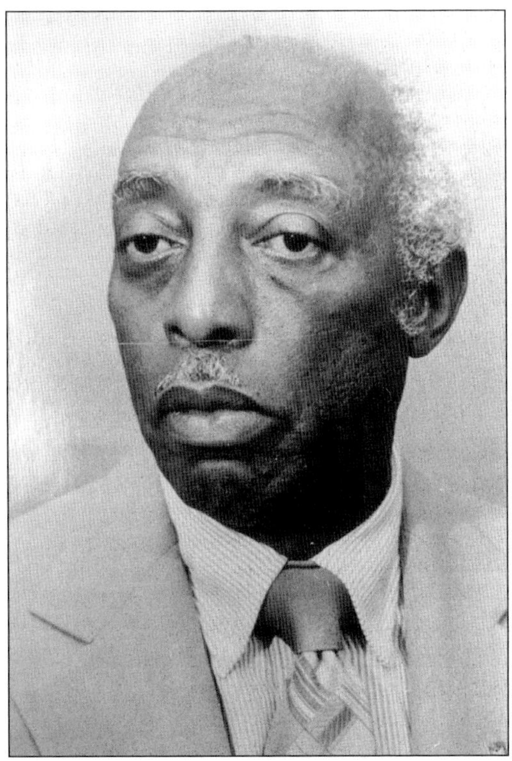

James "Hop" Hopkins is a founder and president emeritus of the United Black Fund of the Midlands, Inc. He is also a member of 100 Black Men of South Carolina, Inc. (Courtesy of the United Black Fund.)

Ernest Henderson Sr. was the first black South Carolinian to become a licensed pilot. He was a flight instructor with the U.S. Air Force at the Tuskegee Institute, where he trained the pilots of the all-black 99th Pursuit Squadron and the 332nd Fighter Squadron who heroically served in Europe. (Courtesy of the United Black Fund.)

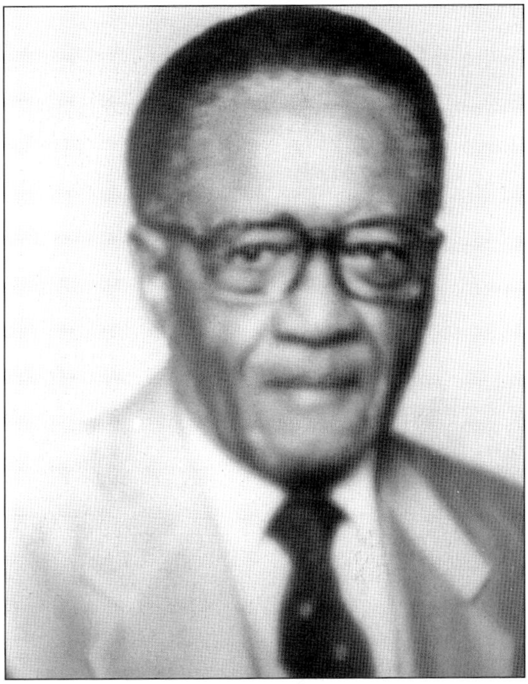

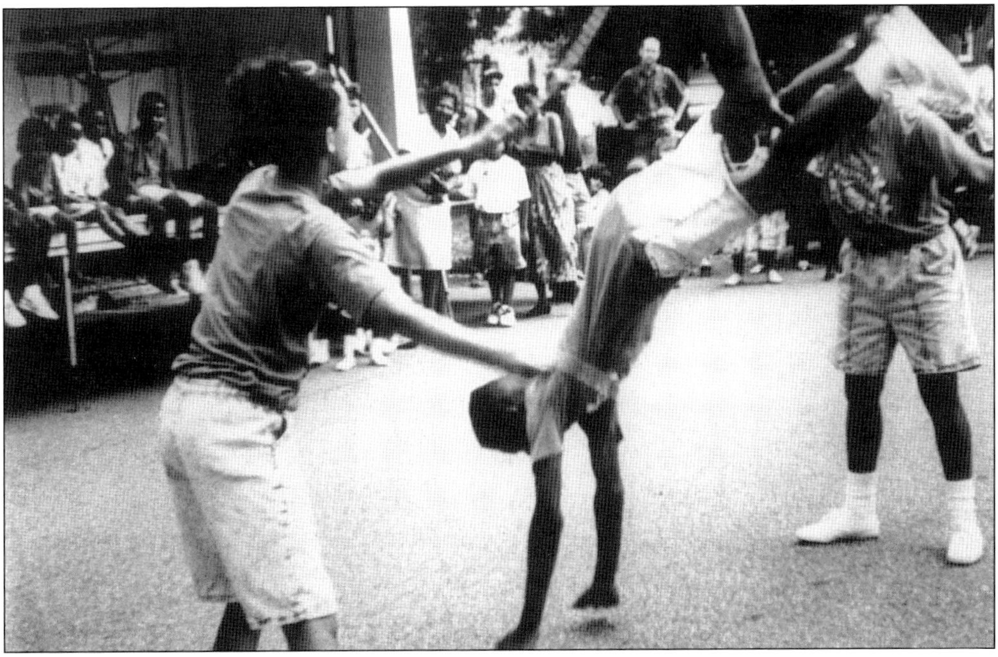

The Double Dutch Forces, made up of more than 85 members, have appeared all over the United States. They have made media appearances on *Jenny Jones* and *Gullah Gullah Island*. This year, the group won the world championship in six events. Double dutch rope jumping requires time, patience, and lots of hard work. Two ropes are being turned at the same time while jumpers do flips and stunts inside the ropes. (Courtesy of the McKissick Museum.)

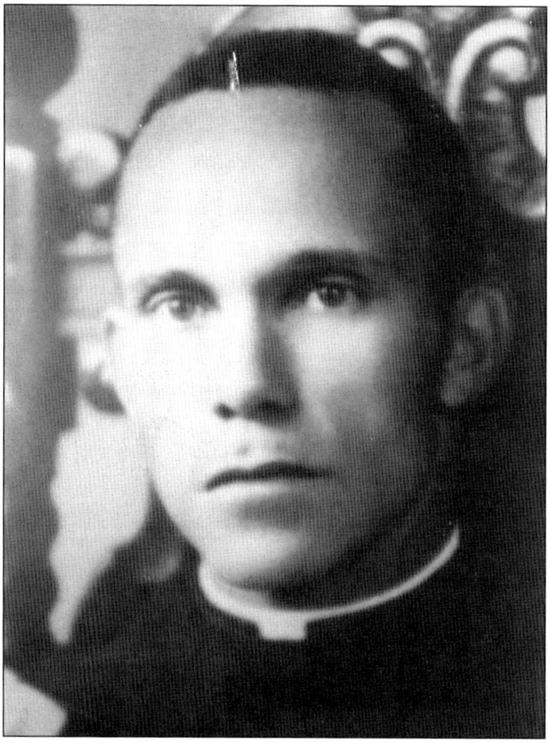

Fr. William F. O'Neal of St. Luke's Episcopal Church was tragically slain. In the turbulent 1960s, O'Neal was a member of Columbia's Bi-racial Community Relations Council that engineered the desegregation of public facilities and local business enterprises. (Courtesy of the United Black Fund.)

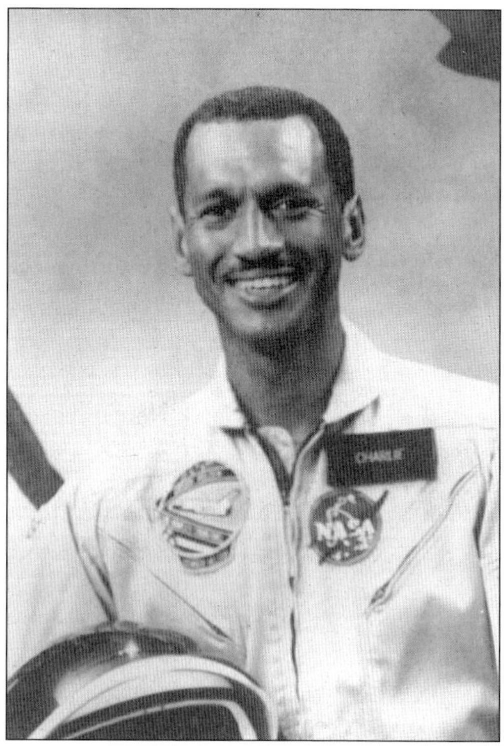

Gen. Charles F. Bolden Jr. became an astronaut in 1980. He has piloted the space shuttle *Discovery* (1991) and the *Atlantis* (1992), NASA's first mission designed to study the earth's environmental and atmospheric conditions. (Courtesy of Black Media.)

Ozie Jackson Sr. owned sandwich shops on Harden Street near Allen University and Benedict College. (Courtesy of the United Black Fund.)

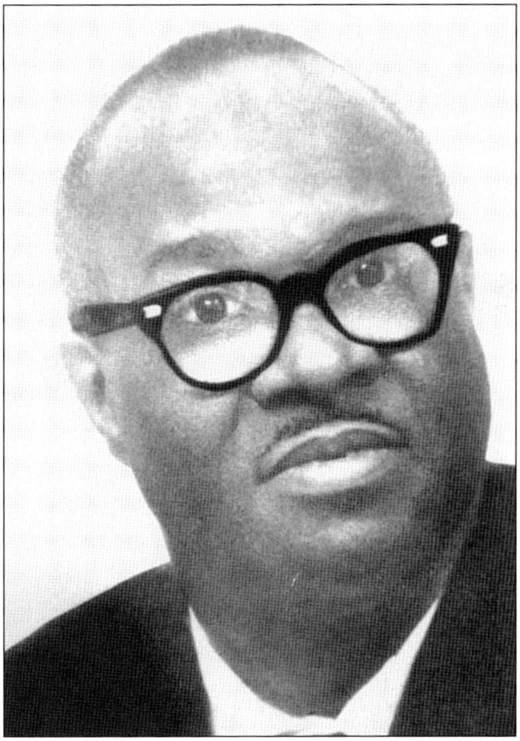

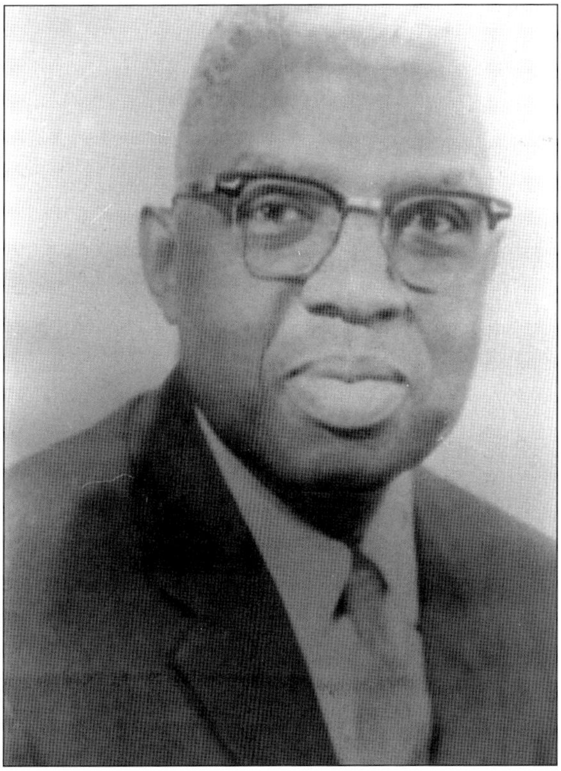

J. Andrew Simmons was a legendary principal of Booker T. Washington High School in the 1930s and 1940s. (Courtesy of the United Black Fund.)

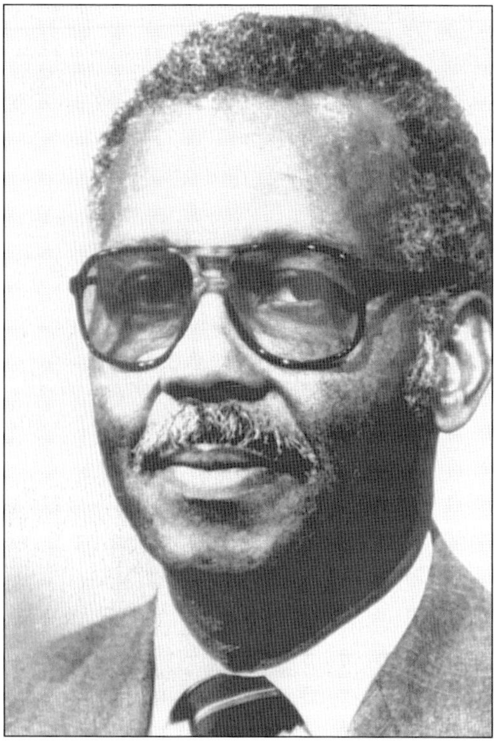

John R. Stevenson was the first black superintendent of the Richland #1 School District. (Courtesy of the United Black Fund.)

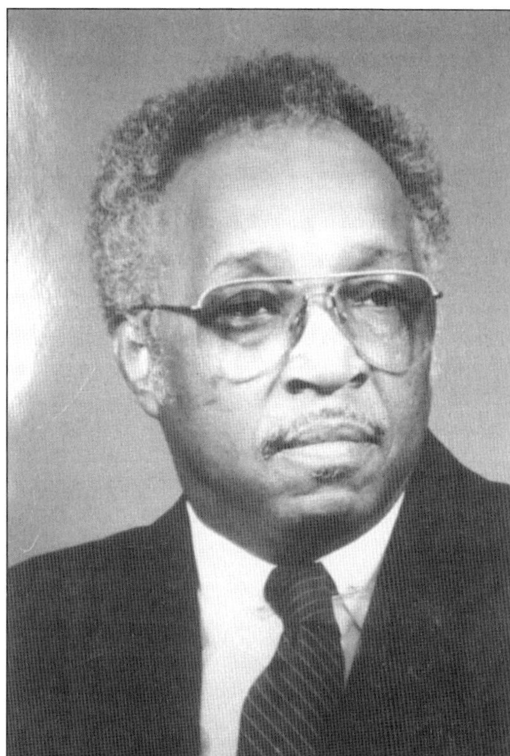

Andrew C. Jackson was a founder and the first pastor of the Bible Way Church on Atlas Road in Columbia. He built the church into a congregation of over 1,000 and a complex consisting of four modern buildings. (Courtesy of the United Black Fund.)

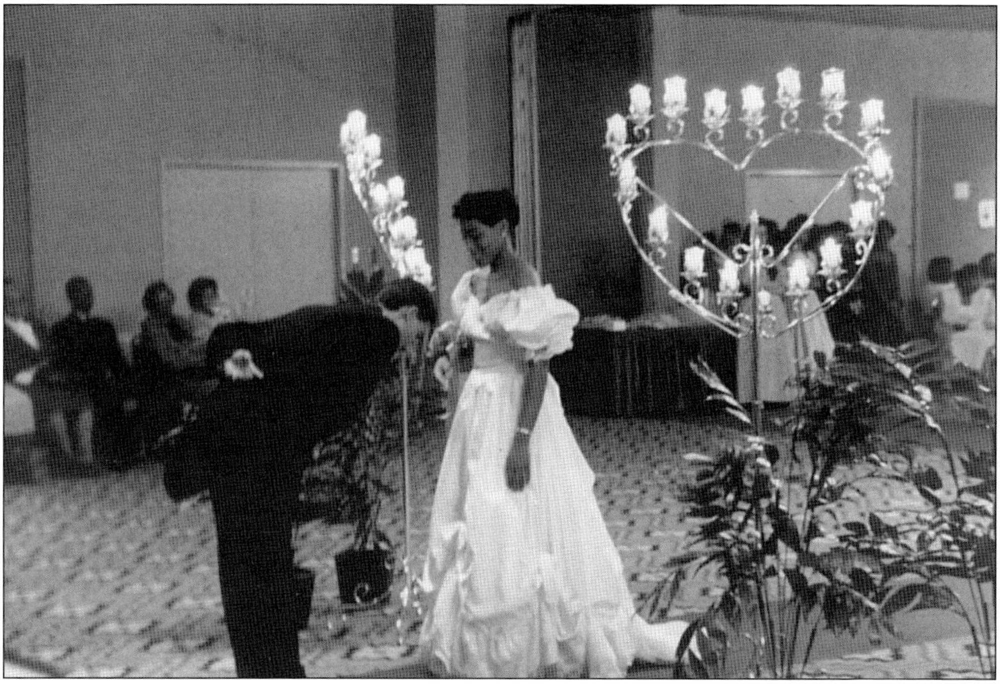

Pictured above is an event at the 81st annual convention of the South Carolina Federation of Youth Clubs; this is the Debutante Cotillion in 1990.

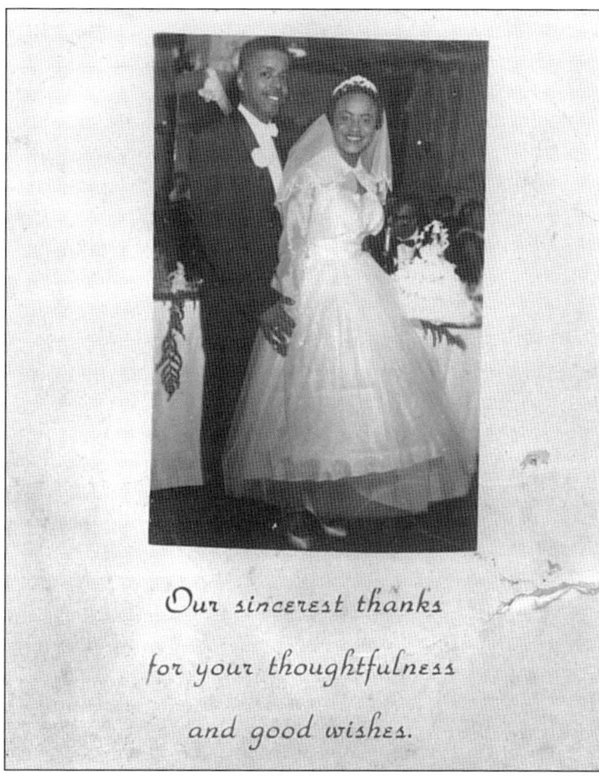

Here is a kind thank-you card for a wedding gift sent to Birdie T. Pompey Bouknight.

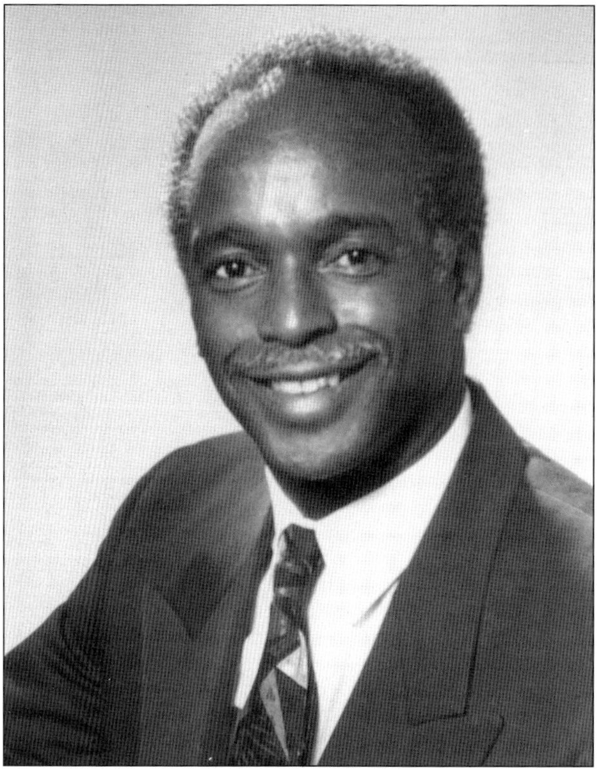

Thaddeus Bell, physician in family practice and a flight surgeon with the rank of major in the Air Force Reserve, serves as the chairman of the Governor's Council on Physical Fitness and Health. (Courtesy of Black Media.)

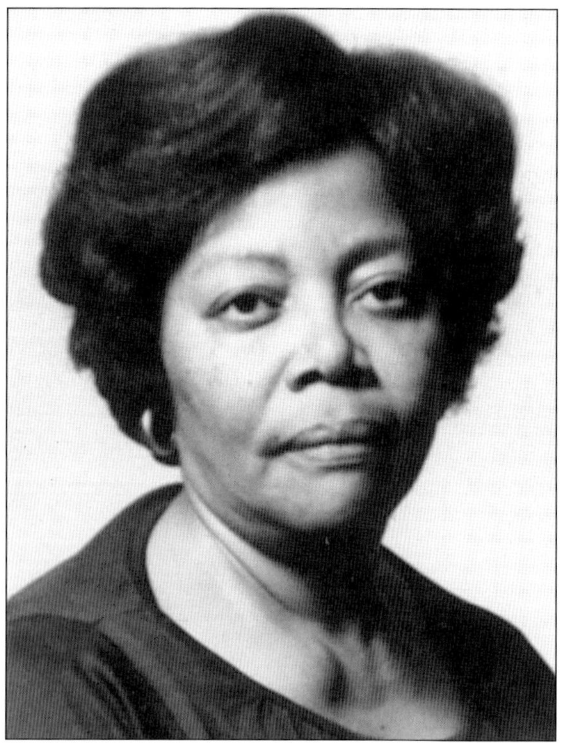

Alma W. Byrd serves in the South Carolina State House of Representatives. (Courtesy of Black Media.)

RESOURCES

CENTER COLUMBIA CONVENTION AND VISITORS BUREAU, audio-visual presentation, brochures. 1012 Gervais Street, Columbia, SC 29201.

COLLABORATIVE FOR COMMUNITY TRUST, civil rights resources, videos, and community projects. P.O. Box 50055, Columbia, SC 29250.

COLUMBIA FIRE DEPARTMENT, located within the award-winning Headquarters Fire Stations, preserves and exhibits the history of the fire service in Columbia. 1800 Laurel Street, Columbia, SC 29201.

EVA P. TREZEVANT MEMORIAL LIBRARY AND RESOURCE CENTER, community resources and assistance. 2300 Laurel Street, Columbia, SC 29204.

HISTORIC COLUMBIA FOUNDATION, brochures, guided tours, self-guided tour information. 1601 Richland Street, Columbia, SC 29201.

MCKISSICK MUSEUM, FOLKLIFE RESOURCE CENTER, created in 1985 as a repository for field notes, photographs, slides, audio tapes, videotapes, albums, publications, and other information of value to Southern folklife scholars and interested members of the general public. The University of South Carolina, Columbia, SC 29208.

RICHLAND COUNTY PUBLIC LIBRARY, historical and bibliographical information, statistics. 1431 Assembly Street, Columbia, SC 29201.

SOUTH CAROLINA DEPARTMENT OF ARCHIVES AND HISTORY, government records, genealogical information, publications, workshops, exhibitions. 8301 Parklane Road, Columbia, SC 29223.

SOUTH CAROLINA STATE LIBRARY, historical and bibliographical information, statistics. 1500 Senate Street, Columbia, SC 29201.

SOUTH CAROLINA STATE MUSEUM, exhibits, workshops, lectures, publications, tours. 301 Gervais Street, Columbia, SC 29201.

SOUTH CAROLINIANA LIBRARY, manuscript collection, photographic collection, South Carolina imprints, historical and genealogical data. University of South Carolina, Columbia, SC 29208.

UNITED BLACK FUND OF THE MIDLANDS, INC., manuscript, photographic, video collections of notable African Americans in South Carolina. 1919 Hampton Street, Columbia, SC 29201.

ACKNOWLEDGMENTS

This book is a part of an ongoing research effort to preserve Columbia's African-American history. This photographic collection, with permission, will be donated to the Main Branch of the Richland Public Library for educational purposes.

The author would like to thank the community of Columbia for its support. Special acknowledgments go to the *Black Media* newspaper, the Columbia Fire Department, the Eva P. Trezevant Memorial Library, the United Black Fund of the Midlands, Attorney John Harper, the Summers Family Collection, the City of Columbia Police Department, the City of Columbia Department of Parks and Recreation, the USC Archives, the Bicentennial Office of USC, the South Carolina Department of Mental Health, the McKissick Museum, and the South Carolina State Museum for their generous donation of photographs, and the Bell South African-American History Calendar and Dr. Grace Jordon McFadden for biographical profiles.

My sincere thanks to the McKissick Museum for providing continued support, office space, and the use of a darkroom, the African-American Studies Department of USC for academic support, and the Historic Columbia Foundation for resources, guidance, and editing.

Individual thanks belong to Brandy Hamilton, Andrena Davis, Regina Monteith, Dr. Barbara Jenkins, Doris Trezevant, Lucretia M. Cayruth, Lynn Robertson, Jay Williams, Gordon Brown, Zack Weston, Ginetta Hamilton, Christine Castaneda, Sarah S. Benson, Ethel Bolden, Dr. Tom Johnson, John Heiting, Arthur F. Jones, Mark Berry, and Christine Riley.

Thanks also to the *Columbia Star* newspaper for publishing portions of Black Society in Columbia. Funding was provided by the Richland/Lexington Cultural Council.